Love and Power in the
Peasant Family

Love and Power in the Peasant Family

Rural France in the Nineteenth Century

Martine Segalen

Translated by Sarah Matthews

The University of Chicago Press

The University of Chicago Press, Chicago 60637
Basil Blackwell Publisher Limited, Oxford OX4 1JF

Typeset by Oxford Verbatim Limited
Printed in Great Britain

83 84 85 86 87 88 89 90   54321

First published in French as *Mari et femme dans la société paysanne*
© 1980 by Flammarion, Paris

Library of Congress Cataloging in Publication Data
Segalen, Martine.
  Love and power in the peasant family.
  Translation of: Mari et femme dans la société
paysanne.
  Includes index.
  1. Family – France – History – 19th century.
  2. Marriage customs and rites – France – History.
  3. France – Rural conditions.   I. Title.
HQ737.S4313   1983   306.8'5'0944   82-50495
ISBN 0-226-74451-5

The endpapers show the interior of a peasant house by De France de Liége
(photograph: Roger-Viollet)

Contents

List of Illustrations   vii

Acknowledgements   xi

Introduction   1

1 Marriage Rituals and Conjugal Relations   11

2 Couple, Household, Community   38

3 The Household at Work   78

4 The Man, the Wife, and the House   112

5 The Man, the Wife, and the Village   137

6 Male Authority – a Folklorists' Tale?   155

7 The Rural Household and Change   173

Conclusion   188

Bibliography   194

Index   201

Illustrations

1 Pottery plate from Nevers, 1774, showing a couple leading three pigs to market. The man holds a whip in his hand, the woman a bottle and a glass   40

2 Print from Pellerin in Épinal, nineteenth century. The man holds a stick, the woman a distaff, while the children and animals try and stop the quarrel   48

3 Interior of the main room-workshop at Saint-Jean-la-Poterie, Morbihan   50

4–5 Communal living of men and livestock, the main room opening onto the byre, in the Landes and in Brittany   54–5

6 Plan of a dwelling-house in Villevieux, Jura, in which two brothers each have a separate kitchen for their households, but farm in common   57

7 Plan of a farm at Imbsheim, Lower Rhine: a well-off household with separate dining-room, and where the bedrooms have been moved up to the first floor   60

8 Plan and section of a dwelling-house in Ploudalmezeau, Finistère. Several generations, numerous children, and the servants all share the same area   67

9 Plan of the ground-floor at Heugas, Landes: here the generations sleep separately   76

10 Harvesters in the Beauce region: the men carry the large scythes, the women use sickles to collect the sheaves   100

11 The *'Taste Poule'* or 'hen feeler', an engraving by Weivix,
late sixteenth century   114

12 Route covered by man on a farm at Riche, Moselle   119

13 Route covered by woman on a farm at Riche, Moselle   120

14–15 Division of male and female territories during a
wedding in Lower Brittany. The 'men's side' and the
'women's side'
                                                                  145–6

16 Role-reversal in a print by Robier-Boulard, Orléans,
c. 1820. The woman bears the insignia of masculinity: hat,
pipe, walking-stick, gun; the man, wearing a wig, is spinning
and nursing the baby   156

Acknowledgements

The publishers are grateful to La Bibliothèque Nationale, Paris, for premission to reproduce figure 11; and to Le Musée national des arts et traditions populaires, Paris, for permission to reproduce the remaining figures.

Introduction

We are constantly fascinated by peasant society, by what it is and what it means to us. Is it familiar or remote, unique or comparable to others, has it gone for ever or will it always be with us? Questions such as these, and the light they throw on our understanding of the rural family, are particularly relevant today, when the concept of the family is so much a focus of discussion.

The family, they say, is going through a crisis; it has changed, but from what sort of earlier family? Ideological discourse has long set the image of an urban family, reduced through the consequences of industrialization to the triad of father–mother–child, against that of the open rural family, in which grandparents and married children share the responsibility for running a farm, in which the old rule, for the good of all, transmitting the 'right' values to their descendants. Even though this schematic opposition between the old extended rural family and the modern nuclear urban family appears to have been gradually abandoned in recent analyses put forward by anthropologists and historians, who denounce the falsity of such a dichotomy, its corollary stereotype continues to be universally accepted.

The rural family is no longer assumed to have been extended; the fact that it was often made up, just as in our towns today, of only the parents and their children, has been conceded. But that it was 'patriarchal', that the authority of the husband over the wife was absolute, and the wife's subordination universally accepted, that old cliché is alive and well. Whether they are seen as the good old days, a model for resolving the crisis of contemporary society, or whether such an attitude is violently rejected – as in feminist pronouncements – there remains a persistent belief in the absolute authority of the husband over the wife, and, more generally, in the domination of the female group by the male group. One might well ask why such a belief should be so long-lived.

For the feminists, the model of male imperialism serves to bring out the promise of a better future for women, while the traditionalist view is fuelled by nostalgia for a bygone order. In fact, we do not know a great deal about the nature of relationships within the rural household, and there is nothing to support the view that the husband's authority over his wife was absolute. Our aim, on the contrary, is to enquire into the nature of this married life, in agricultural families and, to a lesser extent, in the families of craftsmen. In thus restricting our range, we have assumed that there is a very particular relationship between those three aspects of agricultural life made up by the man, his wife, and the land; that this relationship remains fundamentally unchanged in contemporary peasant society, despite the changes to which it has been subject, and, finally, that the permanence of this relationship makes it possible for us to understand and to interpret the documents which are available to us in order to study the family of bygone days.

The relationship between two people and their farm, between two humans and the land is spelled out in the cosmic universe, in the cycle of the seasons and the weather. It is a unique relationship. Despite the progress made by technology, we do not yet know how to stem floods (indeed, on occasion, our untimely interference in the natural cycle even provokes them), nor do we know how to combat drought. The majority of our farmers still live by the skies, even though economic measures may lessen the consequences of the most extreme weather conditions, at least on a financial scale, there cannot be a farmer who does not still suffer the consequences in the health of his beasts and the state of his fields. Just as in the past, the rural family is closely linked to the world of animals and nature.

Woman's place in the rural family is unique, too. It will become evident that, though the law made her an inferior, she was, in fact, viewed as a producer, and, as such, had a special relationship with the soil. Whatever the economic level of the farm, its future largely depended on the woman's labour. Thus any study concerned with the rural couple must also entail an analysis of this involvement with the biological, human, animal, and cosmic universe. We would maintain here that a certain familiarity with the field and the study of day-to-day life in family relationships on a contemporary farm has made it possible for us to evaluate folklorists' accounts, to decode rituals, and to interpret proverbs – all documents which serve as sources for the study of the 'traditional' nineteenth-century family.

The aim of this work is to establish the nature of relationships within the rural household, not so much in terms of the 'happiness' of the couple, which, in the final analysis, is impossible to gauge, but more in terms of the systematic content of relationships of labour, authority, and respect, so that this model can also serve to clarify the nature of the crisis which the institution of the family is undergoing in the twentieth century.

It is perhaps this present crisis in the family (or the development of an ideology of crisis) which has contributed to the recent adoption of the family as an object of study. Previously there were the separate disciplines of anthropology, history and sociology. Now there is a field which is illuminated by the cross-fire of these various sciences, which have perfected the tools of analysis and unearthed new sources in order to comprehend better how the unions were formed; how many children an average couple might have, and why that has changed; whether the sons inherited from the fathers, and whether married brothers and sisters lived together or not.

Let us just recall for a moment the contribution of anthropologists, which has so dominated this field of study in recent years. The fertility of the concepts which they use in their analysis of exotic societies, kinship, descent and marriage, has been tested in complex societies, and even if these concepts cannot be directly transposed, they have considerably enriched the problematic, with the historians, sociologists and ethnologists of European societies seeking to find in them the regularities observed in exotic social systems.

In the domain of history, the most outstanding contribution has been made by demography, the most reliable facts having arisen from improved systems of analysis such as the method of reconstructing families:[1] the first problems relating to the family which aroused the interest of historians being questions raised by a rising curve of marriages, a lowering of the marriage-age, a fall in the fertility rate, or a rising curve for illegitimate births. Social history, prompted by these questions, has turned towards being a history of mentalities, and towards uncovering sources capable of explaining the why of the phenomena brought to light by the demographers. Various archival

[1] Michel Fleury and Louis Henry, *Nouveau manuel de dépouillement et d'exploitation de l'état civil ancien.*

sources – legal, ecclesiastical and notarial – trace the behaviour of the family, and, thus illuminated by the different movements of history, the family of yesterday is becoming better known. There have even been some attempts to synthesize all these sources. It is open to question whether these attempts have not been premature: demographic data, for all their apparent rigour, are no purer than other sources. The classic method for family reconstitution relies on an observation of the entire family, over the whole period of the wife's fertility, in the same locus of observation, in the same village. This method favours stable households, while masking the important question of mobility, and contributing to the creation of clichés about the human group being rooted to the soil in traditional society.

The increase in the number of prenuptial conceptions or illegitimate births remains incontestable, but it is difficult to find the root cause. Where are the documents that can tell us whether these peasants and craftsmen of the villages of France married for love, and what was the emotional content of their relationships? The difficulty arises from the fact that the people involved are no longer here to speak to us and that, in any case, their relationships were more ones of gesture than of speech. Historical documents have been substituted for this vanished (or non-verbalized) peasant speech: we catch it only in the interrogations of priests and judges, and thus indirectly. Though another spokesman can be found in the work of the folklorists who, from 1820 onwards, and in the second half of the nineteenth century in particular, undertook to depict a society which they saw changing before their very eyes. A number of their accounts concern the family group, most often observed through its rituals. These descriptions were gathered together under the headings of 'beliefs' and 'customs', which imply no sort of value-judgement, but also, frequently, under the heading of 'curiosities, superstitions and prejudices', which does. Whatever the heading, let us treat these narratives with care, however much certain historians have been prepared to take them at their face value, without questioning the validity of their contents, the manner in which the account was put together, or the ideology underlying the description. How can one give any sort of weight to this quotation from Abel Hugo?

> The wives are the first servants in the household: they plough the soil, care for the house, and eat after their husbands, who address them only in harsh, curt tones, even with a sort of contempt. If the horse and the

wife fall sick at the same time, the Lower Breton peasant rushes to the blacksmith to care for the animal and leaves the task of healing his wife to nature. Without, however, remarking that the absence of a doctor makes disasters occur more frequently. Though one must confess that the Lower Breton female is by no means a seductive specimen; her complexion, occasionally a coarse red, lacks pallor and freshness; her stature is short and hunched, with heavy limbs, a rough, dried skin, and a pronounced bust. All this, joined with a native lack of cleanliness, explains, without justifying it, the indifference of her husband.[2]

What sort of credence can one give to such a commentary? A hasty traveller, unfamiliar with the local languages, Victor Hugo's brother judged whatever was told him about local customs in terms of his own moral code, and on the basis of knowledge deriving generally from a specific social category, that of the 'notables', who also tended to reproduce a particular ideology. The value of these documents will be investigated in chapter 5, particularly in relation to Brittany, where the status and image of the wife seems totally alien to the description offered by Abel Hugo. It is by using such documents more or less uncritically that historians have made such brutal assertions as 'on the farm, man and wife got along in quiet hostility and withdrawal'.[3] We will attempt to show the opposite. Let us by all means make use of the folklorists, but let us do so with care. Moreover, the family group has only rarely been the object of their observations, and the study of this area was for a long time distorted by the ethnocentrism of the observers, who projected their own bourgeois standards on to a subject certain aspects of which were completely taboo. Seeking 'curiosities' – phenomena which implied both something distanced from the observer's own culture, and something picturesque – the folklorists often described rituals which have since been systematized by Arnold Van Gennep.[4]

Thus family life was filtered through the once classic prism of the 'stages of life' and 'rites of passage'. The family was observed through the medium of the rites of baptism, marriage, and death. This meant that a large part of non–ritualized matrimonial life was excluded from the field of observation, and yet does this not constitute the supreme

---

[2] Abel Hugo, *France pittoresque*, II, pp. 29–30, quoted by Edward Shorter, *The making of the modern family*, p. 56.

[3] Edward Shorter, *op. cit.*, p. 57.

[4] Arnold Van Gennep, *Manuel du folklore français contemporain*.

period of family life? The material concerns of the life of the couple are treated for the most part in technological chapters dealing with work in the fields or in the home, and the question of the distribution of tasks and of roles is never systematically tackled.

Nonetheless, folklorists' accounts will constitute the main body of our information, since the wealth of their testimony is incomparable, and fills, in the nineteenth century, the place held over the preceding centuries by ecclesiastical and civil archives, which had given a voice to the peasants, a voice which had fallen silent. In the sixteenth, seventeenth and eighteenth centuries, there are many recorded accounts of young peasants coming before religious courts to plead their case about a fiancé(e) who had not kept their promise to marry, or to explain why they had to marry their first cousin. Such documents are lacking in the nineteenth century, the Church's control having moved elsewhere.

The voice and behaviour of the peasants will be perceived according to the subtle observation of the folklorists, depicting by pen and palette the rural society around them. The first, the writers, are legion; the second are far less numerous and, among them, we will make use of those analyses painted or sketched from life and presented in the works of Jean-François Millet and, to a lesser extent, of Gustave Courbet. They make up a body of ethnological material which enables one to grasp, on an almost intuitive level, the totality of a situation or a gesture in a way that only the best pen could never capture (though many of the folklorists have a real talent for writing). Millet's works, supported by his correspondence with his friends, provide a source of the first order for our purposes. We will also use the primary sources provided by popular proverbs, which are, in their own way, the voice of the peasants.

The peasants of the nineteenth century speak to us, by courtesy of the folklorists, through the multitude of proverbs which criss-crossed their daily lives, surrounding them with wisdom from the cradle to the grave and providing them with precepts for all the seasons of the year, for every moment of work or rest. The popular proverbs collected by folklorists also concern every aspect of life, and there are over a thousand dealing with marriage, from the formation of the couple to the place of the wife in the household, and the relationship between man and wife. They put forward a philosophical consideration of men and women.[5] As long as one knows how to evaluate them,

[5] Martine Segalen, 'Le mariage, l'amour et les femmes dans les proverbes populaires français.'

and how to interpret their meaning in terms of a sound knowledge of rural society, they can be considered as a finished series whose contents merit analysis.

We will refer to them often since the wealth of symbol in their discourse tells us a great deal about a society whose culture was characterized by the predominance of the oral over the written, of gesture over speech, and by the assimilation of the subjects into the environment in which they developed.

A final source which will serve to support particular stages of this work is research into rural architecture. Over and above the obvious interest they provide for a study of the peasant habitat,[6] the '1425 sites' of rural architecture deserve to be taken out of their boxes. Carried out at the instigation of Georges Henri Rivière, this research covered every department of France. The architects were instructed to note down everything concerned with the rural dwelling, whether in its material aspect, in terms of the construction and distribution of buildings, or in relation to the social life of the people living on that farm. The unevenness of the findings is a matter for regret. Some reports contain a wealth of information on the history of the construction of the house; on the history of the relation between form (buildings) and function (type of economic activity); and, above all, on the family and the social life of the inhabitants. For our purposes, the most interesting are those that deal with the composition of the household, its size and structure, describing the tasks and roles of the inhabitants, and the family organization of labour. They show where everybody slept, and how they moved about. Unfortunately, complete sites are rare: only 64 remain at the date of the present study, out of a total of 1,759 mono-graphs studied.

With the help of all these sources, we will attempt to deal with that aspect which has so far received least attention in family studies up to the present time: the content of matrimonial life; relationships of labour and authority; the relationship between the couple, and be-tween the couple and the village community. Mother–child relations are excluded, however, since these are dealt with in another volume.[7] We will attempt to cover the concerns of man and wife in terms of

---

[6] These studies, taken up again and brought up to date in 1969 under the direction of Jean Cuisenier and Henri Raulin, are in the course of publication, in the form of a collection in 23 volumes: *L'architecture rurale française*, to appear from 1977 to 1985. So far, fourteen volumes have appeared.

[7] Françoise Loux, *Le jeune enfant et son corps dans la médecine traditionelle*.

tasks and roles, in so-called traditional, that is to say, pre-industrial rural France, over a period starting after the Revolution and continuing sometimes as far as 1945–50.

Over the last hundred and fifty years or so, statistical and demographic studies of the family have been numerous and reliable. During this time the family underwent a period of stability which contrasts with the state of the family under the *ancien régime*. In the nineteenth century it ceased to be 'fragmented'; mortality, and above all infant mortality, began to come under control, as did the fertility of couples, over a large area of France. It was a period in which there was scope for more far-reaching family strategies, once the survival of the individual and of the family group had been ensured, and in particular the strategy of increasing wealth. Strategies of coming into property, extending landholdings, and transferring land without breaking it up, make up the framework of the economic and social behaviour of the peasants. There was also scope for matrimonial stategies which fitted into these broader family strategies.

After long centuries of agricultural pauperization, ownership of the land came into the hands of the peasants, who profited from the relative agronomic progress. The nineteenth century is now recognized as the apogee of French rural civilization, as perceived through popular art, furniture and costume, the disposition of rural dwellings in relation to the rural landscape, and the development of communication routes. The study of the nineteenth-century family nevertheless appears as a poor relation compared to that of earlier centuries. It is too contemporary for the historian, too historical for the sociologist.

Nonetheless, one might well think that a better understanding of the family during this period would be a help in understanding the changes and difficulties which the rural family is undergoing in the twentieth century. How and why has there been the massive female exodus which is an aspect of the present crisis in the rural world? What is the future for a family involved in agricultural work? At the cost of what adjustments will it be maintained or lost? In order to compare today's family with that of yesterday, therefore, we must have a clear understanding of what the nineteenth-century family was like.

In this work, we will be speaking less in terms of the family and of kinship than of the *ménage*, the household, a polysemous term covering at one and the same time the couple's life together, the couple itself, the house and its interior, and also the upkeep of the house.

Originally, the 'maisnie' meant first of all the administration of domestic affairs (*ménagerie*, which has now come to mean housework, used to cover the entire administration of a farm), then the entirety of domestic things, and, finally, everything to do with the upkeep of a family. In this old meaning of the word, there were *ménagers*, that is to say, managers, administrators. This term, subsequently losing its immediate connection with the family and the household, came to designate day labourers. Thus the masculine meaning of the word, and its 'noble' connotations of administration have been lost, while the feminine meaning of the carrying out of household tasks has been maintained.

As early as Olivier de Serres, this semantic distinction was clear: 'the term *mesnage* . . . is understood to mean the whole family: in several parts of the kingdom grandchildren especially are called *mesnage*. *Mesnage* also applies to the furniture and the tools of the house.'[8]

This semantic confusion is here taken to be significant, and the household will be studied as a whole by considering the relationship between its members and the house itself. The complexity of the links binding them together, the variability of situations, and the development of households will all provide the principal framework of the book, while there will at the same time be an examination of the relationship between the married couple, and relationships of tasks, roles and territory.

The central hypothesis of the book is that the man–wife relationship in peasant society is based not on the absolute authority of one over the other, but on the complementarity of the two.[9] This relationship is determined by the particular nature of peasant sociability: before being a couple, the man and wife form part of the male and female groups which make up the basic framework of human relationships.

This hypothesis leads to an emphasis in this work on the condition of women in the rural environment, and recent developments can only justify such an approach. In effect, in certain contemporary family arrangements, the wife is deprived of her role as producer: there follows an imbalance within the couple, a disappearance of the man–wife complementarity on which the traditional organization of work

[8] Olivier de Serres, *Le théâtre d'agriculture et mesnage des champs*.
[9] This work is the expansion of a theme and the development of thoughts put forward in the mounting of an exhibition organized by the Musée national des arts et traditions populaires (ATP), in Paris, from September to November 1973, and entitled *Mari et femme dans la France rurale traditionelle* (Man and wife in traditional rural France).

was based, and a crisis which the emergence of the couple and the disappearance of traditional village solidarities can only accentuate. Clarifying the present in the light of the past might help to resolve this specific crisis in the rural family.

1

Marriage Rituals and Conjugal Relations

Ceux que se marient s'assemblent pour la vie
Those who marry are joined for life (Gascony)

Baisers, taquineries, coups, voilà les trois saisons du mariage
Kisses, jokes, blows, these are the three seasons of marriage (Gascony)

Première année nez à nez, deuxième année bras à bras, troisième année ôte-toi de là car tu me dégoûtes
First year eye to eye, second year arm in arm, third year get out of here you make me sick (Provence)

Each union carries within it its own destiny of incidents and misfortunes, and, even before marriage, the relationship between the couple is determined by the way in which the marriage is carried out. At the time of the wedding ceremony, they are the objects of passionate interest on the part of the village community. Does the girl look as if she will rule the roost? Is the young man so in love with his wife that he will obey her hand and foot? Is she a shy little thing who won't dare contradict her husband?

While marriage is undeniably the central subject of this book, it is less what goes to the formation of the couple than the content of matrimonial life which is the object of study. Nonetheless, a backward glance at how the couple was constituted is necessary in order to understand the specific nature of the rural family in the nineteenth century. The relationship between rural household and farm is shown in the marriage figures for the nineteenth century. In a way hardly seen in preceding centuries, where the family was often nothing more than a framework for survival, there was finally an end to the high mortality rate, and the development and emergence of a familial economic strategy.

What are the quantifiable characteristics of the marriage rate? In the first place, one can observe that its rate is stable, from 1800 on, varying between 16 per thousand and 14 per thousand, if one discounts the disruptions caused by the war years. Secondly, the average age at marriage goes down steadily, especially for males, descending from 28.4 years of age in 1826–30 to 26.2 years of age in 1901–05,[1] while for females, it descends from 25.8 years of age to 23.1 years of age over the same period. If these figures appear to lend a modern air to the nineteenth century, others retain the demographic characteristics of the *ancien régime*: the average length of unions in France, calculated between 1861 and 1865, is still only 28 years 6 months – probably rather closer to what it was in the eighteenth century than to the 42 years 4 months of the period 1960–64.[2] One can thus see, throughout the nineteenth century, a substantial proportion of marriages broken up by the death of one or other partner, and swiftly followed by remarriage, thus continuing to create families with half-brothers and sisters. This complicated relationships between members of the household by setting up relationships of alliance between the generations, relationships which were often marked by a tension which our terminology is unable to cope with, but which is often echoed in proverbs.

The third characteristic which seems to mark marriage in the nineteenth century is, as Dr Sutter has noted, the greater frequency of endogamy, that is to say, of marriages within the community. One can also observe an increase of marriages between kin, termed consanguineous marriages. This increase can be measured by following the degrees of consanguinity, established on the basis of the marriage dispensations granted by the Church. Jean Sutter and Léon Tabah have shown that, in Loir-et-Cher, the number of consanguineous marriages made up over 3.5 per cent of marriages, frequently rising to 5 per cent or 6 per cent; in Finistère, it was higher, even at the beginning of the twentieth century.[3] The authors draw attention to the demographic causes of such a phenomenon, which is due to

[1] Louis Roussel, *Le mariage dans la société française*.

[2] *ibid.*, p. 307.

[3] Jean Sutter and Léon Tabah, 'Evolution des isolats de deux départements français, Loir-et-Cher et Finistère'.

the conjunction of three factors: varying fertility (depending on the family), the decline in the mortality rate, and emigration.[4] But is it not also possible to see, in the rise of consanguinity, the consequence of that fundamental rule of marriage in rural society, no matter what the class: the rule of socio-professional endogamy?

The profound desire to control future cultivation shapes the family's economic strategy, which is aimed at creating alliances which ensure accession to ownership of the land, or its development, or yet again to prevent its being broken up.

These three characteristic statistics of marriage in the nineteenth century – the stability of the marriage rate, the lowering of the marriage-age, particularly for girls, and the increase in the number of consanguineous marriages – have consequences on the relationship between the married couple. If late marriages tended to favour the autonomy of the couple and their economic independence, and thus to increase the value of the wife's role and harmony between the couple in a spirit of equality and equilibrium,[5] one might well assume that, on the other hand, the lowering of the marriage-age, the decline in mortality and the increase in longevity would militate against the rise of the couple. It has been said that, in the demography of the *ancien régime*, the generations succeeded each other relatively swiftly, since the young, marrying late, could immediately take over the cultivation of a smallholding left without anyone in charge due to death. In the nineteenth century, on the other hand, though one cannot generalize, was is not necessary to wait until the death of a father or mother (or both) before being able to take over a family smallholding? Early marriage does not thus necessarily imply accession to adult status and economic independence. Frequently, marriage contracts simply regularized a temporary situation (Normandy, Brittany), with installation in a smallholding only coming later.

Thus, the marriage contract drawn up in Plonéour-Lanvern (South Finistère), 23 July 1854, between the couple Jean-Louis Péron and Marie-Jeanne Lagadic stipulated that the parents of the young man should undertake to have the betrothed couple living with them for two years 'where, in return for their labour on the smallholding, they would receive two hundred and forty kilograms of wheat and two hundred kilograms of barley, in marketable grain; that during their stay with their parents, they would enjoy the use of a dozen ares of

[4] Jean Sutter, 'Fréquence de l'endogamie et ses facteurs au XIXᵉ siècle', p. 57.

[5] Jacques Solé, *L'amour en occident à l'époque moderne*, p. 27.

land in which to plant potatoes and six ares suitable for growing
hemp.'

Thus young people could get married earlier than they had been able
to in preceding centuries: they would serve as labour on their parents'
farm for a period which could be structurally extended, if the co-
residence of generations was the rule, or brief, if the co-residence of
the old and new households only represented a passing stage while
starting out in life. Because of these demographic factors, there tended
to arise a household which stayed dependent on its parents and grandparents for longer than they themselves had done. This situation was a
source of tension and could lead the couple to seek external support
amongst age peers and groups of a similar sexual category. This would
be a possible explanation for the development, or at any rate the
maintenance, of male and female groups, which depended above all on
the collective organization of labour, but which also served as outlets
for couples who were dependent on their parents for too long.

Individualization would be achieved by the void left in a household
by brothers and sisters leaving to get work as domestic servants, or to
gain employment in the developing industrialization of society. Rural
emigration combined with the decline in the birth rate thus gradually
eased the pressure on the land, and the succession of generations was
able to proceed with fewer conflicts, the household designated as the
heirs managing the goods which constituted the essential determining
factor of its existence.

Does this mean that the search for a balance between household and
smallholding is the only value controlling the formation of the couple?
What place did personal feeling play in the strategy of the formation of
couples? This has been a popular question among historians and
anthropologists over recent years, and it is our intention to put
forward a hypothesis on this subject before proceeding to focus our
attention on those marriage rituals which are relevant to the content of
the relationship between man and wife.

MARRYING FOR LOVE AND MARRYING FOR CONVENIENCE

A positively Manichean vision seems to have grown up in recent
writings on the subject. For some, 'anxiety to maintain the integrity of
the patrimony was a dominant factor in family behaviour and attitudes. This preoccupation particularly determined family strategy . . .
Given that, how can one be shocked that the choice of partners should

be the affair of the head of the family? The logic of the system could not confide so serious a decision to any other other than the manager of the patrimony.'[6] On the other hand, the historian Jean-Louis Flandrin puts forward the hypothesis that the history of 'peasant loves' from the sixteenth to the nineteenth centuries was that of an explosion of amorous feelings, and that, if one follows the curve of births occurring six to nine months after marriage, one can establish that 'from the seventeenth century onwards young men were much less subject to their parents than in the past: they had freer access to girls; they more often chose their wives through sexual attraction and more frequently imposed their choices on their parents.'[7]

For the first time, a thesis makes room for peasant speech and thinking. Nonetheless, Jean-Louis Flandrin might be criticized for a misleading indentification of love with sexual relations, and, on another level, for having overlooked regional differences. The one thing we can be sure about, where romantic behaviour is concerned, is that there are wide regional variations. The Vendean *maraîchinage*, which symbolizes a relatively free choice of partner, based on mutual attraction and prenuptial sexual experimentation, would not be applicable to the whole of peasant society. Is it possible to reconcile Louis Roussel's vision of a union dictated by the parents with the freedom of choice and sexual relations which Flandrin finds implicit in the figures for prenuptial conceptions and illegitimacy?

It is a question that must be examined, as far as the present work is concerned, for it is clear that the relationship between man and wife would not be exactly the same if it was a love-match, and as such, a choice which they imposed on their parents, or if it was an arranged marriage. One might assume that the union would be happier, and that husbands would impose their authority over their wives less, if they had reached an understanding, if they had had or maintained an affection for each other, or if they pleased each other physically. A discussion of the role of affection in rural society would be appropriate here. The hypothesis being put forward is that love exists in the rural environment, but that its affective value is received differently according to the organization of the rural groups concerned.

Love is recognized in rural society; they speak it and make it. It is a love whose gestures and speech might appear strange to the eyes of nineteenth-century folklorists who, imbued with bourgeois morality,

[6] Louis Roussel, *op. cit.*, p. 26.
[7] Jean-Louis Flandrin, *Les amours paysannes*, p. 243.

condemned as brutal any code of love gestures which differed from their own. The lovers rarely embrace each other, but throw pebbles at each other, thump each other on the back, give each other hefty blows on the knee or shoulder, squeeze each others' fingers so hard as occasionally to dislocate them.[8] The force of the blow is supposed to correlate to the intensity of the emotion. In Cornouaille, 'two lovers court each other by holding hands; and at all major gatherings one can see a host of couples taking each others' hands, and squeezing them, and twisting them, their tenderness being measured by the degree of energy lent to these brutal embraces.'[9]

Courtship by blows would surely be an effective way of measuring the physical capacities of a future wife, capacities which are of primary importance in traditional rural life.

> On summer evenings, at nightfall, they go out to take the air, sitting on benches or behind a hedge . . . First they exchange glances, then casual remarks, then heavy witticisms. The young man shoves at the girl, thumps her on the back, takes her hand and squeezes it in a bone-cracking grip. She responds to this tender gesture by punching him in the back. The young man rubs his shoulder, sniggers half-wittedly, and notes that the maiden has got a fair right hand and would make a pretty solid housewife.[10]

These 'brutal embraces' sometimes appear totally incongruous to the folklorist. Thus it was conscientiously noted that in upper Brittany 'when a young man and a young woman wish to demonstrate their affection for each other, they spit into each other's mouths.'[11] It appears that this exchange of saliva seals the beginnings of betrothal between the young couple.

How can one know what courting couples say to one another? Observers have remarked that they often courted each other in silence. All the same, some declarations of love have been set down in engravings and on postcards. Their metaphors are often borrowed from the world of peasant objects, from the domain of food or vegetables, as in the following declarations taken from early

---

[8] Arnold Van Gennep, *Manuel du folklore français contemporain*, vol. I, p. 264.

[9] Alexandre Bouët and Olivier Perrin, *Breiz-Izel ou Vie des Bretons de l'Armorique* (ed. Tchou), p. 220.

[10] Hugues Lapaire, *Le Berry vu par un Berrichon*, pp. 38–9.

[11] Paul Sébillot, *Coutumes populaires de la haute Bretagne*, p. 105.

twentieth-century postcards, illustrating stages in the celebrated Vendean *maraîchinage*.

> *Si t'savo ma m'goune, l'plaisir qu'o m'fait d'te biserr. T'a la face si tindre, si tindre qu'o mait avis qu'quint y t'bise ma goule se cale din in morcia d'beirr*
> If you knew, my girl, the pleasure it gives me to kiss you. Your face is so soft, so soft that when I kiss you it seems as if my face is sinking into a pat of butter.

Or

> *Y t'trouve si jolie ma grasse bienche; et pi d'ine si baëlle fraichur qu'y paeu ja meille t'quimparrer qu'à t'chié chimps d'junes chaoux avin qu'les ch'neuilles y seillejin passer*
> I think you're so lovely, my great big darling; and then you're so fresh, that I can't do better than compare you to a field of young cabbages before the caterpillars have been through it

Or, again,

> *Veux-tu m'bisaille? Non, t'as la goule trop sale*
> Do you want to kiss me? No, I don't want to, your face is too dirty

And so on.

This sort of behaviour and language has to be seen against the context of the aesthetic criteria current in traditional society.

As proverbs show, the sense of what is beautiful is guided by considerations of a world in which physical vigour and health are the essential prerequisites of a society based on manual labour applied with both strength and skill. 'Beauty consists in being well-fleshed, glowing, plump and large. A *ben groussière* (buxom) woman, a *ben rougeaud* (ruddy) man, this is the criterion of beauty.'[12]

A folklorist speaks of a woman from his region thus: 'She's a bit uncouth, the mistress of the house in Brie! But nearly always "hearty", well-fleshed, chubby and plump, doutless fairly strong and well set up.'[13]

Feminine beauty – seen solely from the aesthetic point of view – counts for little in the marriage market, and often enough proverbs associate it with a fault.

---

[12] Hugues Lapaire, *op. cit.*, p. 59.
[13] Henri Massoul, *Au bon vieux temps, Souvenir du Gâtinais et de la Brie*, p. 18.

Fille belle est haute comme la moitié du diable
A pretty girl is waist-high to the devil (Upper Brittany)

Belle fille, bête et vaniteuse
Pretty girl, stupid and vain (Catalonia)

On the other hand, capacity to work and quality of judgement,

On connait la femme au pied et à la tête
You can tell a woman by her foot and her head (Languedoc)

and technical knowledge are more important when choosing a wife:

Quand une fille sait pétrir et enfourner, elle est bonne à marier
When a maid knows how to knead and bake bread, she is ready to wed
(Bordelais)

Feelings of affection are also expressed through a variety of objects,
which are usually offered by the young man to the young woman,
objects ranging from the humblest to the most imposing, covering the
whole gamut of feelings and stages which may or may not end in
marriage.

These various objects derive from an ancient convention in which a
gift, even of a simple object, accompanied by a vow, had the force of
an engagement. Sixteenth–century *créantailles*, which were a sort of
rude betrothal, without benefit of clergy, depended on a ritualized
code of an exchange of objects and vows between the young couple.
This constituted a ceremony so binding that the ecclesiastical court
could oblige a defaulting suitor to fulfil his undertaking.[14]

Rustic rings made of twisted glass bought at Beaucaire fair, as fragile
as the budding love which proffered them; so-called 'troth' rings
(*bagues de foi*) with the bezels decorated with two hearts topped with
flames and crowns which the young men offered their sweethearts
during the promenades where they might meet; Breton wooden
spoons carved by the young men during the long hours spent looking
after their beasts; clogs from the Bethmale valley in Ariège, the length
of whose points was proportionate to the intensity of love,[15] kerchiefs,
etc. All these are examples of ritualized gifts whose offer is part of a
code. This gesture of gift-making is part of peasant behaviour, which

[14] Beatrix Le Wita, *Les fiançailles à Troyes de XVe au XVIIe siècle*.
[15] Violet Alford, *Les sabots de la vallée de Bethmale*, p. 181.

characteristically often prefers gesture to speech, making for economy in any breach in relations.

The lover can be refused without any spoken word causing a breach in relations between his own family and the family of the girl he had had his eye on. No breach, no offence. The language of little gifts avoids unnecessary words and serves as mediator in relationships which would otherwise be difficult to establish.

> There is in the country a fairly common way for the young men to find out whether their tender regard for a young girl is returned: that is to offer them one of those brightly coloured silk scarves which the young men and young women alike so often wear around their necks as a sort of kerchief. The young man, who will have been wearing a coloured scarf for several Sundays so that its design might become known, will find some way of meeting the girl who will, herself, be wearing a similar sort of kerchief, and in a carefully contrived conversation he will suggest an exchange. If the exchange is accepted, it expresses much better than any verbal agreement what they wished to say to each other.[16]

In the same way, later on, during the process of establishing relationships between the families, the acceptance or refusal of a suitor is carried out silently: when he comes to the house, and before he has been able to say anything, some object will have been set out to let him know whether or not he can make his request. Various household objects may signify a refusal; for example, a broom, or a cooking-pot, clearly on view in the room. Alternatively they might have recourse to the symbolic language of the fire: it is stirred up, or a burning brand is placed upright in it to signify acceptance; for a refusal, it is damped down, or covered with cinders.[17] As it says in the proverb: *Tisons montants chassent galants* (Smoky embers send off the suitors) (Poitou).

This language of objects as a substitute for speech may appear codified, and thus formal. It does not, however, in any way exclude the sincerity of the sentiment: never before has there been so much marrying 'for love' as there is today, and never before has there been so much giving of engagement rings or 'love tokens'.

One can thus establish that a relationship of affection did exist between young people, expressed in a different way from ours, and

---

[16] L. J. B. Bérenger-Féraud, *Réminiscences populaires de la Provence*, p. 183.
[17] Arnold Van Gennep, *op. cit.*, vol. I, pp. 272–3.

leading most often to marriage. But that affection was as unquantifiable then as it is now, embedded in human nature, like a mother's love for her child or the fear of dying.

One must not, nonetheless, reduce it solely to its sexual dimension. The question of prenuptial relations in a society must to a great extent be connected with the degree of freedom accorded to the young. In the nineteenth century, there appears to have been a great diversity among the models of behaviour, and it is in this domain that the proverbs appear to contradict each other. Most of them refer to the young girl who, having succumbed to the advances of her suitor, brings all sorts of criticisms down upon her head, and ruins her own honour and the honour of the household to which she belongs.

> *Fille sans bonne renommée, paysan sans ferme*
> A girl without a good name, a peasant without a farm (Provence)
>
> *Brebis apprivoisée de trop d'agneaux est tétée*
> A sheep who is too good-natured will give suck to too many lambs (Languedoc)
>
> *Une fille qui perd la face, un huissier qui perd les jambes, un notaire qui demande quel quantième du mois, cela va mal pour tous les trois.*
> A girl who loses face, a bailiff who loses his legs, and a clerk who has to ask the day of the month, it goes ill with them all three (Provence)

On the other hand, the Savoyard proverb does not deal harshly with the liberty of the young girl, particularly when it aims to console her:

> *Jamais fille qui s'est fait trousser le cotillon n'a déshonoré une maison*
> Never has a girl who has had her petticoats lifted brought dishonour on a house (Savoy)

The taboos imposed by the Church on the code of morality during the seventeenth and eighteenth centuries were even more reinforced in some regions, while in others sexual relations among the young were condemned in vain by the clergy and continued to allow the young the possibility of trial before marriage. To be sure, throughout France opportunities existed for the young to meet each other: during the winter evenings, during the great summer agricultural undertakings, at local fairs, sometimes coming out of Mass or Vespers on a Sunday. But the socialization of young people was carried on within very different frameworks: in Languedoc, for instance, separation of the

sexes was almost total;[18] elsewhere, young people found themselves
linked in couples on particular occasions, as in the East of France, in
the *donages* and *saudées* – parodies of Church banns which publicly
paired two young people during a village fair, during which flaming
discs were occasionally thrown.[19] The code of honour, which always
relates to the young girl (the girl only, though perhaps also to her
family), varies from place to place: in one region remaining virgin was
fundamental to the strategy of making up a couple, whereas elsewhere
sexual relations were allowed, and a pregnancy simply brought
forward the date of the wedding. In fact, though, we know little about
this area, since the observers refused to allow themselves to enquire
into these practices.

Observations such as the following, noting the freedom of behaviour, are rare, and as such are all the more precious:

In Upper Brittany

> Rustic virtue is a highly relative thing, the girls freely allowing the
> young men to 'cuddle' them, which means holding them by the waist
> or breast. If caresses are confined to *au-dessus du sa (sac)*, that is, whatever
> is covered by clothing, then not much of a fuss is made, and the girls
> only protest for form's sake . . . At the time of marriage, the bride's
> virtue is not always intact; there are even communities in which those
> who married a virgin could easily be counted. One hears folk say: 'so
> and so's been *chiérie* by her young man', which means that she is
> completely his mistress. If a child does not come along, the girl's capital
> has not gone down in value and she can easily get married, even to
> somebody else.[20]

The question is all the more complex in that differences in attitude are
not confined simply to the regions, but can vary from one district to
the next. Thus, rather than piling up folkloric references which are in
any case partial and biased, we would like to advance a hypothesis to
account for such diversity. Hierarchized societies which have a social
organization of class to defend would be much more severe towards
free intercourse between young people than societies which are based
on an egalitarian organization, in which the social order would not be

---

[18] Daniel Fabre and Jacques Lacroix, *La vie quotidienne des paysans de langue d'oc*,
p. 171.
[19] Arnold Van Gennep, *op. cit.*, vol. I. 1, pp. 298–304.
[20] Paul Sébillot, *op. cit.*, pp. 94–95.

endangered by a marriage which had to be hastened because of an impending pregnancy.

The opposing examples of social organization and visiting customs in the society of Cornouaille and that of the Maurienne region illustrate this thesis. In Cornouaille, farming landowners, a rare group, were at the top of the social scale; beneath them, and hoping to gain access to the land through well-arranged marriages, farmers and tenants (who, following longstanding tradition, were owners only of the farm buildings, the land remaining in the hands of town-dwelling bourgeois) carried on a fairly meagre agriculture, except on the edges of the marshes, with the help of an abundant, and above all a family-based labour force. Still lower on the scale were the day labourers, employed by the day or by the task, making up a lower class, without personal possessions, or land, or even farming capital. They were excluded from the matrimonial strategy which, at the end of the nineteenth and beginning of the twentieth centuries, made it possible for the majority of farmers to become owners of their land. Marriage here is thus an essential element in the business of patrimony, and a middleman was often needed to put two families of equivalent economic status in touch with each other.

> Marriage in rural areas is even more of a commercial affair than it is in the towns. Sometimes, even often, the fiancés are two beings who suddenly find themselves yoked together, without their ever having seen each other, and without their having had the opportunity to discuss this impromptu marriage, though impromptu only from their point of view.
>
> The labourer [here, Bouët, writing in 1836, still uses the archaic term, which has since been replaced by farmer] who has a son to marry off will, without consulting him, contact the father of the young girl he would like him to have for a wife. His first consideration in this matter is the social and pecuniary proprieties, and then his own interest; he determines his choice so that his son may keep the farm, and so that, thanks to the daughter-in-law he has chosen, he may get rid of one of the servant girls. But the two fathers would need to have been long acquainted in order to enter directly into negotiations with each other, and it is nearly always the *bazvalan*[21] who is commissioned to make the initial overtures. When the proposition has been accepted, the two families get together in a local inn, and the young couple-to-be, seeing themselves set side by side at the head of the table, finally begin to

[21] Literally, the sprig of gorse worn by the middleman.

understand that they are to be married, that is to say that they are to be
made to meet through an indissoluble union.[22]

These constraints were internalized by the young themselves. There
might well have been a feeling of affection, but frequently affection
and social necessity went hand in hand. Prenuptial sexual games, on
the other hand, could not be taken very far. In societies such as Brittany,
where contraception arrived fairly late, in the nineteenth century, a
girl would not be allowed to become pregnant, since this would ruin
all chance of her marrying, and would condemn her to raising her
child alone, depriving her of her rights to the farm, even making it
impossible for her to work as a servant for a married brother or sister,
who would, themselves, now hold the farm. One sees these 'unmarried mothers', rejected by their family in the village, taking up the
only work now open to them – washerwoman, seamstress, laundress
– and the reputation for easy virtue attached to these callings is perhaps
due to this recruitment of female misfortune.[23] In a particular Breton
village in Finistère, the hierarchy was so firmly entrenched in customs
and behaviour that, even in the 1930s, the young men preferred to
remain unwed on the farms rather than marry the daughters of
agricultural day labourers, who had become factory girls, and might,
equally, have refused the offer.

In contrast to this rigid society, which contains its young in order to
ensure its social reproduction, the economic organization of the
village of the Maurienne valleys seems to be characterized by a long-
standing tradition of egalitarianism.[24] A significant collective land-
holding, comprising sometimes up to 90 per cent of the land, placed
small and medium smallholders on an equal footing, and excluded the
presence of wage labour. It was important that the endogamy of the
village be respected, but there was no preferential strategy between
certain families. Any union was valid to ensure social reproduction.
Under such conditions, one can more easily understand the existence
of a custom like that of the *Trosse*, a Savoyard variant of a Swiss or
German custom called *Kiltgang*:

[22] Alexandre Bouët and Olivier Perrin, *op. cit.*, p. 379.

[23] Paul Sébillot, *Légendes et curiosités des métiers*, p. 231.

[24] Placide Rambaud and Monique Vincienne, *Les transformations d'un société rurale, la
Maurienne (1561–1962)*.

Young peasants, on Sundays and holidays, were in the habit of staying up late into the night with nubile girls, and then, on account of the distance to their homes, to ask them for hospitality with the aim of sleeping with them, familiarly known as *alberger*. But the girls, even though they had vowed to remain chaste, and without asking their parents' permission, did not refuse this proposition. On the contrary, though keeping on their outer garments, they each climbed unthinkingly into bed with one of the young men and abandoned themselves to his discretion. There, in the heat of passion, it often happened, despite the feeble barrier of clothing, that both their frail vows and the hymens of their virginity were broken, and that those who shortly before had been virgin reached womanhood.[25]

A very ancient custom, in which Van Gennep has sought to find a relation between couples who were secretly engaged. In the final analysis, it matters little whether the young couple were engaged or not as far as our study is concerned.

What matters is the existence of this sort of freedom, which would have been quite unthinkable in the hierarchized social system of Cornouaille.

Marriage for love or marriage for reason? Freedom, or control of the young by the parents? Let us acknowledge the possible variety of models which appear to depend on an economic system putting a value on the family farm and its retention in marriage. For, whatever the nature of the relationships sanctioned between young people, the system of social production functions to protect the fundamental link between the economic unity of the farm and the household. Whether or not there was affection, whether or not there was freedom, the family strategy of alliance re-established the household to ensure the working of the farm.

Marriage, in fact, appears to be an association which immediately confronts the newly-weds with the economic realities of daily life.

Mariage, ménage
Marriage, keeping house (Artois)

Boire, manger, coucher ensemble, c'est le mariage, ce me semble
Drinking, eating, sleeping together, seems to me to make a marriage (Anjou)

[25] Marius Hudry, 'Relations sexuelles prénuptiales en Tarentaise et dans le Beaufortin d'après les documents ecclésiastiques', pp. 95–100.

Mari et femme tiennent dans un pot
Man and wife fit into one pan (Catalonia)

Le jeunes quand ils se marient, au plaisir ils pensent, ils ne pensent pas qu'il faut avoir un berceau à balancer, pot de bouillie, farine de froment dans une boîte, sel blanc dans un tesson
When the young get married, they think of pleasure, they do not think that they need a cradle to rock, a pot of gruel, wheat flour in a box, white salt in a jar (Lower Brittany)

The carrying-out of material tasks, the distribution of jobs and roles has to be regulated between man and wife. Even during the celebration of the marriage, certain rituals suggest to us symbolic keys to an appreciation of what the stakes are in the relationship between man and wife and their farm.

AUTHORITY IN THE HOUSEHOLD: WHAT WEDDING RITUALS REVEAL

It is not our aim here to describe marriage rituals in all their various forms, but rather to study some of them as they occur at certain moments of the wedding, and which evoke work relationships between husband and wife, and their hierarchical or complementary arrangement. One may find in them a symbolic language which provides some key to an understanding of the peasant vision of marriage.

As early as the wedding, a time of important family gatherings, there were all sorts of rituals setting the newly-weds within the sexual and the family community. Naturally, not all the rituals were directed towards this end, there were some which opposed the class of the unmarried to that of married adults, but a good many of them emphasized the community of women and opposed it to that of men. The marriage ritual also showed that relationships within the household itself were not the exclusive concern of the couple, but were socialized and controlled by the community.

Is it not astonishing that the first gesture made by the couple being brought together before the priest (for the civil 'I do' carries no weight in the eyes of the community) should be a ritual symbolically enacting matrimonial authority?

Arrived at the altar, the future couple kneels, and at Fours, near Barcelonette, 'the young woman spreads out her skirt or apron in such a way that the knee of her husband rests upon it, in sign of the superiority of the husband and of the amiable deference due from a wife to her husband.' This, says the folklorist reporting this custom, 'is the clearest allegory of the feeling of respect, of deference and of devoted readiness which a wife should show towards her husband.'[26] In the same way, 'in the Coise and in Astarac, the bride kneels on the first step of the altar, and places a fold of her dress beneath the knee of the husband she has just married in front of the Mayor, who has just said, among other things, that the wife should obey the husband.'[27] In the Basses-Alpes, 'in church, when placing himself next to the young woman, the future husband places a knee upon her apron to signify that he takes possession of her.'[28] Is this necessarily a gesture of authority, as the folklorists would have us believe, and an assertion of masculine superiority? Before going any further, let us note that it is an agreed authority, since the woman spreads out her apron. Now this refers back to a whole symbolic clothing code evoked in such proverbs as:

Une fille sans tablier peut se prendre sans demander
A girl without an apron can be taken without asking permission (Savoy)

Une femme sans tablier, femme à tout le monde
A woman without an apron is anybody's woman (Lower Brittany)

The apron is part of the working clothes, and by extension is a symbol of all work. Even today one may say that one has torn up one's apron (*rend son tablier*) when meaning that one has stopped working. A woman without an apron is thus lazy, a bad housekeeper, vain, and, consequently, a whore, since proverbs do not deal in subtleties. Rather than asserting his authority over his wife, is it not a question of the husband protecting her virtue by publicly demonstrating to the community that she is a good worker? Is it not also a symbolic assertion of his sexual rights over her, who should not remove her apron except for him?

There are other rituals which are enacted before the altar and which demonstrate the principle of an authority to be shared between the couple. A first symbolic struggle for authority is enacted in front of the priest. In a number of regions, folklorists have observed that the

[26] L. J. B. Bérenger-Féraud, *op. cit.*, p. 194.
[27] Dieudonné Dergny, *Usages, coutumes et croyances*, pp. 341–2.
[28] Abel Hugo, *op. cit.*, vol. I. p. 150.

couple struggle with each other during the bestowal of the wedding ring. For a long time only the woman wore one, and 'her fate was intimately linked with that of the wedding ring,' so that when the ring was nearly worn out, the woman too was in her decline.[29] If the groom slips the ring on to his bride's finger, it is said that he will be the dominant authority in the household, whereas if the bride resists, and he cannot get the ring past the second joint, it is said that she will be the mistress of the household. The wedding ring as the material support of ritual has strong symbolic connotations. The wife is the ring, she is the circle which her husband will force. The rite recalls a sexual symbolism of thrust and penetration, and magical formulae about knotting the lace-points have to be spoken at precisely this moment.

Thus, in Perche, for instance,

> The bridegroom in offering the wedding ring to his bride should not push it beyond the second joint of her finger, the bride hastening to push it the rest of the way. In doing this, she believed primarily that she was accomplishing a voluntary act which would go on to ensure her the mastery of the household, and then that she was warding off all the black magic which, according to local superstition, delighted in surrounding newly-weds. They feared above all the black magic called *la nouvie ou le nouement de l'aiguillette*, knotting the lace-points.[30]

The male authority in question here is strongly associated with sexual symbolism, and the struggle around the ring underlines the fact that though authority may be conferred on the man by civil and religious law, it can be challenged by the woman.

The question of authority is also associated with the flame lit on the candles which the couple have brought and which are burnt during the wedding ceremony. 'Whoever's candle-flame burns the higher will be master of the household.'

The symbolic connotation here refers no longer to sex but to death, for the flame foreshadows the death of one or other of the couple. 'If they burn slowly or are always on the point of going out, it augurs ill. The candle belonging to whichever of the couple that burns badly or is burnt up quickly, that one will die before the other.'[31]

In Mortainais, it is the light white veil called the *toilette* which used to

---

[29] Claude Fraysse, *Le folk-lore du Baugeois*, p. 86.
[30] F. Chapiseau, *Folklore de la Beauce et du Perche*, p. 122.
[31] Paul Sébillot, *Coutumes populaires de la haute Bretagne*, p. 122.

be placed over the heads of the couple, which served to predict the distribution of power between the couple. 'People, especially the womenfolk, believed that the one having the larger part of the veil would also have the greater authority in the household.'[32] If the wedding ring is the outcome of a struggle, a ritual in which the couple are active participants, the burning of the candles and the distribution of the veil can be seen more as divinatory rituals, but in both cases there is no balanced, intermediate solution, and the principle of authority is linked with love and death.

The presence of death is everywhere woven into the marriage ritual, which casts around the newly-weds the web of an existence which lasts through life, procreation, and ends only with the death of one or other of them.

Quand on met l'anneau, on prépare le manteau (de grossesse)
To put on the ring is to ready the (maternity) gown (Catalonia)

Ceux qui se marient s'assemblent pour la vie
Man and wife are joined for life (Gascony)

Quand on se marie, à mort il faut penser
In marrying, think of dying (Gascony)

Authority is not the only principle emphasized during the wedding ceremony in church. Sébillot reports that 'towards the middle of the nineteenth century, in Gaillac, in the Tarn, when the couple were kneeling at the foot of the altar, the congregation would let fall a hail of nuts on the backs of the newly-weds, and the first to round on their aggressors was, according to the womenfolk, the one who would be the more jealous in the household.'[33]

Here the ritual makes use of nuts, the symbol of fertility and sexuality. In effect, when a girl has had relations with a boy, they say *Elle a croqué sa noisette* (She's cracked her nut) (Picardy). Equally, after the baptismal Mass, the godparents would throw nuts to children gathered in front of the church, a tradition still maintained with dragees used in imitation of the shelled fruit.

One should not be surprised to see problems which are today regarded as part of private life being dealt with in rituals before the whole community. Management of the household, like adultery,

---

[32] Victor Gastebois, *Légendes et histoires du Mortainais*, p. 74.
[33] Paul Sébillot, *Le folklore de France*, vol. III, p. 401.

involves the whole of the social group controlling them (see chapter 2). On the other hand, it is curious that such profane rituals should take place before the altar: they must predate the imposition by the Church of a wedding ritual, and form part of a lay ceremony which had been incorporated and made sacred over the centuries. Thus, despite the efforts of the ecclesiastical hierarchy to rid the sacred precincts of these popular customs, they hung on for a long time.

Divinatory rites adorn the whole nuptial scenario. Just as the young girls had sought signs of their approaching marriage in springs and sacred fountains, so the community of friends and relations gathered together for the marriage carefully scrutinized the various rituals which predicted the future distribution of authority in the new household.

'In the Haute-Saône, when the couple returned to the house, the cook presented the husband with a wooden spoon containing an egg. He had to throw the egg over the house; if he threw it well he would dominate his wife.'[34] In Mâcon tradition, it is a sign of feminine authority if the bridegroom, on the wedding-night, has difficulty in removing his wife's bridal crown.[35] The act of going to bed is also accompanied by omens predicting both authority and death. In Brittany, 'whoever gets into bed first will die first, and whichever one of the couple sleeps at the front of the bed will be in charge.'[36] Obviously, the couples were just as well acquainted as anybody else with the primary meaning of these rituals, if not with their deeper significance. It was up to them to deal with them according to the kind of relationship which had already become established between them. One might imagine, for instance, a slightly domineering young woman taking great pleasure in fixing her bridal crown with so many pins that her husband would have no easy task getting them all out. In this way the ritual can be analysed on two levels. There is a signifier (the general meaning of the custom), and a signified (the mediating object), and this double meaning is more significant for the social community than the individual accomplishment of the rite by each couple.

The rituals which we have just described are disruptive; they impose

[34] *ibid.*, vol. III, p. 237. A custom which was still to be seen in Frétigny, Haute-Saône, in 1946 (research for the Atlas folklorique de la France, ms. in Musée des arts et traditions populaires).

[35] Gabriel Jeanton, *Le Mâconnais traditionaliste et populaire*, vol. II, p. 37.

[36] Paul Sébillot, *Coutumes populaires de la haute Bretagne*, p. 133.

divisions between sexual groups. But, just as in Van Gennep's typology there are aggregation rituals to set beside the separation rituals, so here binding rituals express the complementarity of man and wife.

'In the Hautes-Alpes, towards 1840, on the table set up at the entrance to each village, when it was known a wedding was about to take place, there were two confectionary nuts, one for each partner, and a glass of liqueur which the married couple could not refuse to drink, symbolizing that they should be united as the two halves of a nutshell.'[37] The nut, symbol of sexuality, serves as a material inter-mediary in a ritual uniting the married couple. The Church's blessing was not sufficient, and popular mentality fed on ritual repetitions. The community would feel the need to renew the symbol to reinforce it. By making the couple drink from the same glass, it offers the classic gesture of alliance which used to seal an oath and binds them yet further, by allowing them, through this shared drink, to know the thoughts of the other. Rituals repeated during the wedding must also be renewed periodically during the course of married life, as if the attribution of domestic dominance had never been settled.

In Brandons, at Carnival time, a period during which young married couples were singled out through ritual, omens of fire refer to marital harmony. Thus, in Perreux, in the Yonne, a large log was placed in the public square, and 'around the base of the log are dug as many little holes as there are people invited to set light to the log. These people would be the mayor, his deputy, and the year's newly-weds . . . They drew omens from the way in which the fire burned in front of the newly-weds. Was the flame clear and strong? An excellent sign for the household. Did the wood smoke? Bad omen, it would be a stormy marriage.'[38]

Every year, the question of the distribution of authority was re-opened by means of divinatory rituals. At Christmas, a log placed on the hearth by the head of the household had to be as large as possible. In Tarn, 'if the log burned until New Year's Day, it was the husband who ruled the household. If not, it was the wife. If the log caught light by the smaller end, and if that end was the first to be consumed, the wife would rule the roost all year.'[39]

---

[37] Paul Sébillot, *Le folklore de la France*, vol. III, p. 401.

[38] Charles Moiset, 'The customs, beliefs, traditions and superstitions which have existed or which continue to exist in the various parts of the department of Yonne', p. 28.

[39] Dieudonné Dergny, *op. cit.*, vol. II, p. 136

Other rituals with the capacity to tell the future concerned the spheres of activity of man and wife. Particularly widespread is the custom of the distaff to be spun by the new bride. 'On the day of the wedding, the future wife was given at Mass a distaff of hemp which she began to spin. She took the distaff and the hank, which had been provided by her parents, home with her, and she was expected to spin the entire supply of hemp and then to place it as an offering on the altar of the Virgin. The yarn would be auctioned off for church funds one Sunday after Mass.'[40] In Montauban, 'when the new bride came into church for the first time after her marriage, she was given a distaff with a hank of hemp, and a piece of bread which had been blessed; she took the piece of bread and gave in exchange a piece of silver.'[41]

The young wife had to undergo a sort of test in these quasi-initiatory rituals; she had to demonstrate her qualities as a housewife, and to pass the test of being able to spin in order to be accorded the adult status of a married woman. The transformation to which she subjects the yarn symbolizes the transformation to which her own body is being subjected. She too has been worked. Marriage has made of her both a housewife and a woman. The material itself carries a sexual connotation. Thus, with regard to the Breton custom of mutual aid between widows, an observer noted that the widow distributed hemp to be spun through the intermediacy of four boys. They gave 'the female hemp to the young girls and the tow to the married women'.[42] Spinning is also associated with the crucial moments in female life. For instance, in the Yonne, towards 1830, 'when the mother of a new-born child came to the end of her lying-in, the first place she went to outside the house was church; she gave the priest a ball of yarn (a skein of yarn weighing about half a pound). This yarn would have been spun by the mother.'[43]

Spinning has a deeply feminine symbolic connotation: even more than washing, it is the special task of women; just as women are subjected to all sorts of periodic taboos (see chapter 5), spinning can only be done at certain times of the year and day. The proverbial saying goes that *ce que femme file le matin ne vient jamais à bon fin* (what a woman spins in the morning will never come to a good end) (Anjou), and when it comes to illustrating a world turned upside down, we get

[40] Claude Fraysse, *op. cit.*, pp. 86–7.
[41] Paul Sébillot, *Coutumes populaires de la haute Bretagne*, p. 139.
[42] Lucie Guillaume, 'Fraternités bretonnes', p. 501.
[43] Charles Moiset, *op. cit.*, p. 58.

images of a man spinning, as ridiculous as a fish angling for a fisherman or a rabbit shooting at the huntsman. *Un homme qui file et une femme qui conduit les chevaux composent un ménage ridicule* (A man spinning and a woman leading the horses make an absurd household) (Picardy).

The ritual marriage distaff expresses the question of authority, this time less in terms of death than of labour.

Van Gennep shows that, in certain communities in the Hautes-Alpes, the young bride was only given a distaff 'if the wedding took place in the autumn or winter, and that she was given a sickle if it took place in spring or summer.'[44] A distaff or a sickle: the symbolism of the object evokes – following the rule of taking the part for the whole – work in the house or in the fields, and emphasizes the relationship between family and agricultural work. But here, there is no need to consecrate the gesture in church. In fact, there are a number of rituals which emphasize the complementarity of masculine and feminine tasks, and the team which the husband and wife will make on their farm.

In Burgundy, as they came out of church, 'the new bride was presented with the tools of her husband's trade: a mattock if he grew vines, an auger, hammer and nails if he was a carpenter, and so on, and the bride was made to use them to initiate her into the work which her husband would do, and for which she would have to provide moral support.'[45] In other regions, this ritual takes place after the wedding supper. Dergny notes that in Feuquières-en-Vimieu, the bride is

> subjected to a test in relation to the work which she will have to do in her new career. If the man she has just married is a farmer, straw is scattered on the ground.

> *All'harnaque in q'vo et all'vo hercher, si chest in sérurieu, all'lème in morcieu ed fer*
> She harnesses a horse and goes out to harrow, if he is a smith, she files a piece of iron.[46]

The man-and-wife association with labour is underlined by these ritual gestures, while other customs emphasize the separation of

[44] Arnold Van Gennep, *Le folklore du Dauphiné*, p. 159.
[45] Arnold Van Gennep, *Le folklore de la Bourgogne*, p. 49.
[46] Dieudonné Dergny, *op. cit.*, vol. II, p. 377.

labour. For instance, in Beauce, 'shovels, mattocks, sickles, scythes, tongs, brooms, and chairs were scattered pell-mell across the threshold, blocking the entrance to the main room. Each partner had to recognize what belonged to his particular sphere and to put them away in their places, or else the household would be badly run.'[47] Occasionally, only feminine implements were there, and, in Beauce and Perche, for instance, the bride had to collect and put away shovels, tongs, brooms and chairs.[48] The almost universal presence of these rituals in different regions of France testifies to the importance accorded everywhere to the division of roles and tasks. Each marriage sets up or modifies a unit of residence which is an economic unit and a unit of consumption. In the nineteenth century, which, to an even greater extent than preceding centuries, was a century of mobility, the organization of labour and the hierarchy of tasks were important. It was also the time when the quality and quantity of the labour were stabilized, and the matrimonial ritual lays particular emphasis on this aspect of the reception rites when the procession arrives at the house, after the wedding ceremony is over. They are most often directed towards the bride, and must underline her new functions as a housewife, the role she will play in the preparation of food, and her place by the hearth and the fireside.

In Joigny, in the Yonne, the godparents would give to their goddaughter what was called *la grand' chaudière*, in other words, a shovel, tongs, a poker, bellows, a warming-pan and a cauldron.[49] The wife would recall these gifts, for, in engravings illustrating 'the great domestic quarrel', she is occasionally to be seen threatening her husband with the tongs (or with a distaff). If the young bride has to co-reside with her parents-in-law, the problem of the distribution of tasks and of authority is less a question of between husband and wife than between the new wife and her mother-in-law. In this case, a ceremonial reception is occasionally given by the mother-in-law, who relinquishes management of the household, either completely or else only in certain sectors, such as the farmyard or the kitchen. The ritual is performed by means of symbolic objects representing this handing over of power. A soup ladle, for example, will be attached to the belt of the young wife. Henceforth it will be she who will prepare the meals, and, even more than this, run the household. Thus, in Dauphiné,

---

[47] P.-L. Menon and Roger Lecotté, *Au village de France, la vie traditionelle des paysans*, p. 108.

[48] F. Chapiseau, *op. cit.*, p. 127.

[49] Charles Moiset, *op. cit.*, p. 57.

the expression *prendre le manche de la louche* (to take the ladle by the handle) means 'to take charge'.[50] It is worth noting that the young bride is taken into the household by her parents-in-law, and not by her husband.

When rich peasants got married in Mortainais in 1735, after the husband, cook, servants and guests had all given their presents, there came

> the taking possession of the household: all the doors were open, doors to the rooms, doors to the cupboards, to wardrobes, and all the drawers open too; and the procession would start, the bride arm-in-arm with her mother-in-law, followed by all the guests, two by two . . . After seeing round the inside of the house, comes taking possession of the outbuildings; but here it is the father-in-law who takes his daughter-in-law on his arm; he leads her to the well, and makes her touch the rope . . . Then they go to the bake-house, where the daughter-in-law touches the kneading-trough and the bread-shovel, looks into the oven, makes a small sign of the cross on the door, and, before leaving this sanctuary of bread, dips a wet finger in a little pile of flour and passes it across her lips. Before the door of the stables she will be shown a white foal . . . At the byre, she will only be shown the best milk cow. She sees the barns full of grain. Finally she visits the garden, the particular sphere of the woman.[51]

Here, taking possession is not confined to the house, but concerns the whole domain, but this description relates rituals of a striking fullness compared to the symbolic receptions witnessed in France as a whole. They are usually more limited, and most often relate to a broom which the young bride has to lift. The gesture can be interpreted in different ways. The young wife is destined for a life of work, so if she steps over the broom she shows that she will be a 'slut'. One wonders what new bride would be so naïve as to bring down on herself the label of a vice so fraught with consequences before the whole community. Her qualities as a housewife are underlined in other rituals in which the young wife has to pretend to sweep the house. But the gesture of lifting up the broom can also mean that she will take charge of the household. Van Gennep also sees in the broom lying on the ground a symbol forbidding passage, and, in the act of

---

[50] P.-L. Menon and Roger Lecotté, *op. cit.*, p. 108.
[51] Victor Gastebois, *op. cit.*, pp. 81, 85–6.

lifting it and using it, a rite of admission to the new house.[52] The handful of grain which she occasionally holds in her hand during this rite can be seen as a symbol both of fertility and of this specifically feminine task, within the household, of looking after the hens. The panoply of symbolic objects associated with the woman gradually becomes clear. Along with the distaff and the broom, the cooking-pot forms the third element in the trilogy. This last links the woman with fire and water. When the new bride entered the house in Brie, 'she was led towards the iron cooking-pot under which she had to light a fire symbolizing the hearth of which she was the guardian.'[53] In Languedoc, 'she was made to go three times round the pot-hook . . . She was told: *aqui restaras, aqui demouraras* (who remains, dwells) . . . and she was made to promise to remain faithful to the house and to fulfil her wifely duties well.'[54] The symbolic meaning is reinforced if one knows that in the same community in the Languedoc, 'when they buy a chicken, it is made to go three times round the pot-hook in order that it should get used to the house and should stay there.'[55]

If the wife is the hemp symbolically worked by the husband she is also above all, in the animal domain, associated with the hen.

We will see how care for the animals in the farmyard falls to her, and in the parallel thinking which the popular mind draws between the human and animal worlds, she is definitely associated with the poultry. Rites and proverbs are based on the same symbols.

We have already referred to the grain, which, through its association with poultry, signifies fertility. An even clearer rite was observed in the Orléanais towards 1806: 'The fathers and mothers of the married couple, after having led them into the nuptial chamber and shut the door on them, made the husband sit with his behind in a bowl of water, and call Cock-a-doodle-doo three times, while his bride was made to kneel in front of him and answer Chuck-chuck three times, being the song of the hen after she has laid an egg.'[56]

The hen is associated with fertility and sexuality. Thus there are numerous proverbs promising death to those hens who play the cock: that is, substitute themselves for the man and make amorous advances. Rural society fears those women who need love, who destroy

[52] Arnold Van Gennep, *Manuel du folklore français contemporain*, vol. I, 2, p. 496.
[53] P.-L. Menon and Roger Lecotté, *op. cit.*, p. 108.
[54] Claude Seignolle, *Le folklore du Languedoc*, p. 123.
[55] *ibid.*, p. 267.
[56] Eloi Jouhanneau, *Mémoires de l'Académie celtique*, pp. 305–10.

the 'natural' order (that of their passivity and submissiveness in this area), and bring about the arrival of a world turned upside down.

Marriage rituals, where they are concerned with authority, are also implicitly concerned with sexuality. They are mediated through everyday objects: yarn, a broom, a cooking-pot or the domestic animals. The microcosm of the farmyard reflects the household. It is not only masculine and feminine work tools which are involved. Breeches, which are deeply symbolic of male authority, figure materially in the marriage rites described by Fortier-Beaulieu in the deparment of the Loire. These rites take their place among the customs barring entry to the house in which the wedding supper is to take place. On their arrival, the married couple behold a pair of men's trousers attached to the shutters of the house and a broom resting against the closed door. It is a race and a genuine struggle to get hold of the trousers: if the man gets hold of them, the woman must take up the broom and show that she knows how to use it.[57] In the same region, Fortier-Beaulieu mentions a cradle rite which takes place at the same moment in the wedding rituals. The bride is shown a cradle, and she must pretend to rock a child in it. 'When she intends not to have any children and to pay scant attention to the cares of the household, she leaps over cradle and broom at one bound ... The leap has a magical power which, under those circumstances, enables the wife to keep her independence.'

Any rite is polysemic and all the different levels of interpretation are closely interrelated, with some serving to mediate between other levels of the reality concerned. Right from the wedding ceremony the married couple is linked by a web of customs which emphasize the question of authority between the couple. These customs demonstrate that, beyond the framework of civil and Church law, the question of authority between the couple is still an open one. And yet, it lies at the heart of the life of the newly formed couple, and the rituals concern all levels of existence, from the most material activities to sexual life, and to death. Marriage in a traditional society is a dramatic moment, unlike our marriage today in which everything is directed towards an idealized conjugality. Death is an essential dimension in a peasant marriage.

Through each couple, the order of things is called into question and ritual imposes on each new household the fundamental questions, Will the young wife be able to carry out her duties? Will the couple get on?

[57] Paul Fortier-Beaulieu, *Mariages et noces campagnardes*, p. 273.

The rituals are ambiguous and, as with proverbs, anyone can read what they want into them. In picking up a broom, the young wife can demonstrate her qualities as a housewife, but she may also be unmasking her desire for authority. The young wife may also assume authority by maintaining her husband in his position thanks to the violence of his sexual appetites. Thus, the ritual emphasizes gestures of the broken ring, together with fears of male impotence.

While the rites are sometimes mediated through objects in domestic life, they do not always have any material mediation, and are by that token bearers of portents which are even heavier in consequence. The first occur within the context of the happy atmosphere of the wedding, the second in a serious setting, with all the participants knowing what is at stake.

In these rites, young people are very infrequently involved, in contrast to the other wedding customs in which the couple is surrounded by the young unmarried men and women. They have in front of them the church or the house, the two poles of peasant life.

The rites take place before the group of relations and friends invited to the wedding, who take charge of controlling relations between the couple. For although the proverb says: *Entre mari et femme, ne t'y mets pas, même pour un bien* (Do not come between man and wife, even in a good cause) (Catalonia), the village community, acting through the young or the adults, will oversee relations between man and wife, watching to see that the social order is not disturbed by a complaisant or weak husband, or by a shrewish or idle wife.

Often the ritual involves only the woman. It asks her to prove her aptitude for housework, while the qualities of the husband appear to be taken on trust. Can one not see in this a constant questioning of female qualities, linked to the fear inspired by women? Can it not also be explained by the central position of the woman in the 'home', by the symbolic recognition of her crucial position in the organization and future of the household, which is astonishing in a society which sees itself as being based on masculine superiority?

2

Couple, Household, Community

In traditional society, problems that would today be considered personal, whether to do with the intimacies of the heart or of the body, were the responsibility of the community. The formation of the couple, as well as concerning the young people themselves, involved the two families and the entire social group. The community took note of the new alliance through marriage rituals and continued to exercise control over the relationship between man and wife.

The 'happy ending' films of the 1960s which finished with a shot of a car carrying the couple off towards the closed world of their intimacy were conceived in an urban, bourgeois environment. In nineteenth-century rural France the newly-weds went back to work the day after the wedding ceremony, even in well-off peasant families. They often started their married life in a crowded house in which their only personal space would be their bed, their only shared possession a linen chest.

The validity of the notion of the couple in a rural environment should therefore be questioned. Does it have any meaning in a village setting which is deeply imbued with wider affiliations? Was there in the nineteenth century, as there is today, an area of interaction belonging solely to the man and his wife, which was separate from the context of the wider family and allowed scope for emotional relationships? When a historian enquires into 'married life under the *ancien régime*,[1] is he not artificially circumscribing the scope of his field of

[1] François Lebrun, *La vie conjugale sous l'Ancien Régime*.

observation by cutting the married couple off from the wider social framework to which they belong.

Is it not the case that the 'making of the modern family',[2] the emergence of the nuclear family and of the sense of being a couple has occurred particularly slowly in the rural world because the social organization and the organization of labour there are fundamentally communal? We would like to show here the pressure of the weight of these wider affiliations bearing down on the man-and-wife unit and the general socialization of a number of factors which today belong to the private domain.

First, we would like to substitute for the notion of the couple the notion of the household, whose validity is related to the economic function of the house. The term covers such a wide variety of situations, however, that we will attempt, in the second place, to analyse the factors determining its variability and influencing the content of relationships of labour and authority between man and wife.

DOES THE NOTION OF THE COUPLE HAVE ANY MEANING?

Ethnological studies have shown that the inhabitants of rural communities were united by a network of more or less close family relationships which underpinned the whole of social life. Local political figures, religious and para-religious organizations, groups for mutual economic aid, leisure organizations, etc., are made up of the families of the village or of adjacent villages linked together for generations. In the nineteenth century, this situation was reinforced by a twofold process: the decline in mortality, and emigration.

This is no longer the age of the 'static village' of Sennely-en-Sologne in the eighteenth century,[3] in which the family framework was broken up by both the ever-present factor of death – making for numerous widows and widowers, and children from different unions – and by acute poverty, which sent children out from the family home at ten years of age, and sometimes even earlier. In the nineteenth century, couples were less often victims of these demographic accidents: the notion of a family strategy stretching over several generations made sense.

[2] Edward Shorter, *The making of the modern family*. He places this development in mid nineteenth century, with the possibility, it seems to me, of it being a century earlier for the rural family.

[3] Gérard Bouchard, *Le village immobile, Sennely-en-Sologne au XVIIIᵉ siècle*.

1 *Pottery plate from Nevers, 1774, showing a couple leading three pigs to market.*
The man holds a whip in his hand, the woman a bottle and a glass.

The beginnings of emigration reinforced this development. First of all, the departure of the less favoured in economic terms relieved pressure on the village community. Although it was no longer the emigration caused by acute poverty and famine of previous centuries, it was still emigration for economic survival, like that of agricultural labourers from Lower Brittany who gradually, from 1850 onwards, exchanged their village status and precarious livelihood for employment round Nantes, in the Beauce, and in the Paris region, or later left to populate the emptying agricultural areas like the Dordogne. To this class emigration one can also add the more traditional emigration determined by family policy: that of children excluded from inheritance of land or from the tools of craft production and who, willingly or of necessity, went elsewhere to gain their bread in other ways.

These were gradually followed by the craftsmen, tailors, wheelwrights, saddlers, and cobblers, and all those who lived from a combination of domestic industrial activity (such as weaving) and the income from a smallholding.

The rural village, in the nineteenth century, was more agricultural than ever, and remained so right up until recent times when agriculture became an industry in itself.

Up to now studies have tended to concentrate on the stable family, since the method of reconstituting families on the basis of the parish registers aims to describe 'whole families', and so eliminates mobile households on principle. Even though our information regarding family migrations is still very thin, the image of the rural family as being static and rooted to the soil is one which must be corrected. Families were more or less stable according to the times. The nineteenth century appears to have been an age of resumed mobility, often over great distances, for economic ends, as seen in the emigration of younger sons debarred from inheritance, and seasonal migrations which became permanent, etc.

In these demographic and economic contexts, the nineteenth-century village family is seen to be all-powerful at the levels of the community and the members of the household. Family considerations weigh heavily on individuals who tend to disappear in the face of the wider aims of economic and social improvement of the family line. In these terms the couple is merely a link in the chain leading to the growth of patrimony or resisting the fragmentation of landholdings through inheritance. The individuality of the couple, or rather, its tendency towards individuality, is crushed by the family institution, and also by the social pressure exercised by the village community as a whole, and the neighbourhood in particular. Anything that might endanger the household might also prejudice the village community, and the community therefore reacts, occasionally violently, to punish those who contravene the rules. This intrusion of the community into every aspect of family life is very noticeable.

The formation of the couple is carried out before the eyes of the village: there are the familiar 'May branch placing' rites on girls, declaring love or insult in vegetable language. Without words, through the symbolic medium of the plant or tree, the young men praise or condemn the girls. This right of social control which the young men appropriate to themselves in the name of the community and exercise over the young girls, is exercised equally over the community of women as a whole, and over the couple. Thus they maintain a sexual right over the young married couple which is expressed at Carnival, a time of licence. 'In the Roannais and Berry regions, a *figot*, or traditional fire, is lit on the occasion of the feast of the Brandons (usually the first Sunday of Lent). A rabbit's tail tied to a red ribbon is fastened to the end of the husband's trousers. First the young married men leap over the flames; the "Novia" makes all the young men, and then the married men, jump over the fire, while the husband does the same with the young women and wives.'[4] Another ritual, practised in Touraine on Carnival day, is called *tricotage de la mariée* (the bride's race): in the afternoon a group of young men and a few young women, all armed with sticks or staves, would go to the house of couples married since the previous Carnival. The young wife would have obtained a wooden ball as big as her fist, which, when her adversaries appeared, she threw as far as she could into the most inaccessible spot: a pit or bushes.

> Immediately the sticks or staves set to work. The ball had to be driven back and under the bed of the young couple: there was an absolute ban on touching the ball with the hands. But the young wife would have hastened back to her house. Armed with a broom she stationed herself before the wide open door, in accordance with custom. The ball, having been brought back to the house, was thrown into the interior of the room. The bride swept it with her broom. The struggle could sometimes go on for hours, and young wives have been known to faint with exhaustion. Once the ball had been pushed under the bed, the players would eat pancakes together, and drink a glass of wine . . . A woman who had had a baby during the year was let off: she was held to have *gagné son tricot* (won her race).[5]

The group's right of control is not only of a sexual nature. It is also concerned with the woman's qualities as a housekeeper and is expressed in specific rituals.

In the north of France, it was the custom to put up a post insulting a housewife who had failed in her duties. If she 'had not hoed her garden

---

[4] Paul Fortier-Beaulieu, 'Coutumes et cérémonies des Brandons dans le Roannais et en Berry'.

[5] Jacques-Marie Rougé, *Le folklore de la Touraine*, p. 61.

before the end of April, she could be sure that during the night of the first of May a straw man would be put up in her garden, a ladle in his hand.'[6] We know that the garden, like the farmyard, is the special, almost exclusive domain of the woman; there are proverbs which frequently identify her with the fruits and vegetables which she grows there, and with their qualities and failings.

Au moi de juillet, ni femme ni chou
In July, neither woman nor cabbage (Provence, Languedoc, Gascony, Anjou)

Une femme et une poire qui se taisent sont bonnes
A soft pear and a silent woman are both good (Anjou)

The tribunal of young people exerts its control over conjugal relations – and it is very much a question of conjugality here – nowhere more strongly than in the rituals of charivari and *asouade*.[7] If an old man wishes to marry a young woman, or if a socially ill-matched couple intend getting married, then the young people express, in their own way, their disapproval of alliances which go against the social order. If a husband beats his wife too hard, and, above all, if he is beaten by her, or if two lovers let their adultery become known, then the charivari, being led about on a donkey, or an insulting scattering of vegetables, will punish the wrongdoers. Neighbourhood solidarity and the publicizing of deviant conjugal relations characterize these rituals. They took place, either at the time of the event, or during Carnival.

During the week preceding the intended marriage, the young people would gather together every evening and make a noise with all sorts of paramusical instruments, thus producing a true sort of counter-music[8] under the windows of the future bridegroom. The noise would go on until the compensation provided in money or wine by the victim was judged sufficient.

The charivari also condemned husbands who had been beaten by their wives, and occasionally inflicted on them a donkey-ride, known as an *asouade*. The beaten husband usually had to ride the donkey in a ridiculous manner, mounted backwards, and holding the donkey's tail in his hands. Being mounted backwards was supposed to both under-

[6] Dieudonné Dergny, *Usages, coutumes et croyances*, vol. II. p. 300.
[7] *Le Charivari*.
[8] Claudie Marcel-Dubois, 'La paramusique dans le charivari français contemporain'.

line the absurdity of the situation and to upset the established model: it is a world turned upside down, both literally and symbolically. Sometimes the charivari was accompanied by a masked procession, and a figure was made to ridicule the husband in the village. One noteworthy example of all these rituals was that of the town of Valenciennes, in the North, where there was a day for the *durmenés*, the name given to husbands dominated by their wives. On that day, which was the last day of Carnival, 'willy nilly, the man who allowed his wife to beat him mounted a donkey, holding the donkey's tail in his hand, while his wife, mounted on the same animal, held the bridle and guided it. In this manner they were obliged to go all around the village preceded by music and young people.'[9] Certain kinds of *asouade* demonstrate the interdependence of neighbouring households. Thus, when a donkey-ride has been organized, the culprit's house is surrounded, whether it is a question of upsetting authority or of an illicit couple, and if the culprit has fled, his closest neighbour is taken as a 'substitute'.

It was thought, in effect, that the neighbour's responsibility was implicated in the scandal, since he had been a witness to what had been going on during the year without intervening. 'This practice highlights in a very striking way the close interdependence of different households in traditional peasant society. Not only were facts and deeds well known, just as they always are, but everyone was answerable for everyone else, and the community depended in this respect, either on those nearby in terms of distance, or on the young people, who were usually commissioned with punitive expeditions.'[10]

Thus, in Upper Brittany, men who beat their wives were victims of the whole community and the entire domestic quarrel was fully brought out into the open.

> When a husband has beaten his wife, the young men provide themselves with a barrow, and getting up on to it, crack their whips. The word goes round: 'So and so has beaten his wife, he'll have to be taught a lesson.'
>
> The young men gang together and surprise the husband, who is put in the barrow and paraded round the village, while around him they discuss the quarrel which brought about the blows, using as far as possible the same terms as were used by the couple themselves.[11]

[9] Arnold Van Gennep, *Le folklore de la Flandre et du Hainaut français*, p. 98.
[10] André Varagnac, *Civilisation traditionelle et genres de vie*, p. 104.
[11] Paul Sébillot, *Coutumes populaires de la haute Bretagne*, p. 143.

The ritual form of the procession spotlighted not only the husband who was beaten. In Saint-Jacut-de-la-Mer, in the Côtes-du-Nord, the woman who beat her husband was paraded round in a barrow, and a pair of trousers was attached to one of the handles of the barrow. The man was put on a barrow decorated with a petticoat. They were taken round the village, and 'the young men sang *par ma fa, mon fu, c'est elle qui porte les brées* (my word, my friend, it's she who wears the breeches).'[12]

Sébillot reports that, on the island of Guernsey, this donkey-ride took place on the occasion of quarrels between husband and wife, or when role reversal took the form suggested in the expression 'the hen who sings louder than the cock' – that is to say, a woman who takes the initiative in sexual matters. We have already referred to his comparison between woman and hen which corresponds to a very deep-seated trait in the peasant mentality, in which symbol and reality merge.

The woman is in charge of the farmyard, she is the hen and must submit to the law of the cockerel. When she 'sings like a cock', she is upsetting the world order. Such women were powerful and much feared, and language and rituals alike were uncompromisingly harsh towards them. *A poule qui chante le coq, il faut tordre le cou* (The hen who sings like a cock should have her neck wrung), etc. In Guernsey, a collective remonstrance was delivered to the household contravening the order which was held to be the norm. Thus, even in the most intimate areas, nothing is secret and 'the hamlet rises up in a body. It is too austere an observer of the proprieties of the bedchamber not to serenade this all-matched couple. Then two young people, a girl and a boy, back to back as at a witches' Sabbath, sitting astride a donkey, represented the guilty husband and wife.'[13]

In another sphere of conjugal life, adultery was equally a motive for charivari, *asouade* or other forms of ritual repression, which usually took place on the Saint's day or at Carnival time. The cuckold, or his effigy, was paraded round the village, bringing everyone up to date with his sexual misadventures. Frequently his wife alone was judged to be guilty, and suffered the charivari, while a figure was placed on the roof of her house rigged out with so many emblems that it constituted 'a positive public outrage to shame'.[14]

[12] Paul Sébillot, 'Additions aux coutumes, traditions et superstitions de la haute Bretagne', p. 99.

[13] Paul Sébillot, *Coutumes populaires de la haute Bretagne*, p. 143.

[14] Charles Poette, *Histoire d'Holmon*, pp. 67–8.

Adulterers were also the subject of insulting vegetable-scattering. In the night, to the sound of a horn, or sometimes in silence, the houses of the lovers were joined together by an alleyway of straw (Oise); in the Gers, trails of weevilly beans, or feathers were laid. Rotten vegetables are a sign of derision, while feathers might refer to the woman–hen. Some vegetables are a direct reference to sexuality. At Loudun, in Vienne,

> In the Sainte-Eutrope, on 30 April, young people of both sexes, wearing masks, went the round of the houses of cuckolds who had had public conjugal difficulties, and of those of the cuckoos who had installed themselves in 'the nests of others'. On the threshold of the one they placed bouquets of dandelions, which the Loudenais call *cocus* (cuckolds), while on the threshold of the second they placed bouquets of primroses or cowslips, singing appropriate songs to each.[15]

While today one would be more likely to try and suppress the scandal, and have friends and relations limit themselves to private discussions of the goings–on, in traditional society the deviant relations of husband and wife are subject to public control. The neighbourhood plays a crucial role in this repression, either as substitute for the victim, or as making public the behaviour of the deviants. There is no such thing as private life. In the popular engravings of the nineteenth century entitled *The Great Domestic Quarrel*, the couple fight over a pair of trousers, the symbol of authority. The neighbours know what is going on: in the engraving there is always a neighbour watching the scene through a window. Moreover the commentary on the picture refers to her:

> *Allons courage et bientôt les chaudrons*
> *Les casseroles nous donneront de la musique sur tous les tons*
> *Pour les commères, quelle aubaine!*
> *On n'en tarira pour toute la quinzaine*
> *Tout le quartier, ma foi, le saura*
> *Tout le monde à la ronde en jasera*
> *Et de cette grande querelle la*
> *Longtemps encore on parlera . . .*

[15] All these examples are taken from the *Atlas folklorique de la France*, ATP enquiry, and analysed in our article 'Les derniers charivaris'.

(Not long now and
the pots and pans will give us a tune in every kind of tone. What a gift
for the gossips!
No-one will tire of it for a fortnight.
The whole neighbourhood will know about it, believe me,
everyone all around will gossip about it
and everyone will go on discussing this great quarrel
for ages to come . . .)

The abundance of descriptions of charivari nonetheless masks an
enormous ignorance about the social context in which it occurred. The
charivaris were all the more vigorous in that they opposed kinship
groups or rival households within the heart of the community.
Remarriage or adultery were perhaps only pretexts for much deeper
rifts, with implications going beyond particular targets. We would
have to know more about the relationship between husband and wife,
the reasons for their quarrels, their relationship with the rest of the
community (Were they hated landowners? Had their family already
suffered 'dishonour', etc?). In England and Germany similar traditional practices are continued under a variety of names: 'rough music',
'Skimmington', 'riding the stang', an insulting ride in which a beam
replaces the donkey, '*Katzenmusik*',[16] but during the nineteenth century, the English charivari was most of all concerned with husbands
who beat their wives. Was this a sign of growing respect for the wife, a
development in the equality of roles towards that of the modern
family? Nothing could be less certain. 'The proliferation of charivaris
in which the victims are husbands who beat their wives could be
interpreted either as an indication of the growing brutality with which
wives were treated, or else as the women's lack of available defence in
such a situation.'[17]
Nor is the French charivari whose victims are beaten husbands a
sign that the community is protecting them and condemns such
behaviour. Quite the reverse: it is the husband's inability to regulate
his household which is being criticized. His weakness is in effect a
danger to the whole social order of the village. Finally, 'the importance
of the rites of charivari resides in the fact that they are an extremely
sensitive gauge of changes in the definition of sexual and matrimonial
roles.'[18] The community's control is so acute that one could advance

---

[16] Edward P. Thompson, 'Rough music: le charivari anglais'.
[17] Edward P. Thompson, 'Rough music and charivari: some further reflections'.
[18] Edward P. Thompson, 'Rough music: le charivari anglais'.

2 Print from Pellerin in Épinal, nineteenth century. The man holds a stick, the woman a distaff, while the children and animals try and stop the quarrel.

the hypothesis that these rituals in fact compensated for an excessive intimacy between man and wife: the social group would suffer from too extreme an emotional relationship between the married couple, since it might run the risk of endangering the wider bonds on which the community depends.

On the contrary, however, it appears that this public control in fact extends and provides external support for a private control. The house shelters several generations, occasionally brothers and sisters, and often servants. The couple does not exist, principally because it has no space dedicated to it. The communal room, which often enough is the only room in the house, is the place in which one sleeps, cooks, eats, works, and entertains one's neighbours. There is nowhere for two people to be alone together. The folklorists were shocked by this communal living, fearing that this promiscuity might have harmful consequences for the 'morality' of children who often slept several to a bed, even when they were quite old, no matter what their sex. That the husband and wife might regret not being alone in their own room does not seem to have entered the heads of these observers: the couple is not frustrated by a lack of intimacy, having always lived in a fairly overcrowded environment. Besides, the folklorists saw in this transmission within the family of the tradition of collective sleeping arrangements a guarantee of moral protection. In the houses in the Hautes-Alpes, 'morality does not suffer from the promiscuity of the inhabitants, either in the stables, or in the family rooms. One can attribute this good fortune to the highly developed religious feelings of the Alpine people, to the watchfulness of relatives and elders, whose presence inspires respect, and finally to the constant habit of living, from earliest infancy, in the midst of a family of patriarchal customs, and whose least aspect of behaviour has nothing immodest about it.'[19]

This lack of intimacy which would seem to us today so hard to bear did not bother them then. One observer who knew how to stand back, and who made some effort to understand the peasant mentality remarked with regard to the Norman household, near Avranches,

> Morality loses nothing through all the inhabitants on a farm sleeping in the same room: on the contrary, it brings about a sort of mutual surveillance. They prefer the dormitory to the cell. Only decency is in any way disturbed, and even that disturbance is less than might be

[19] Alfred de Foville, *Enquête sur les conditions de l'habitation en France. Les maisons types*, vol. I. p. 174.

supposed by those who have always had rooms of their own . . . This intimate communal way of life is not only a habit, but a taste, since those labourers who have exceptionally got houses with more than one room still set up their sleeping arrangements in the same way as those living in the standard houses.'[20]

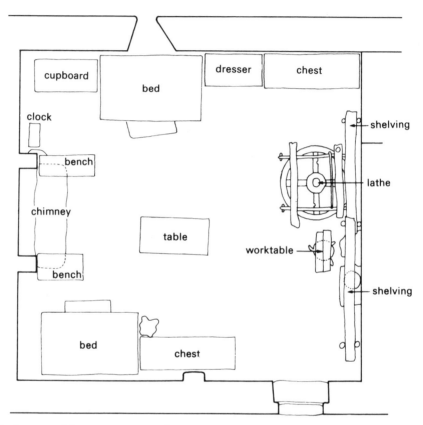

3 *Interior of the main room-workshop at Saint-Jean-la-Poterie, Morbihan.*

This crowding together in the communal room, and the control of the life of the married couple by the whole household, persisted for a long time, since habitat 'is one of the slowest elements to evolve in a rural setting.'[21] Improvements, in fact, were carried out primarily on the outbuildings.

Often, too, the peasant did not own his house and the 'master was

[20] *ibid.*, introd. p. xxxvi and xxxvii.

[21] Maurice Agulhon, Gabriel Désert, Robert Specklin, *Histoire de la France rurale,* vol. III, pp. 321–2.

more inclined to pay over his money to buy new materials, or fodder, or other expenditure which one could assume might bring in a return rather than on improvements which served only to improve the inhabitants' comfort.'[22] It was as much a question of a particular attitude towards conjugal and sexual life as of comfort. The married couple did not feel the need to isolate themselves in a room, or felt it less than town-dwellers. Sexuality could find room for expression at other moments or in other places than that of nocturnal rest. It is no surprise that researchers sent into the field at the end of the Second World War should still have found numerous examples of peasant co-residence.

In 1945, in the Côtes-du-Nord, at Plédran, M and Mme M . . ., their daughter, son-in-law, and the daughter's two young children all slept in the same room, that is, three generations and six people together.[23] At the same date, at Saint-Véran, in the Hautes-Alpes, one can observe an extreme case of 'promiscuity', as the researchers called it. 'The house was a byre/dwelling-house, with the same entrance serving both men and beasts. The two parents and seven children live and sleep there. Within were three curtained beds, side by side. In the centre of the room there was a table, chairs, and the stove. A ceiling-high enclosure served as a cage for the hens, a small ladder making it possible for the hens to get into it. At the end of the room were kept the cows and the ass.'[24] The researcher was even more astonished that the inhabitants of the house declared themselves in no way hampered by this living together, quite the reverse. The presence of the livestock in the room was a source of heating in that very cold area. It made looking after the animals easier, if they were ill or in calf, when it was often necessary to get up several times during the night. There was no need to dress hurriedly and go outside in the cold and damp. The community life of the household thus extends to all the people and livestock which go to make it up. In certain regions, the servants shared the communal room with their masters, but elsewhere, from the eighteenth century on, they were segregated. In the Seine-Maritime, from the eighteenth century onwards, there was no collective sleeping in the communal room, even in fairly modest households. This fact seems to be associated with the wealth of the region and the mildness of the climate, which did not necessitate close living between beasts

[22] *ibid.*, p. 322.
[23] *Enquête d'architecture rurale* (EAR), no. 11.
[24] EAR, no. 5.

and men. Thus, on an average farm at Harcanville (Seine-Maritime) in Caux, built between 1760 and 1770, the bedrooms were on the first floor, over the communal room, with the children and servants having small rooms of their own. But the male servants, the two cowmen, the two carters and the labourers slept in the barn and the stable, on wooden beds which were hung up on the beams by day.[25] Here, these separate sleeping arrangements are not solely based on exclusion, or distinguishing between masters and servants; they are also dictated by a desire for efficiency, by the idea of putting those responsible for the care of the animals near their charges, so that they can keep an eye on valuable property.

The existence of a separate bedroom, however important it might be (and it is a subject to which we will return later), does not signify the breakdown of the communal life of the household. Meals were generally taken in common, masters and servants together. The main room was often the site of craft-work: it functioned, for instance, as a dairy, for the making of the cheese which the woman sold at market. It was also the place for meeting together in the evening. Thus, at Idaux-Mendy (Basses-Pyrénées), in a small house built in 1765, the share-croppers would gather together in their house in winter, two or three families, making between 20 and 25 people, for stripping corn.[26] From morning to night, and from night till morning, the life of the household is concentrated in the communal room, where cooking, eating, sleeping, loving and working are all carried on. It is, besides, the only room which is called *maison* in some parts of Normandy, the Seine-Maritime, even in dwellings which have several rooms. This overlapping of social and private life is particularly marked in the households of weavers, such as the *cacheux* of Caux who wove cotton imported through le Havre.

The modest dwelling was principally made up of a *chambre à cacher* which served as bedchamber and dining-room: in it were found the loom and the spinning-wheel, that is to say, the means of production, and also the bed, table, sideboard and stove. The separate kitchen was used only during the summer. The whole life of the family was concentrated in the work-room, the only room warm enough to ensure agile fingers.

If one is looking for signs of the development of the modern family, based on the couple, the existence of separate bedrooms within the

[25] EAR, no. 10.
[26] *ibid.*

rural dwelling is not particularly significant. The central aspects of life are conducted in the communal room, where the integration of the members of the household is carried out above all through eating and working together. Separate dwellings, 'decoresidence', are today a crucial demand of young couples working with their parents on a farm. It is not so much a question of sleeping separately (which goes without saying these days) as of cooking and eating on their own. Nowadays, husband and wife wish to lunch and dine alone with their children, with the aged parents doing their own cooking for themselves. Even where the afternoon break is concerned, the desire is for each individual to be in his own home.

The notion of the couple has no great meaning in the nineteenth-century rural family; the matrimonial relationship must be restored to the context of the village community and habitat. The areas which today are considered the most intimate were controlled by the villagers, the arbiters of the collective norms. The couple was also based on wider networks which criss-crossed the organization of work and which were still to a large extent based on mutual help between neighbours and kin (see chapter 3). In daily life, the couple was integrated in another entity, the family, which was itself merged with that of the household and served as mediator between the individuals and the village collectivity. What role did kinship networks play in terms of relations between man and wife?

We know that they were the determinants in a variety of spheres: through the constitution of couples, particularly in the increase of endogamous and occasionally of consanguineous marriages; at the moment of the rites of passage which punctuate individual life; through the distribution of goods; through the organization of groups living together; through the control of power in the village, and not only political power, etc. However, above and beyond the group of very close relationships who live specifically within the household itself, distant kinship has no distinct influence on conjugal unity and merges with the influence exerted by the community as a whole. It might be assumed, although there is no description to tell us so, that the donkey bearing the beaten husband was led by a cousin. This fact could denote a family rivalry which was part of the rivalry between village groups; in the same way, town councils throughout the nineteenth century were fraught with confrontations between groups of relations, and family political rivalries were merely symptoms of wider rivalries.

4 *Communal living of men and livestock, the main room opening on to the byre, in the Landes.*

5 *Communal living of men and livestock in Brittany.*

We have seen certain couples in the materiality of their habitat; but did the framework of the house always contain the same human group? On the contrary; nothing fluctuated more than this association of men, women, children and animals. We will now try to determine which characteristics modify the household and, therefore, might have a bearing on matrimonial relations.

HOUSEHOLD: DEFINITION AND TYPES

The household, defined as being a group of people linked (or not) by ties of consanguinity and/or alliance living under the same roof and working at the same undertaking, has for some years been the object of scientific debate. After the war, sociologists saw it in terms of a Manichean opposition: industrialization and urbanization led to the nuclear family – a horrible term designating the mother and children focused on the father – rather than the 'traditional' extended family, which was above all a rural phenomenon, while historians have shown that the rural household in past times was also often made up of the couple and their children. The ethnologists then accused the historians, imprisoned in their sources (primarily consisting of population censuses), of omitting the whole substance of social life, which was embodied in the relationships between households. Even if there used to be a nuclear family, it maintained social relations which were interwoven with the whole of its existence. Historians now agree in recognizing the diversity of models of the household, both in time and in geographical area, and also the coexistence of different types of family within the same geographical area.[27]

In order to analyse the question of the variety of composition of the family group, a classificatory framework had to be found, and most researchers adopted that put forward by the English historian Peter Laslett. According to him three categories of household can be distinguished: so-called simple households, made up of the father, mother and children, which today we call 'nuclear families', and two kinds of complex household – the extended household, containing one of the kin of the couple, either older (widowed mother or father), or collateral (brother or sister), and multiple households, made up of two or more couples who are generally linked by ties of consanguinity.

These ties can be vertical, as in the case of parents who have a

---

[27] Jean-Louis Flandrin, *Familles, parenté, maison, sexualité dans l'ancienne société*, p. 68.

married son or daughter under their roof, or horizontal, as in the case of two or more married brothers or sisters.[28]

Laslett may have been able to demonstrate that the nuclear family has been the rule in England for centuries past, but it is more difficult to make any such categorical assertion with regard to France. Jean-Louis Flandrin has given us a highly varied picture of the French household under the *ancien régime* which must hold true for a large part of the nineteenth century as well.

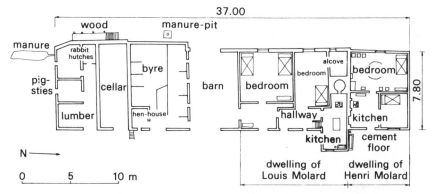

6 *Plan of a dwelling-house in Villevieux, Jura, in which two brothers each have a separate kitchen for their households, but farm in common.*

Although the demographic conditions favourable to the nuclear family prevailed all over France just as they did in England, it appears that in southern France the structure of households was very different (from a nuclear structure). In Limousin, in Périgord, in Rouergue, in Provence, in the area of Nice, and in Corsica, apparently in most of the central and southern regions of the kingdom, there existed a sufficiently significant proportion of families with complex structures to make one question the normalcy of the conjugal famly.[29]

Having established that this variety in the kinds and structures of households exists, it is not our intention here to add further arguments to the debate, but, rather, to analyse the factors of this variability, and their consequences at the level of matrimonial relations. How is the work organized when there are several men and several women? Who is in charge? Who carries the honour of the family and the house? etc.

[28] Peter Laslett and Richard Wall, *Household and family in past time.*
[29] Jean-Louis Flandrin, *Familles, parenté, maison, sexualité dans l'ancienne société*, p. 74.

Let us put demographic factors to one side. One can postulate that the age of the head of the household, that of his wife, the difference in age between them, and the wife's age at the date of the birth of their children must condition, in part, the type of relationships established in the household. Our data are still too thin to make it possible to build up a coherent picture, but it is clear that the problem of the respective ages of the married couple was a deep preoccupation in peasant mentality, and several proverbs deal with the subject. If they mention age differences, it is in terms which better ensure male control of the household: *Fille de 15 ans, homme de 30* (Girl of 15, man of 30) (Provence). Proverbs reject the marriage of couples who are ill-matched in age, with a young man marrying an older woman:

> *Mariage de jeune homme avec jeune fille est de Dieu, mariage de jeune homme avec vieille femme est de rien, mariage de vieillard avec jeune fille est de diable*
> The marriage of a young man to a young girl is from God, the marriage between a young man and an old woman is nothing at all, the marriage between an old man and a young girl is from the devil (Pays Basque)

> *Jeune gars, vieille guenon, mariage du démon*
> Young lad, old hag, devil's union (Normandy)

An ill-assorted marriage, made by the devil, in which the woman might perhaps be the devil herself. Holding the reins of the household, and the more so because the young man has married the old woman for her farm, her cows and her money, the woman can lord it over her husband, and reverses the natural order of things.

On the other hand, proverbs speaking of couples in which the husband is the older – even if much older – praise the fertility of the union:

> *Femme jeune et homme vieux, enfants en série*
> Young woman and old man, children one after another (Gascony)

> *Jeune brebis et vieux bélier ont vite fait un troupeau*
> Young sheep and old ram have soon made a flock (Languedoc)

Let us, rather, look into the social or cultural factors which determine the variety of different types of household. And the first factor of all is time. A household is never a fixed unit and it changes over the years: its numerical status (its 'size') varies, the people who go to make it up change, its 'structure' goes through stages of 'simplicity' or 'complexity'. To make these ideas less abstract, we intend to follow several households through what sociologists call 'the cycle of family life'.[30] By studying the population censuses in a village of South Finistère, carried out every five years, the movement occurring within a household working the same farm over 25 years can be judged. Let us first of all look at a stable household.

It was in 1855 that Henri Le Berre, a farmer, married Marie Corcuff, who was older than him by two years and the widow of Isidore Le Bleis, by whom she had already had three children. One can see the new couple between 1856 and 1861 living with Marie Corcuff's parents. Then, from 1866 to 1906, the couple are alone on the farm. In 1866, the household is made up, above and beyond Henri and his wife, aged respectively 33 and 35 years, of the three children from Marie Corcuff's first marriage, aged 17, 15, and 14, and of the three children she has had by Henri, aged 10, 6, and 2. With them lives Marie's father, Jean Corcuff, a widower, and aged around 65 years. In 1872, Jean Corcuff, probably dead, is no longer there. Only the six children remain, with their parents. In 1876, the four youngest children are present, those from the first marriage having left the household (regional or distant emigration?). In 1881, there were present in the household, apart from the two youngest children, a daughter of the couple, Catherine Le Berre, who is married to Guillaume Tanneau, who has now become a member of the household. Five years later, the young couple have left their parents' house to set up independently, and they are replaced by another young household made up of Louise Le Berre, another daughter, and her husband, Corentin Marc, and their twin children Corentin and Marie, aged six months; but there still remain under the old parents' roof a bachelor son and two grand-daughters, Marie Bargain, 5, and Marie Tanneau, 3, the children of two daughters who have married and who live elsewhere. In 1886, nine related people cohabit: five adults, and four young children. Moreover, two servants complete the make-up of this household which can be seen to be, according to Laslett's classification, both 'complex' and 'extended'. In 1891, Henri le Berre and Marie Corcuff's houshold contracts: only Sébastien, still a bachelor at 31, remains with them. On the other hand, in 1896, apart from Sébastien, three other grandchildren are in their charge: the children of Corentin Marc and Louise Le Berre, who had left the village in 1896: Henri, 9, Yves,

[30] Jean Cuisenier and Martine Segalen (eds.), *Le cycle de la vie familiale dans les sociétés européennes.*

8, and Sébastien, 7. At this point the Le Berre grandparents employ three servants. In 1901, one can see the household made up in the same way, minus the servants, the children being old enough to replace the hired help.

Finally, Henri Le Berre and his wife are seen for the last time in 1906, aged 73 and 75. They are alone apart from Sébastien, probably having retired from their farm. Knowing as we do that the household lived its entire life in the same house, on the same farm, we can see that its history is a succession of complex phases, with phases of co-residence between generations – parents, married children, grandchildren – alternating with some simple phases.

In our modern household, once the children are grown up and launched into the outside world, the couple finds itself alone. Here,

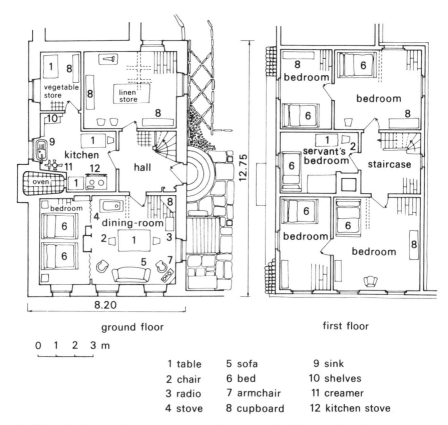

ground floor   first floor

0 1 2 3 m

1 table	5 sofa	9 sink
2 chair	6 bed	10 shelves
3 radio	7 armchair	11 creamer
4 stove	8 cupboard	12 kitchen stove

7 *Plan of a farm at Imbsheim, Lower Rhine: a well-off household with a separate dining-room, and where the bedrooms have been moved up to the first floor.*

there is nothing of the kind: granted, the children leave early to become servants on other farms, freeing the family from having their mouths to feed; but as Breton households are very fertile, births are staggered over several years, and the task of bringing up and educating the young children continues at the same time as the apprenticeship of the older ones.

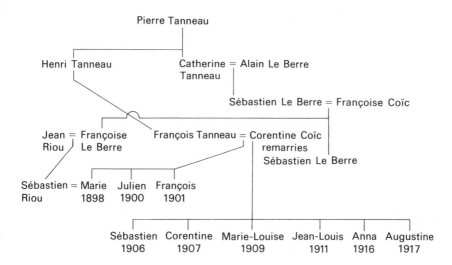

There are constantly young children in the house, since once the youngest have been brought up, the grandchildren, confided for a while to their grandparents' care, arrive to replace them. The task of bringing up and educating a child, which is traditionally a feminine occupation, lasts much longer than in our households today. For the young married couple, coresidence with the parents represents an interim period between the time of getting married and acquiring a farm of their own which they will work independently. For the parents, this young couple living with them constitutes a less onerous source of labour than employing servants. An economic arrangement between the two parties can, therefore, both provide a temporary income and enable the young people to build up their capital with a view to their future commitments (see contract, p. 22).

The confusion between house, household and farm is brought out by the constant number of active hands. In our example, the size of the farm demanded the labour of at least five men and three women. This labour was provided at some moments in the cycle by servants (when the children were young). It was subsequently ensured by adolescent

LIFE CYCLE OF THE COUPLE LE BERRE-CORCUFF

(= signifies married to)

1866
Henri Le Berre   =   Marie Corcuff
farmer, 33 years old   35 years old
Sébastien, 6, Marie, 10, Louise, 2, Le Berre; Isidore, 17, Jeanne, 15, Anne, 14, Le Bleis; Jean Corcuff, 65

1872
Henri Le Berre   =   Marie Corcuff
Sébastien, 12, Marie, 15, Catherine, 10, Louise, 8, Le Berre; Isidore, 23, Jeanne, 21, Anne, 19, Le Bleis

1876
Henri Le Berre   =   Marie Corcuff
Sébastien, 16, Marie, 20, Catherine, 14, Louise, 12, Le Berre

1881
Henri Le Berre   =   Marie Corcuff
Sébastien, 21, Louise, 16, Guillaume Tanneau, 27; Catherine Le Berre, 19; 1 servant

1886
Henri Le Berre   =   Marie Còrcuff
Sébastien, 26, Henri, 24, Corentin Marc, 29, Louise Le Berre, 21; Corentin and Marie Marc, 6 months; Marie Bargain, 5, and Marie Tanneau, 3 (granddaughters); 2 servants

1891
Henri Le Berre   =   Mari Corcuff
Sébastien, 31

1896
Henri Le Berre   =   Marie Corcuff
Sébastien, 36, Henri, 34, Yves, 8, Sébastien Marc, 7 (grandchildren); 3 servants

1901
Henri Le Berre   =   Marie Corcuff
Sébastien, 41, Henri, 16, Yves, 14, Sébastien Marc, 13 (grandchildren)

1906
Henri Le Berre   =   Marie Corcuff
Sébastien, 46

or married children living with their parents. Thus, Emile Guillaumin relates how, on the Bourbon farm where *La vie d'un simple* unfolds, 'Catherine having reached twelve years of age, it was her job to replace the servant which my mother had employed up till then. She left the flock to take care of jobs in the house and to work in the fields. I was seven: looking after the flock was entrusted to me.'[31] Elsewhere he explains how and why he had to replace his wife:

> The neighbour who usually helped me get in the corn had to be away on a day when rain was threatening. I got Victoire, who didn't mind at all, to come with me to help load the few stooks we had made the day before on to the cart. She got very hot, then began to shiver under the downpour which fell unexpectedly early: that night she coughed blood, and two days later she was dead . . . To cope with the domestic chores I had to engage an aged widow, who was very deaf, and had hardly any idea about dairying – so much so that I had to stay with her the first few times to help with making the butter and cheese.[32]

Everything is conducted as though the function of the house as residence is by far secondary to its function on the farm. A kinship group whose size and composition varies from year to year settles in a house whose capacity is highly flexible. The only constraint to be respected is the number of active people necessary to run the farm.

Nonetheless, the family cycle which we have just observed does not constitute a model for every type of household. On the contrary, in the same village and at the same date, we can see cycles which present quite a different profile.

Thus, in 1861, the tailor Pierre Le Garrec sets up house at 27 years old in the village where he was born, with his wife Thumette Le Drezen, who is 24 years old, and their young son François, aged 2. From 1861 to 1881, every five years, the family has increased by one or two children, and, in 1881, one can find in this 'simple' household six children aged 17, 16, 13, 10, 5, and 1 years old, the oldest, aged 22, having left home. In 1891, there are still four children aged 25, 22, 15 and 11, the three older children being employed on neighbouring farms as day labourers. In 1896, Jean, 28, and Michel, 27, still live with their parents, as well as their granddaughter, called Thumette like her grandmother, who is 2 months old. In 1901, the last date on which one

[31] Emile Guillaumin, *La vie d'un simple. Mémoires d'un métayer*, p. 19.
[32] *ibid.*, p. 345.

can observe this household, Jean-Marie, 32, and Marie-Jeanne Souron, 29, with their daughter Thumette, aged 5, are living with their parents. In 1906, Pierre Le Garrec having died, the old Thumette Le Drezen, 72, shares the house with her son Jean-Marie and his wife. They are farmers.

LIFE CYCLE OF THE COUPLE LE GARREC–LE DREZEN

1861

| Pierre Le Garrec | = | Thumette Le Drezen |
| tailor, 27 years old | | 24 years old |

François, 2

1866

| Pierre Le Garrec | = | Thumette Le Drezen |

François, 7, Pierre, 1, Thumette

1872

| Pierre Le Garrec | = | Thumette Le Drezen |

François, 13, Thumette, 10, Pierre, 7, Jean-Marie, 4, Anne-Marie, 1

1876

| Pierre Le Garrec | = | Thumette Le Drezen |

François, 17, Thumette, 14, Pierre, 11, Jean-Marie, 8, Anne-Marie, 7, Marie-Josèphe, 4

1881

| Pierre Le Garrec | = | Thumette Le Drezen |

Thumette, 17, Pierre, 16, Jean-Marie, 13, Anne-Marie, 10, Marie-Josèphe, 5, Michel, 1

1886

| Pierre Le Garrec | = | Thumette Le Drezen |

Jean, 17, Marie-Josèphe, 10, Michel, 6

1891

| Pierre Le Garrec | = | Thumette Le Drezen |

Pierre, 25, Jean-Marie, 22, Marie-Josèphe, 15, Michel, 11

1896

| Pierre Le Garrec | = | Thumette Le Drezen |

Jean-Marie, 28, Michel, 17, Thumette, 2 months (granddaughter)

1901

Pierre Le Garrec	=	Thumette Le Drezen
Jean-Marie	=	Marie-Jeanne Souron
32 years old		29 years old

Thumette, 5

The Le Berre household was that of a well-off farmer, within the social hierarchy of the village. Pierre Le Garrec belonged to the community of poor craftsmen. Although the parents' house remained for a long time a shelter for the children, it did not provide a place of work, since the children went out to work as day labourers on various farms.

The phases of coresidence between older and younger generations were also shorter, since the household could not provide work for adolescent or adult children. There was no inheritance to hand on: a small field, perhaps, but a tailor's work is all in his finger-tips, and he has only his skill to hand down. At the death of the head of the household, the widow, left without resources, must be taken in by the household of her son.

The household thus appears to be a temporary fluctuating grouping of kin, working together on a farm and sometimes helped by wage labour, though of a quasi-familial status. Place of residence, work and family are all closely linked together in this situation. The dimension of time modifies these relationships, acting on the composition of the structure of the household which expands or contracts according to the times and demographic contingencies.

Time is also a disturbing element in the household, with occasionally unforseeable effects. There might, for example, be a demographic accident in the form of a husband with a long-term illness, on whose work one can no longer depend. At a time when the division between success and poverty was a very narrow one, fluctuating according to bad harvests, or epidemics, such a young household would 'miss' its economic growth, and would find itself as poor at seventy as it had been at twenty. Most often, it is death which breaks the cycle, depriving the head of the household of his wife and constraining him to remarry; he then confides management of the household to his young wife.

Remarriage was the rule in rural society and would have remained so if the young girls had not fled to the towns. It was especially the rule for the men rather than for the women, except for those women who, while still young, found themselves in charge of a farm which they could not run without a man. Rich widows remarry quickly, declare the proverbs:

Veuve dorée tôt consolée
Widow with gold soon consoled (Gascony)

Jamais de veuve sans conseil, ni de samedi sans soleil
Never a widow without friendly advice, nor a Saturday without sun
(Catalonia)

These new alliances created by remarriage set up between man and wife a different kind of relationship from that prevailing in a first marriage. The men understand that a wife is indispensable to them to look after the farm and to care for the children who have been left without a mother; they remarry more quickly than widows, demographic studies show, but are also ready to allow their new wives greater autonomy:[33]

La première épousée est la servante, la seconde la maîtresse
The first wife is servant, the second mistress (Bordelais)

La première a les pleurs, la seconde les fleurs
To the first the tears, to the second the flowers (Provence)

La première épouse, bergère, la seconde, dame
The first wife, shepherdess, the second, lady (Catalonia)

The new household, occasionally made up of two widowed people with children to look after, is peopled with half-brothers and -sisters joined in a network of genealogical relationships, particularly where those families respect the rule of endogamy and 'reforge' the alliance. Here is an example, in the same village, of the complex family relationships which were often created by these remarriages.

Corentine Coïc married François Tanneau, the son of a landowner, in 1890; there were three children of the union, Marie, Julien and François. François, the father, died in 1903, and Corentine, unable to manage the substantial farm on her own, remarried a distant cousin of her husband's. Six children were born of this new union, whose relations by blood conveyed on them the status of cousins and half-brothers. These relationships can be schematized as shown on p. 61.

Remarriages created particular difficulties for children of different unions, and step-parents and step-children. The tale of Cinderella is a reminder of the antagonism that can be felt in such relationships:

[33] M. Monnier has noted that the ritual struggle at the church at the moment of putting on the ring took place most often on occasions of remarriage: 'it was particularly widows who offered interested onlookers the spectacle of such struggles'. ('Vestiges d'antiquité observés dans le Jurassien', p. 359).

competition between the children for the inheritance, and the strategies employed by father or mother in question to benefit their own children. Remarriages within close family links (within the degrees not forbidden by the Church) sought specifically to lessen this antagonism arising from remarriage, by not introducing a stranger into the household.

Jamais de l'autan un bon abri, ni du deuxième mari de ta mère (payrastre) un bon ami
Never a sound shelter from the stormy wind, nor a good friend to your mother's second husband (Languedoc)

In the eventuality of widowhood and remarriage, matrimonial relations were particularized by this new relationship. But kinship vocabulary in French is fairly thin, since it cannot distinguish terms which deal with this new alliance, which has arisen from the marriage. The *belle-mère* can equally be the wife of the father as the mother of the

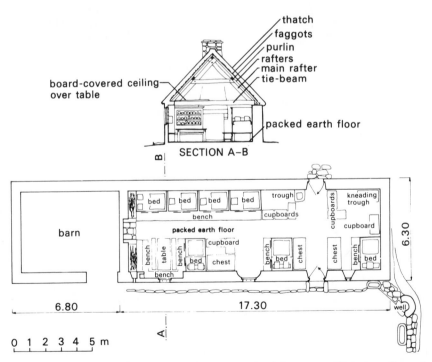

8 *Plan and section of a dwelling-house in Ploudalmezeau, Finistère. Several generations, numerous children, and the servants all share the same area.*

husband; the *belle-fille* the daughter of the husband and the wife of the son. The terms *bru* and *gendre* (daughter-in-law and son-in-law), deriving from another source, have been included in our vocabulary without eliminating others. The semantic confusion is significant; all marriage relationships are seen in terms of antagonism:

> *Amour de gendre, soleil d'hiver*
> Son-in-law's love, winter sunshine (Provence)
>
> *Amour de bru, amour de gendre, c'est une lessive dépourvue de cendre*
> A daughter-in-law's love, the love of a son-in-law are like washing without cinders (Catalonia)
>
> *Qui prend bru ou gendre se met dehors*
> To take daughter-in-law or son-in-law is to put yourself out in the cold (Limousin)
>
> *Tout gendre et toute bru sont gens étrangers*
> All sons-in-law, and daughters-in-law, are strangers (Franche-Comté)
>
> *La mieux mariée est celle qui n'a ni belle-mère, ni belle-soeur*
> She has married best who has neither mother-in-law nor sister-in-law (Catalonia)
>
> *La belle-mère est bonne, mais meilleure quand la terre la recouvre*
> A mother-in-law is fine, especially when she's underground (Catalonia)

Emotional relationships are characterized by coldness: the parents know that the course of life condemns them to be excluded from their own household when they can no longer manage the farm, but the most violent antagonism is reserved for relationships between women, and the step-mother may detest her step-daughter all the more in that she replaces her married daughter, whom she misses.

> *A la fille, pain et chaise, à la bru, croûton et dehors*
> For the daughter, bread and a chair, for the daughter-in-law, a crust and the cold outdoors (Catalonia),

a proverb which echoes the Mâconnais expression: *couper le pain en belle-mère* (slicing the bread like a step-mother), meaning parsimoniously.[34]

In Catalonia, the rule of the inheritance of goods singled out which of all the children should be the inheritor. The wife was thus a stranger

---

[34] Suzanne Tardieu, *La vie domestique dans le Mâconnais rural pré-industriel*, p. 377.

in the house of her mother-in-law. Cohabitation was an acute source of conflict, the area of female activity being, to a great extent, confined to the house; that is, to the territory of the communal room. The men, often father and son, even in the case of father and son-in-law, found more extensive territories, less open to conflict, working in the fields. Marriage rituals ensured only a symbolic transfer of authority from one generation to the next, and in reality the old woman often wished to remain mistress of the household. The proverbs must here be a faithful reflection of female quarrels, and if popular engravings picture the married couple fighting with domestic implements, one wonders whether there are not hidden in such representations other, female battles around the cooking-pot:

Quand il y a deux femmes à la maison, il y en a une de trop
When there are two women in the house, there is one too many (Anjou, Dauphiné, Bordelais, Savoy)

Deux pots dénotent une fête, maix deux femmes grande tempête
Two mugs mean a party, but two women stormy weather (Provence)

Deux femmes au logis, deux chats pour un raton, deux chiens pour un os, fais-les accorder si tu peux
Two women in the house, two cats and one rat, two dogs and one bone, make them agree if you can (Provence)

Which of the two women will impose her authority, and how will she be regarded by the menfolk? Each household must settle its own spheres of influence. Some situations settled themselves. For instance, temporary emigration, wheter seasonal or definitive, could deprive the household of one part of its masculine labour force.

When the husband, a migrant shepherd, went and got a job as a pit-sawyer, or travelled to Paris to seek temporary employment during the winter, it was up to the women to take over. When the First World War broke out, the women were at their posts.

Thus there does not seem to be any such thing as a 'model household' which can be applied to the whole of France, but a variety of systems and attitudes which depend on types of techno-economic organization and specific cultural factors. Amongst these must be counted particular systems of inheritance. There is, for instance, the distinct example of the Pays Basque, in which predominance is accorded the house, which is seen as having an existence in its own right, identified with that of lineage. One of the children is designated to inherit it and everything that goes with it – farm, name, family honour, etc. A specific matrimonial strategy is imposed, whereas other children, excluded from the inheritance, must marry an 'heir' or 'heiress', or emigrate. If the heir chosen is a girl – a possibility allowed in the system – she must marry a younger son, and it is she who receives the ownership and management of the property.

> When a girl is the oldest, she will inherit, and she will become the mistress of the house and of the family holdings. She will be called *Etcheko anderia*, the lady, the mistress of the house. The husband she takes to help cultivate the farm will occupy an intermediate status between master and farm servant: there is, incidentally, no proper word in Basque to express the husband's relation to his wife. The heiress must seek in the young man she intends to marry all the qualities of a good labourer. She needs to ensure the services of a hard worker because it is to her husband that she will entrust the care of her fields and the management of her livestock and, by preference, she will put her trust in some man who has, as farm-servant to some local large landowner, acquired practical experience in agriculture.[35]

The underlying ideological principle of this system is the maintenance and transmission of the house whose name is substituted for the patronymic of its inhabitants. 'For each house there is a corresponding tomb in the crypt of the church . . . When a new house is built it will be erected within the family enclosure.'[36]

The farm-dwelling constitutes the fundamental determinant of the system. For the young man, a 'son-in-law's marriage' is a way of ascending the social scale, but at the cost of losing his own lineage, and even his own name. Elsewhere, this type of union is condemned in facetious rituals. In Savoy, Van Gennep notes the insulting expressions 'son-in-law's marriage, marriage of a goat', 'sheep', 'bull', 'heifer', etc., and in all the regions where they attribute the name of a horned beast, a common farce consists in offering him 'water in a bucket, or hay, or straw.'[37] On the other hand, there is no such system in Lower Brittany. There, when a girl inherits a farm, which is far from constituting such a close-knit unit of house, name and lineage as in the Pays Basque, she hands over its management to her husband.

[35] Mme d'Abbadie d'Arrast, *Causeries sur le pays basque, la femme et l'enfant*, pp. 6, 20–21.

[36] Anne Zink, *Azereix, la vie d'une communauté rurale à la fin du XVIIIᵉ siècle*, pp. 234–5.

[37] Arnold Van Gennep, *Manuel du folklore français*, vol. I. 2, pp. 499–500.

These different types of household appear to be conditioned by the different cultural attitudes adopted towards the possibility of female responsibility for a farm-dwelling. In the Basque case this possibility is allowed, in the other it is not. The 'son-in-law's marriage' depends nonetheless on the latent need in any rural society to help out fathers who have daughters but no sons. What few rural societies can tolerate, however, is an unequal marriage, uniting the farm labourer and the farmer's daughter:

> *Qui se marie par intérêt, de sa femme est le valet*
> The man who marries for money, is his wife's servant (Catalonia)
>
> *Celui qui épouse une femme pour sa dot, mange un double décalitre de sel pour se désaltérer*
> The man who marries his wife for her dowry, is eating two bushels of salt to quench his thirst (Provence)

Let young men seeking to climb the social ladder through marriage beware! While this system worked well for families of craftsmen in which the apprentice became the master's son-in-law, the peasant family repudiates a young man who has nothing to bring to the marriage. As well as his lack of capital (if one can use such an anachronistic term), there is the dominance which the wife might have over the young upstart to be feared.

What do the subtleties of traditional practices tell us about the management of the farm when there are two couples which cohabit? Between father and son, who is it that is entitled to be the *patron* or 'master', and which of the two women is the *patronne*, or 'mistress'? These customs vary widely from one region of France to another, and even within the same region. Thus, in the north Bigouden region, around Plozévet,

> Custom has it that the oldest son or the oldest of the sons-in-law takes over the management of the farm on his marriage. The parents occasionally (but not always) move to a nearby house; their material future is guaranteed by a reserve payment contracted to them from the farm revenues, but they continue to participate in the running of the farm as simple labourers. This type of swift transfer of authority from one generation to the next neutralizes tensions, avoiding a sense of frustration among the young, and of decline among the old.[38]

[38] André Burguière, *Bretons de Plozévet*, p. 80.

The family cycle tends to be a short one, whereas 25 kilometres away, in the households whose family cycles we have described, we can see, on the other hand, the older couple maintaining its farm and its authority right up until the last child is married.[39] An old widow running a farm with her eldest son declares herself to be the 'head of the household' to the census officer; and she is so, in fact, as much with regard to the household as to the outside world: it is she who will be seen going to markets and fairs, visiting the lawyer, or in the office of the mayor's secretary.

In the Basque-type system, cohabitation between generations is institutionalized by custom, as well as by the authority of the father, who holds the name, the dwelling, the farm, and whose power is all the more substantial in that it is he who decides which of the children will succeed him.

In the nineteenth-century, the *Code Civil* had not yet come to introduce uniform methods of handing down property in peasant families, in which ancient traditional practices continued to regulate the succession of generations on the farm.

The size and structure of the household were also profoundly influenced by the diversity of production systems, the socio-economic organization of labour. A direct link between maritime and pastoral activity and type of household cannot be firmly established: the ways of thinking, the way in which the family is represented in society remain factors relatively independent of economic considerations. There are, nonetheless, a certain number of links which contribute towards one aspect of this variety of households which we are seeking to explain.

The economy of the farm is primarily a function of the family cycle. Over several generations, on fairly small farms, periods of investment and technical and economic improvements have corresponded with periods during which the adolescent members of the family could provide effective help for their parents. After such a time of plenty, there is always the difficult question of succession, of dowries, and of the eventual division of goods. Secondly, one might ask whether dwelling, household and farm are entirely overlapping notions in traditional society. We can probably say that they are, if 'farm' is not restricted to mean simply a self-supporting unit. In the eighteenth century, the equation was more integrated than in the nineteenth,

[39] Martine Segalen, 'Cycle de la vie familiale et transmission des biens; analyse d'un cas'.

during which time, despite the existence of a majority of farms whose production was intended for home consumption, there were also a growing number of farms producing for the market, such as the great cereal-growing farms of northern France, in Picardy and Artois. The 'sites of rural architecture' have the merit of showing us, at one particular instant, the variety of situations prevailing at the same date, and the coexistence of these very different types of household. From the modest labourer's dwelling to the great cereal farmer's domain, there were a whole range of situations, which could be observed, from one region to another, and even within the same region – sometimes within the same village. How do the system of economic production and the types of household appear to be linked?

M and Mme B . . . and their five children living in the Gironde, at Saint-Étienne-de-Lisse,[40] were *prix faiteur,* tied workers – that is, servants receiving a contract sum which included housing, heating, a certain amount to drink, a small garden and a sum of money in return for looking after about three hectares of vineyard. The household is a unit living and working together, but not a unit in the framework of the economic and social advancement of the house and its inhabitants. The children must seek housing and wages elsewhere. The rural household here is nothing but a precarious framework for economic survival.

The system of sharecropping, in which the farmer owns nothing – not even his materials (unlike the farmer who owns his tools of production) – and shares half the fruit of any harvest with the owner, hardly constitutes a favourable family and economic framework for a strategy of family advancement.

At Lavit, in the Tarn-et-Garonne, M and Mme L . . . and their two children farmed, with the help of Mme L.'s father, a sharecropping holding of 23 hectares given over to crops and livestock.[41] At Vieux, in the Tarn, M and Mme D . . . and their three children, helped by a servant, worked a sharecropping holding of 30 hectares of vines and cereals.[42]

The tenant farmer benefited from quite a different juridical system. As the owner of the production tools, he settled his accounts once a year (most often Michaelmas) in cash or in kind. Sometimes, as in the case of a smallholding worked by its owner, the farmer would combine the two systems of tenancy and direct ownership in order to extend his farm.

[40] EAR, no. 9.   [41] EAR, no. 24.   [42] EAR, no. 4.

The borderline between the status of tenant and owner-farmer was sometimes a narrow one in systems of smallholdings. Unlike the day labourers, and the sharecroppers, tenant farmers and/or owner-farmers' households could be the bearers of a family ideology, and an economic strategy. Farm leases, like property itself, could be transmitted from one generation to another, with the households which inherited them having the responsibility of handing on the patrimony, either increased or intact: in 1945 some of these farms were extremely small. For instance, in the Lower Rhine, at Treuchtersheim, M and Mme H . . . and their three children (under ten years old), with the parents of Mme H . . . worked a mixed farm of 17 hectares, with the help of two servants.[43] At Plédran, in the Côtes-du-Nord, it was still possible to find agricultural holdings of 2 hectares and two cows worked by a farming couple, their daughter and her husband, and their two grandchildren,[44] and, at Saint-Véran, in the Hautes-Alpes, a household made up of father, mother and seven children lived in the highest village in Europe on a holding of 5 hectares, with 3 cows and 10 sheep, in a house built in 1772, and hardly changed since.[45]

In contrast to these households, which were reduced to self-sufficiency on land which might or might not belong to them, some very large farms are occasionally to be found in the same regions. Thus, at Harcanville, in Caux, a traditional *cour masure*, with its scattered buildings, was made up of 66 hectares devoted to mixed farming (15 milk cows and 43 stock) – 48 hectares of grazing, and 18 of crops. It was worked by a couple and their children and a range of workers composed of two carters, two cowmen, two yardmen and a domestic servant. Hoeing and raising the beet was paid for as task-work. For harvest and threshing, a supplementary labour force of two women and a man was needed temporarily.[46] At Riche, in the Moselle, a mixed farm of 147 hectares, with 37 cows and 500 hens, was worked by a farming couple helped by their four children, six living-in servants and 13 seasonal workers.[47] In the Eure, at Gouville, 112 hectares were worked by the owners, with their children, a domestic servant and five permanent agricultural labourers.[48]

In our description of the diversity of households, let us note that the rural world still includes a number of craftsmen comparable, in their poverty and in the structure of their households, to day labourers. Their production made up part of an economic activity which was not

[43] EAR, no. 19.　　　[44] EAR, no. 11.　　　[45] EAR, no. 5.

[46] EAR, no. 22.　　　[47] EAR, no. 22.　　　[48] EAR, no. 15.

self-sufficient, and which was directly dependent on the vicissitudes of the market economy. Thus the nineteenth century saw the development in Normandy, on the banks of the Seine, of a weaving trade which had important links with the cotton imports at Le Havre, The *cacheux* wove at home cotton brought to them by a trader, who then bought the piece back again once it had been made up. There was a small garden for growing vegetables for domestic consumption, and one or two cows for milk. In summer the weaver would leave his trade and become employed as an agricultural labourer during the periods of intensive activity requiring an extensive labour force.

In the weaver's household, the craft performed involved the entire family, a family often smaller in size than that of the agricultural worker. Two trades worked together in the 'shop', in the weavers' households of the cloth regions of Elbeuf and Louviers, in which the men wove linen and the women lighter fabrics. The children, from an early age, were involved in winding the yarn. This household was based not on an association of land, but on an association of two weaving trades.

Finally, it seems from this description that the manner of ownership is predominant when explaining the variety of peasant households. Direct ownership weaves a series of emotional ties between household and dwelling: the aim is to keep it or extend it; its possession reinforces and justifies family strategies which, in their turn, tighten the ties between the family and the land they work; it imposes particular responsibilities in maintaining its status and honour. Thus one can explain that the apogee of a particular type of rural situation can be located during the nineteenth century and at the beginning of the twentieth century, when accession to property became first an ideal and then a reality.

In the second place, it is necessary to attribute due importance to the organization of work: we can see types of activity which make very different demands at the level of seasonal activity. Farms could employ servants throughout the year, or they could have recourse to a communal form of labour, which was either informal, relying on neighbourly mutual help, or else institutionalized in the form of a common shepherd, or of cooperative production.

The variety of forms of household depends on the times, on traditional systems and on the organization of production. No typology which can relate all these factors is possible at the present stage of our knowledge. Nonetheless, it is possible to posit the hypothesis that

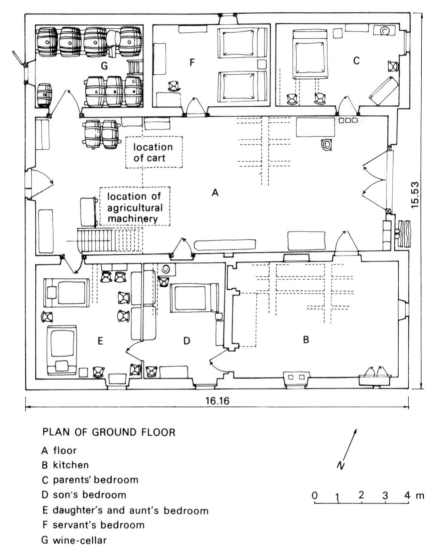

PLAN OF GROUND FLOOR

A floor
B kitchen
C parents' bedroom
D son's bedroom
E daughter's and aunt's bedroom
F servant's bedroom
G wine-cellar

9 *Plan of the ground floor at Heugas, Landes: here the generations sleep separately.*

relationships within the household would be relatively different: a couple alone (day labourers) as against a household (of tenants or owner-farmers) crammed with elders, with married or bachelor brothers and sisters, with young children everywhere, and servants, permanent or seasonal, to organize. Not only does the distribution of tasks and roles in a household depend on such variables, but equally the household's relationship with the village community depends on them.

The owner of a large farm does not have the same status as an agricultural day labourer on the social scale in a rigidly socially hierarchized village, whatever the cultural integration of all its members. The entire family life depends on this status. The man going to market to sell his stock is surrounded with prestige. His wife has the privilege of being 'mistress' of an important farm.

The study of nineteenth-century family life, even if confined to households all living under the same roof, still comprises a whole range of variations, from the wealthy couple of Norman farmers one can picture surrounded by domestics and farm servants, the wife with her head-dress and her Rouen cross made of rhinestones, to the labourers of Millet's 'socialist' paintings, in clogs, and dropping with fatigue. This is not to deny a certain unity of rural family culture. On the contrary, the following chapter is aimed at demonstrating the main spheres of activities and the relationships between inhabitants of the dwelling.

But we are far from a single model of family systems for the same region. Do cultural oppositions carry more weight than techno-economic factors? If there is no equivalent in the South to the master and mistress of the large livestock farms of Caux, could this not be simply because there are no large livestock farms in the South? And the question might be posed whether, despite the cultural distance, the households of small Norman tenant-farmers are not closer to the sharecroppers of the Tarn than to the large Norman farm.

3

The Household at Work

The solidarity of house–household–farm gives rise to a family-based organization of labour which plays an important role in kinship relations: The extended family, cousins, uncles and aunts, are called upon in times of family crisis such as childbirth or sickness, and their help may also be asked for during threshing-time or harvest, on a reciprocal basis. But the daily life of labour rests most often on the shoulders of the man and his wife, the parents of one of them, with the help of the children and sometimes of servants. The narrower family unit for the daily work which closely identifies the household and the farm; the more extended family grouping for important social occasions: accession to political power, the handing-on of goods, and marriage strategies.

The organization of labour also places the man and his wife within wider solidarities which merge with or complete the kinship network. The men or women meet and help each other on specific occasions, so that a family organization of labour, often based on a principle of separation of the sexes within the house, is reinforced by the solidarity and the sociability of men and women in a way that emphasizes their disunity.

Before making a detailed examination of the tasks carried out on the farm, it is important to ask whether the destination of production had any significance for the organization of labour.

The household had to produce in order to live, and often only lived in order to produce, production guaranteeing the perpetuation of the human grouping. There was some interaction between the two functions, though living often came closer to surviving in the poorer households. Was the organization of work affected by whether production was for home consumption or for an external market? It seems that, more often that not, farms producing for the second category left the organization of the market to specialized intermediaries. The example of Norman butter from Isigny is well-known. The commercial vocation of the region was evident as early as the twelfth century; the inhabitants benefited from the right of *franc salé*, which gave them salt tax-free, making possible the long-term conservation of butter.[1] Specialized merchants took butter thus preserved to the markets of the capital. From 1850 onwards, in South Finistère, the so-called Bigouden region specialized in growing new potatoes for export to England, but the growers did not have any hand in the trade, which was organized by the bourgeoisie in the towns. In the same way, the raising of livestock was aimed at markets in which the producer-farmer was involved at the first stage of the commercial circuit, but without controlling the subsequent phases. Thus, production for commercial sale has little effect on the organization of labour within the household, since the commercial activity is undertaken by a particular social category of professionally organized merchants. Today, on the other hand, new organizations and structures of production have broken up relations between members of the farm, and have created a crisis in certain agricultural families.

Having settled the question of the independence of the family organization of work according to type of production, it is now possible to enquire into the structure of its organization in traditional society. Folklorists studying this rural world which is at once familiar and remote, and historians of attitudes and behaviour – usually more interested in the working-class family than in the rural family, whose specific nature they overlook – have settled the question between them. As far as they are both concerned, it is an established fact that the man works in the fields, the woman in the house, the man produces and the woman takes on the non-productive domestic tasks.

An analysis of the distribution of tasks has not been systematically carried out, and researchers have been more interested in a technological study of work rather than in the people actually doing it, and the articulation of these different tasks. It is even possible that certain categories of analysis have been misleadingly open. Is the concept of domestic life, separate from the life of production, a meaningful

[1] Armond Frémont, *L'élevage en basse Normandie, étude géographique*, p. 64.

concept in terms of the peasant household? Does it not lead to an artificial separation of operations which merge with each other in the cycles of work on the farm?

Let us listen to two folklorists observing a peasant couple at work. One can already note in these sensitive observations some differences from the current stereotype.

> Tasks within the farm are reserved to women. They take care of the stock. In order to get feed for the animals, they go out in the fields, gathering huge bundles which they carry balanced on their heads. They keep the fire going under the pot where the soup is cooking. They look after the farmyard, they force-feed the geese which are being fattened. The sharecroppers' wives take the sheep and turkeys out to graze on the stubble. They present the calf to its mother to suckle. They milk the cows and make butter and cheese. If necessary, they put hay in the mangers for the cattle and horse. In the right season, they hunt in the woods for mushrooms. They hoe and till with a strong right arm, then winnow the corn, and thresh; they tie up the vines and gather in the crop.
>
> In the winter, the women dress the pig, salting it or storing it in fat. They preserve hams and stuff sausages with pepper for the meals to be taken in the summer on the sweet meadow grass under the peach-trees, to the sound of grasshoppers. They preserve the fattened geese in their yellow fat; the poorest of households will keep a couple by to season their soup. Slightly rancid portions of goose would be served up for meals on feast days, and on important occasions there would be the famous *pâté de foie truffé*. Finally the mistresses of the houses prepare *galantines* of turkey and chicken, with truffles in, obviously. They maintain the time-honoured fame of Périgord cooking.
>
> The men do the heavy jobs: they load the carts with manure and spread it, they do the carting, the mowing, dress the vines, carry on their shoulders the panniers full of grapes; it is they who tread the grapes, they who work the land. Rising before dawn, they gaze at the sky for signs of coming weather.[2]

From this slightly confused description, tinged with romantic idealization (charming nature: sweet meadow-grass, singing grasshoppers, etc), and put together by a *gourmand*, there appears to be a contradiction between what is said and what is done. At the beginning, the author asserts that work within the farm is reserved to women,

---

[2] Georges Rocal, *Le vieux Périgord*, pp. 161–3.

yet shows the same women running over the field and vineyard. The men have the 'heavy' jobs, yet the women wield agricultural implements 'with a strong right hand'. Finally, force-feeding the geese is described as a domestic task, while it is, in fact, an important product of the farm.

Let us listen to another folklorist, who compiled an analysis of tasks and roles within the household in a rather more significant manner:

> Sunrise is the eternal clock presiding over this activity (of the household). The moment it becomes light, life begins. The men go and feed the stock and bed them down, then see to the first milking. Meanwhile, the women light the fire and prepare the meal. It is they who go to the village pump if there is no well or spring at the house, which is often enough; they return again to fetch more water at dusk.
>
> On the farmstead, the father is the head. He is in charge of looking after the interests of the household; he tells the servants and day labourers what to do; he has responsibility for the stock; he directs the major agricultural undertakings, and decides what should be grown. If he is on his own, he also has responsibility for the garden, for wood supplies, for repairs, etc. The wife is in charge of the upkeep within the house, of the kitchen, of washing the linen, and its care, making bread, milk products, provisioning, the farmyard, and also of the education of the children until they are old enough to help her, if they are girls, or to aid their father, if they are boys.[3]

From this text one can see the intermeshing of a number of tasks carried out on the farm, which forms a whole, dwelling and farm being most often indistinguishable. The house, the byres, the barn, and the cart-shed are emphatically associated with the fields, whether or not they stand nearby, just as the animals are associated with the men. There is no distinction in kind drawn between cultivation and cooking. Preparing a meal, or giving the pigs their swill, all come under the household; men, women, children, servants and animals are all equal beneficiaries of this work. Thus, work in the kitchen should no more be considered part of a strictly defined category of housework than tilling the soil should be excluded from the category of 'production' insofar as it is an activity of preparing the soil. The preparation of a meal is an important task on the family farm, and the making of cheeses and force-feeding of the geese can be seen as parallel to the

---

[3] Ulysse Rouchon, *La vie paysanne dans la Haute-Loire*, vol. III, pp. 25–6.

grain production which is the source of revenue. Not only should our analytical categories be revised, but the classification of male–female work should be re-examined in the light of a greater number of concrete instances.

The two principles on which the organization of family labour is based are the division of tasks and complementarity in certain undertakings. Despite their apparent contradiction, they fit together, but in different ways according to different regions. It is perhaps this diversity in the way these two principles are fitted together which explains the variations observed between these types of household.

Certain kinds of work are always reserved for women, others are carried out, depending on the region, by either men or women, while a third category, of predominantly male tasks, intermittently or regularly calls upon a female labour force.

Some examples drawn from particularly detailed researches into the rural habitat show the constant intermingling of the activities of men and women. In 1945, on a sharecropping farm in the Tarn-et-Garonne, Saint-Projet, worked by a young couple with two children, the 23-hectare farm was given over to stock-raising and mixed farming.[4]

Work in the fields was shared between the sharecropper and the owner, who used his tractor to cultivate the soil, to harrow, and to pull the reaper and binder. The master of the house was particularly associated with looking after the animals; he cleaned and fed the stock before he had a meal himself. The mistress of the house gave the house a quick clean first thing; she prepared food for the family, and swill for the pigs, which was cooked on the same stove before or after the men's meal; she looked after the hens, which she fed once or twice a day on grain and vegetable marrows. In November and December, force-feeding the geese was her concern. Her three geese were force-fed for six weeks, twice a day, for 20 minutes at a time. The sale of farmyard produce, the fruits of specifically female labour, covered the running costs of the house. On a farm of comparable size, in the Orne, at Tinchebray,[5] the organization of work was quite different. On this 22-hectare farm, mostly given over to grazing, with 15 milk-cows and ten calves, lived and worked a farming couple with their three daughters, helped by a servant.

The woman, with her daughters' help, performed the main domestic duties, since it was they who cared for and fed the stock, milked the

4 EAR, no. 35.
5 EAR, no. 4.

cows twice a day, made the butter and went once a week to sell it at Tinchebray market, as well as vegetables and fruit. The man looked after the meadows, which required much less attention than the fields in regions of intensive culture. From the Tarn-et-Garonne to Normandy, work was organized differently, the care of the stock being in the one place the concern of the man, in the other a woman's work. Another example, that of a smallholding of 6 hectares in the Vaucluse,[6] worked by the owner as a mixed farm: wheat, barley, hay, alfalfa, grapes, beans, and potatoes, which went for consumption, either animal or human, and the production of tomatoes, melons, millet, vines (stool) for sale. The father, mother, son and two daughters worked on the stools for several days during the winter. The man looked after the vines and maintained them, and worked in the fields. The wife worked in the fields to gather the tomatoes and melons. In the Aube,[7] on a large farm worked by the owner, which was made up of 80 hectares belonging to the farm, with an additional 34 hectares of rented land, on which were kept 77 head of cattle, the owner, helped by three agricultural labourers, looked after the housing and feeding of the stock (distribution of forage and beet). The summer was given over to the harvesting of forage. Here there was no wife, but a niece in charge of cooking, housework, looking after the labourers' rooms, and their washing, the farmyard, the poultry, and the milking of two cows, for domestic consumption. The owner was above all a businessman, moving about a lot, buying underweight beasts in Nivernais and in Normandy and fattening them up to sell to the butcher. This example, which represents one possible extreme of the organization of family work, shows the most clear-cut division of tasks.

As far as grazing farms in Normandy are concerned, a geographer analysing the development of production in the Auge was struck by certain extreme cases.

> The wife in the Auge works, and she alone milks the cows, the husband not knowing how to milk. She makes the butter and cheese. She must look after the vessels in the dairy. She cares for the calves and the pigs. She picks dandelions for the rabbits. She oversees the farmyard. She helps with the hay-making and gives a hand in changing the litter for the stock. Every week she goes to market and while her husband talks to his cronies she sells the products of her poultry, of her garden, and occasionally some butter, cream and cheese.

[6] EAR, no. 20 (Piolenc).
[7] EAR (Briel-sur-Barse)

The author links this organization to the development of the cultivation of apple-trees.

> For the man has become gradually more and more detached from the demands of this world. Right up to the middle of the nineteenth century he was active and sober. Then came the great age of profits from cider and from the 'hard stuff'. He looked after that as well as dealing with the livestock. His whole mind was taken up with the contemplation of barrels and of rumps. Between the wars, just selling the apples was enough more or less to cover the costs of the farm, and a good harvest could ensure two to three years rent. Now there is a proverb from the pays d'Auge which says, 'sell an apple and you sell it once, mash it and you sell it twice, let it go ropey and sell it three times.' For half a century the apple was an essential product, frequently accounting for more than half the net product of the farm. As well as hay-making, the man was thus above all concerned with his cellars and his cider-press, with maintaining the still and with selling his product at market. In short, it was the man who looked after the main money-bringing crop, and left the woman to cope with the secondary concerns ... These secondary concerns, i.e. milk production, have now become the main product. The Auge peasant has not, for all that, changed his habits. The wife continues to bear the full load of the farm. The 'father' goes to market, chats with his cronies, trims his hedges when he remembers, and ritually makes his cider.[8]

In another region of Normandy, the Bocage, the organization accentuates the complementarity of man and wife in daily life in which spending on purchases for the farm – purchase of stock or maintenance of materials – and spending on members of the household was mixed together in the same accounts, or rather lack of accounts. 'No-one on the farm receives a wage. The man and his wife share the financial concerns following a simple rule: the wife spends current income on day-to-day expenses; the man keeps "large sums" for major undertakings ... Nobody accounts for his time. Every day, the mother fills the dishes. She renews the work-clothes when she has money in hand. The father might contribute something towards restocking the wardrobe at time of important family ceremonies.'[9]

The husband, a producer who fills the granary once a year, the wife a consumer who empties it every day? In the light of these few

---

[8] Armand Frémont, *op. cit.*, pp. 145–6.
[9] *ibid.*, p. 350.

examples, such a schema appears over-simplistic, and roles and tasks are occasionally reversed. By drawing up a catalogue of tasks on the farm, noting who carries out each job, we will gain a better understanding of the organization of work in the family.

ACTIVITIES RESERVED TO WOMEN

In the chronological succession of these daily acts, the first was to light the fire. The woman daily gathered her supply of wood, and, every morning she relit the fire under the cooking pot. A physical act, but an act charged with symbolism. The woman was the guardian of the hearth, with all that that could mean in protective or maleficent terms for the household (see chapter 4). Just as she is responsible for the fire, so also she is responsible for the water.

Woman Returning From the Well is a picture which Millet painted between 1855 and 1862. The way the woman is standing with arms stretched out by the weight of the water immediately gives some indication of the importance of water in the life of the family and on the farm. The painter wrote about this picture:

> I have tried to paint her so that she seemed neither a water-carrier nor a servant; that she had been to draw water for her household, water to use in cooking for her husband and children; that she did not appear to be carrying a weight which was either lighter or heavier than two full buckets; that through the kind of grimace which was almost forced from her by the weight pulling at her arms, and through the way the sunlight makes her half-shut her eyes, one can make out an air of rustic goodness on her features . . . I wanted . . . her to be accomplishing with simplicity and cheerfulness, without considering it a burden, an act which, with the other household duties, is a daily task and her life's habit.[10]

A task to be performed daily, and even several times a day. It is hard to imagine what a life without running water must have been like, and the important responsibility which this laid on the woman in looking after the precious liquid. Water is necessary to prepare and cook food for men and beasts; it provides drink for people and animals; it is used for washing and bathing. The size of the house and farm thus determines how much water will have to be fetched every day. In the

[10] Jean-François Millet, Catalogue of the exhibition of *Jean-François Millet*, p. 135.

nineteenth century, says Bougeâtre, speaking of Vexin and Mantois, provision of water always posed a serious problem. 'Gutters running along the roofs of the buildings collected the precious rainwater into cisterns, troughs, sluices, or barrels; but there it either stagnated, or was quickly used up, and then it was a question of turning to the well or to a pond.'[11] A number of farms visited between 1944 and 1946 did not have any water, and the description of the tasks which this entailed is as relevant to the nineteenth century as to the centuries before that.

In the Eure, at Vannecroq, Mme C . . . fetched water from a small pond dug near the entrance, called the *mare nette* (clear pond) or *marnette*, and protected from the sun by willows. In the Morbihan, at Thèse, water was fetched from the spring in buckets; in the Tarn-et-Garonne, in Lavit, water was still a problem of prime importance. There were two springs from which water had to be fetched in two buckets twice a day. In the Basses-Pyrénées, in Alcay, drinking water was fetched in buckets from the village well 50 metres away from the house. In the Corrèze, at Bugeat, the source of water was a 150 metres from the house and a 125 metres from the byres, which meant frequent, tiring trips, since the road was uphill.

In the Haute-Vienne, at Rochechouart, the farmer's wife went to fetch water from a stone well with a winch. The water was carried back in buckets hung from a wooden 'carrier', a sort of yoke which spread the weight over the shoulders. One bucket stood permanently on the draining-board by the sink; drinking water was taken out with the help of a ladle, a sort of large spoon made of wood or metal with a hollow handle. The other bucket stood on its own shelf under the sink. This was water for doing the dishes, for washing, and for the laundry.[12]

The emptying of used water posed a second problem. It was not always wasted. In the last house mentioned, in the Haute-Vienne, used water was emptied out of the house through a hole in the wall, under the sink, the *bassi*; a large flat slate, leading to the outside wall and gently hollowed in the centre, took the water away from the wall and emptied it into a little granite trough which the ducks and hens could dabble in. On this farm, it was also necessary to fill the water-troughs for the piglets and the fat pigs with water drawn from the well. Water which was precious and rare, and always difficult to get in

[11] Eugène Bougeâtre, *La vie rurale dans le Mantois et le Vexin au XIXᵉ siècle*, p. 29.
[12] EAR, no. 12 (Eure), no. 2 (Morbihan), no. 12 (Pyrénées-Atlantiques) no. 13 (Haute-Vienne).

the nineteenth century, and even, on some traditional farms, right up to 1946, this was one of the essential physical elements determining the shape of household tasks; devolving entirely on the woman, shaping the rhythm of her daily life, fetching the precious liquid was crucial to running the farm. It was so fundamental that it was one of those mechanical acts of which one ceases even to be aware: women, when asked about their daily tasks, forgot to mention it!

The woman went to fetch water or went to the water. The great launderings which periodically occurred were organized within the framework of mutual female help. The heavy linen – that is sheets, cloths, and work-clothes – was washed with ashes in a big wash-tub, then brushed, beaten and soaped at the spring or in the wash-house. It was a long and exhausting process which took place during April and October, and a third time, if necessary, after the harvest. Smaller and less spectacular launderings were regularly necessary to deal with the day-to-day washing; especially if there were little children.

There is a deep-seated affinity between the woman and water which appears in rituals as a symbolic element ensuring the passage from life to death. Analysing the acts of the woman who 'came in' to help at births and deaths, washing the new-born child and laying out the corpse, Yvonne Verdier remarks that 'washing appears to be an act laden with symbolic powers ... Over and above the Christian symbolism of purification, washing offers an image of the passage from life to death, a passage of which water will be the vehicle, and the image works in two ways: to pass on, but also to come into the world, as if the child too had to pass through water ... In this double passage, the washing-women could thus act as guide.'[13] The woman handles the water, consumes and manipulates the liquid. She accomplishes physical tasks and production tasks; contact with the purifying liquid confers on her a symbolic power, the power to put the world back in its place, to turn back the clock of life and death.

With the water the woman cooks, boiling and stewing the meals. It is the privilege of the mistress of the house since she knows that its reputation, with neighbours and servants, depends on it. The servants only play an auxiliary role in this task. The number of meals and their composition vary according to the seasons and the length of the working day. Bougeâtre describes it, in an example taken from Mantois and Vexin, but which summarizes the general situation in a rural environment.

[13] Yvonne Verdier, 'La femme-qui-aide et la laveuse', p. 180.

In summer, the peasant has five or six meals, two breakfasts, the first a snack about five in the morning, the second between about seven and seven-thirty; lunch at midday; a snack about five in the evening and supper at dusk, usually about eight or eight-thirty . . . In the winter, two meals were not taken, the snacks early in the morning and late in the afternoon. The single breakfast is then carried forward to between six and seven in the morning, and supper is at seven in the evening at the latest. The early morning snack is made up of bread and cheese; it is taken standing, a hunk of bread in the hand, after which, in the larger households, the carter goes and feeds the horses. At the second breakfast, to the cheese is added either a slice of salt lard, or a round of sausage, or a piece of liver pâté, locally called *fromage de cochon*, pig's cheese. At midday, the woman of the house will serve a fat soup followed by boiled pork with vegetables, a salad and cheese. The evening snack is taken wherever the worker happens to be employed at the time . . . Finally, the last meal of the day is made up of soup eked out with leftovers from midday's soup, an omelette or a dish of potatoes boiled with lard, and fruits in season, cherries, plums, apples or pears.[14]

Was the preparation of meals a very time-consuming task in traditional cooking? Meals for feast-days, made at the end of the major agricultural undertakings, or for a wedding, brought a lot of guests together, and presented quite a different array of dishes from usual, dishes which took a long time to cook. Their preparation was based on cooperation between the women: it was an occasion for mutual help between neighbours and kin; but everyday meals were not so time-consuming as in nineteenth-century bourgeois society, where culinary etiquette demanded two elaborate meals a day. Meals like that demanded a lot from those working in the kitchen. By contrast, in the rural environment, the daily meals remained for a long time, during the nineteenth and twentieth centuries, monotonous menus, in which every day resembled the day before, and where all that was required was to add a piece of lard or a few potatoes to the pot which was kept constantly on the boil. Cooking was thus a very different task from what it is today, in town or in the country. It was in a very fundamental way associated with the woman, and not just any woman, not the servant, nor the daughter of the house. It was the responsibility of the mistress of the house; it was her privilege in the same way that sexual relations were her privilege, and she learned about both at the same time when she got married.[15]

---

[14] Eugène Bougeâtre, *op. cit.*, pp. 51–2.
[15] Yvonne Verdier, 'Le langage du cochon', p. 151.

As well as cooking food for humans, food also had to be prepared for the animals, particularly the pig-swill which had to be made up and boiled twice a day before or after the men's soup.

This female cooking was based on boiling and simmering, a product of the relationship between food and water. When the men cooked, they would grill, demonstrating a contrast between day-to-day cooking and feast-day cooking, a contrast which is continued to this day in the barbecue at the end of the garden – an American custom recalling a long-standing organization of labour. In addition, men were involved in the food process, although usually at the beginning; they supplied the grain to be made into soup or bread; they killed and salted the pig which the women were to cook.

In this rapid enumeration of the tasks reserved for women, and account devoted to feeding, some mention must be made of bread, but its preparation varies from region to region, and in any case involved the other principle of organizing labour which we mentioned, that of male–female cooperation. We will thus discuss it later. To complete this treatment of tasks relating to meals, let us mention the making of preserves, in fruit-growing areas, a task which only petered out relatively recently, and partially, at the end of the nineteenth century and the beginning of the twentieth, with the takeover of this domestic production by industry.

The domain reserved for women also comprises all the jobs aimed at the upkeep of the house, and one must add to them the general list of tasks usually included under the heading of 'housework': sweeping, dusting, making the beds, etc. The amount of time spent by the mistress of the house on this sort of task depended on the number of little children in the house and the number of servants. (Although it is not clear from available descriptions, servants seem by and large to have been assigned to production tasks such as milking and working in the fields, rather then looking after the house itself.) These maintenance tasks were also related to particular cultural environments. Thus, in some regions, the interior was regarded as 'sordid' or 'dirty', although observers testified to carefully polished furniture. In Brittany, for instance, the housewife prided herself on the shine of the nails which decorated her cupboards and enclosed beds, and a sort of local competition enforced cleanliness. In a novel situated in the Bigouden region, the heroine, Thumette, polished every Saturday in anticipation of the visits of the morrow 'all the copper on the cupboards, all the locks, nails and hinges; and Saturday night, her forehead shining with sweat and her cheeks ablaze, she gazed with pride at her clean and shining house, with its pleasant smell of wax.'[16]

Nevertheless, the upkeep of the house and the housework did not make up a substantial part of the mistress's tasks. The earth floor only needed an occasional going-over with a broom; the beds could be made more or less speedily. The cleanliness of the interior was a function of the time the mistress of the house wished to dedicate to it, if she had no servant to help her: housework came after working in the fields, and caring for the children and animals.

A whole range of activities which were production tasks, though secondary ones, also became part of the women's sphere. The making of cloth by spinning and weaving, for example, was carried out by the woman, if it was for domestic consumption only. Naturally, the importance of this activity depended on how comfortably off the family were, and the degree of urbanization of the region concerned, where certain kinds of cloth or pieces of clothing could be bought at market. It is true that these activities gradually disappeared with the growth of the textile industries during the second half of the nineteenth century but they nonetheless maintained their importance in peasant thinking, even though they were performed increasingly less often. In the first place, these tasks could be carried out only at certain times of the day, during the evening, which was a time of relaxation and social contact: *Ce que femme file le matin ne vient souvent à bonne fin* (What a woman spins in the morning does not often come to a good end) (Anjou).

Marriage rituals emphasize the symbolic relationship between tow, yarn and sexuality; but unlike cooking, which the woman learns to do alone, just as she must encounter her sexual experience alone, spinning is an activity which a young girl can carry out and which can be performed collectively; it is conducted concurrently with her apprenticeship in romantic relations. Often, the young girls would spin during the evenings while the young men came to pay them court: it was, moreover, their trousseau which they were getting ready.

Knitting and sewing were supremely feminine activities, handed on from mother to daughter, and provided a means of socializing the young girl. The boys were sent out into the fields and the girl was kept at home so that her mother could teach her how to handle a needle. Let us observe the mother which Millet painted giving her daughter

---

[16] Anna Selle, *Thumette Bigoudène*, p. 54.

The Knitting Lesson. Everything is quiet in the poor, but well-kept house, with its flagstone floor. The woman and the little girl are seated, and the mother is tenderly guiding her daughter's hand as she leans over her shoulder. There is no better illustration of the feminine transmission of techniques, gestures and attitudes than this painting imbued with tenderness. Knitting was often the occupation of shepherdesses in Millet's work, where, far from the house and looking after the sheep in the fields, they managed to preserve, even in the open air, their feminine bearing. For needlework was also a question of bearing. Even more than a technique, it was a whole controlled attitude of the body which the mother was teaching to her daughter.

The community school would take up this instruction of a quiet and proper bearing, a system which was continued by housekeeping schools which sprang up between the wars, specifically for the daughters of farmers. As an example, here is a text given to the pupils as a dictation exercise, in 1886, in a country school at Vieux-Rouen-sur-Bresle in the Seine-Maritime:

> Young girls must be taught needlework at a early age. But, up until the age of twelve and even later, whatever their parents' fortune, they should not be allowed to work any of the imaginative pieces beloved of rich women. The pleasure taken in such work is sufficient to teach a skill in it, whereas it is important that one should learn, at an early age, to perform those tasks which cannot be learned later. Young girls must be taught from their earliest years that calm, self-possessed bearing which is at once a mark of modesty and of grace. They must early be taught those habits which will make them sedentary. I believe thus that, as early as six years of age, sitting next to her mother, the young girl should begin to use her needle for an hour a day, in two sessions, for one must be careful to guard against her becoming put off the most precise and most consolatory of all women's occupations. Hemming, stitches to be worked on coarse canvas, a piece of tapestry-work should be her first undertakings. It is also important to teach knitting when they are very young.[17]

This is an illustration of the belated recovery (at the end of the nineteenth century) of family instruction. It contributes to the reinforcement of the specifically feminine, by imposing a model which, although deriving from bourgeois morality, links with the traditions

[17] 'Cahiers d'histoire de l'enseignement', p. 18.

transmitted within the family. One can see the difference between what is learned unconsciously and that which is taught externally and is enforced.

Over and above all her other functions, the peasant wife is also a mother. She is responsible for bringing up and educating the young child, tasks which she shares with the female world of the household: grandmother, mother-in-law, older daughters, and servant-girls. Once again, it is Millet who shows us the tenderness with which the mother could blow out *The Child's Candle*. In this society where infant mortality was still high and in which, even when it was decreasing, one was still constantly aware of it, the mother had to try and keep her child healthy through a variety of practices, more or less related to official medical practice, according to the social class and the particular region.

An entire book has recently been devoted to this subject, and all we need do here is to recall that his heavy responsibility was part of the tasks which fell to rural women, who used a body of magical and empirical rules, es which were integrated into a rationale suited to the peasant mentality.[18] It was crucially important for the mother to preserve her children's lives, so that, above and beyond life given and maintained, she could ensure the continuity of her household. In the same way as she appears to be the lynch-pich of the household when her husband goes off to fish or travels to Paris to become a water-carrier during the winter, so too the woman has the fundamental task of keeping healthy and educating the children who will one day succeed the couple. From every point of view, 'the mother ensures the continuity of human life within the life of the family.'[19]

Nor is the domain of women entirely confined to the inside of the house. Fetching water at the well or at the spring, or doing the washing at the river took the woman out of the house. Less distantly, within the sphere which constituted her particular domain and which she has symbolically appropriated in the marriage-rites, the mistress of the house had responsibility for the farmyard and the garden. These were domestic activities since they were intended for domestic con-sumption, but they were also productive since they were often the only activities which could bring a small regular income into the house, since any surplus produce was sold at market.

Though the farmyard was primarily intended to satisfy the needs of

[18] François Loux, *op. cit.*
[19] André Varagnac, *op. cit.*, p. 186.

the house, the farmer's wife still had the chance of selling at market any surplus eggs or poultry as well as products from the dairy or the garden. Sometimes, as we saw at Lavit, in the Tarn-et-Garonne, the farmyard provided not a secondary but a primary source of production within all the productive activities of the farm. But, whether secondary or primary, the care and the produce of the farmyard are a specifically feminine concern which controls every stage of the operation.

The symbolic relationship between poultry and the woman is perceptible in numerous proverbs linking woman and hen. We have already seen the sexual parallel which was drawn, but that is only one aspect of a wider homology. Hen and woman have the same characteristics, the same qualities, and the same faults.

Just as the hen knows how to pick up grains, so the woman knows how to be economical.

> *Le coq a beau éparpiller, si la poule ramasse, elle remplit le grenier*
> The cockerel can scatter grain as much as he likes, if the hen picks it up, she'll fill the barn (Franche-Comté)

The farmyard marks the limits of the territory reserved for women:

> *Quand la poule reste au poulailler, c'est signe que tout va bien pour le coq*
> When the hen stays in the hen-house, it is a sign that all is well for the cock (Provence)
>
> *Poule et femme qui s'écartent de la maison se perdent*
> The woman and the hen who stray from the house are lost (Val d'Aosta)

The garden is, as we have seen through a number of rituals, highly feminized. In effect, it is cared for daily by the woman. Day after day, she prepares the soil, sows, waters, hoes, and harvests, and this cultivated area, close to the house, appears as a tiny replica of the fields which the man looks after. In this garden, a vision of future provisions lies before the housewife's eyes: the household soup is growing ready there, waiting to be out in the pot. In proverbial speech the woman is often compared to fruit or vegetables, and the quality of the garden's produce determines to some extent the family reputation: *A la maison et au jardin on connaît ce que femme vaut* (You can tell what a woman is worth from her house and her garden) (Gascony).

For what is emphasized most of all through this gardening are the qualities of patience and hard work, and the ability to carry out the appropriate action each day. Gardening is a productive activity, but also an eminently social one: a housewife who neglects her garden runs the risk of the insult of a charivari.

ACTIVITIES RESERVED TO MEN

While feminine activities are more or less identical throughout all French peasant society, even throughout traditional society – everyone has to be clothed, and fed, to bring up and socialize children – and are also identical throughout the year, since they are the fundamental daily activities, activities reserved to men, on the other hand, are dependent both on the economic setting to which they belong and on the period in the productive cycle in which they occur. It is not within our scope here to describe these activities in their technological detail. We seek rather to summarize their principal characteristics in order to compare or contrast them with the tasks carried out by women.

Within the house or with regard to it, the main male activity is to provide the wood. In dead periods of production, during the winter, 'the man chopped the wood and . . . in March he would bring in the faggots and the bundles of wood which finished "weathering" in the wood-shed ready for the next winter.'[20]

In general, the man is only rarely indoors, except to eat and sleep. He is out of the house throughout the summertime, the time of major work in the fields, while in winter, when tasks in the fields are fewer, he devotes his time to repairing his tools and to mending things about the house. It is during the long winter evenings that he does his basket-making with willows and rushes.

The principal labour of preparing the soil, whether for agriculture or viticulture, is performed by the man. For agriculture, if one looks at the tools employed, it is the man who handles the spades, picks, hoes, bill-hooks, pruners and other hand tools which were still widely used during the nineteenth century.[21] As soon as one goes on to equipment drawn by animals, it is no longer a question of an exclusively male domain, but rather of cooperation between the sexes, since, although the plough may be led by a man, a woman may often guide the equipment harnessed to it. The activities linked with planting and sowing are also male tasks: hoeing, and sowing the seed from sacks, or

[20] Eugène Bougeâtre, *op. cit.*, p. 30.

[21] Mariel J. Brunhes-Delamarre and Hugues Hairy, *Techniques de production: l'agriculture*, pp. 9–19.

baskets, or bushels. These activities have symbolic connotations: the farmer opens the soil and sows his seed, and the soil, the female womb, brings forth and bears all the hopes of the household.

The preparation of the soil and the work around the plant, in the case of viticulture, are also male tasks: grafting, pruning the vine, putting in props, trimming the shoots, and sulphuring.[22] But, as with cereal harvests, the operations associated with the major tasks of summer, the grape harvest calls for the help of all the members of the household and often also of other men and women who find themselves drawn together in these tasks.

In the animal sphere, one can oppose to the farmyard the care of animals which feature as means of production in the organization of labour, such as milk-cows or horses. These animals are valued because they are costly, and proverbs emphasize how much the men are attached to them. One should not, of course, take such expressions literally. They show, rather, the relative importance attached to the labour of animals and of people:

> *Bon Dieu d'en haut, prends ma femme, laisse mes chevaux*
> Good God on high, take my wife, but leave my horses (Upper Brittany)

> *Mort de femme et vie de cheval font homme riche*
> A dead wife and a living horse make a wealthy man (Brittany)

> *La mort de sa femme n'est pas une ruine, mais la mort de sa vache en est une*
> The death of a wife is not a disaster, but the death of a cow is (Alsace)

In the South the same kind of statement is made about the beast used for traction and transport: *Homme riche si sa femme meurt, pauvre si sa mule meurt* (A man is rich if his wife dies, poor if his mule dies) (Languedoc).

Draught animals distinguish the farmer from the sharecropper and the day labourer. They are the sign and the means of achieving particular social and economic status, and, just as the hen and the woman, so the horse is the man leading and controlling the equipment of the household.

The state of technology in the nineteenth century meant that male tasks demanded considerable physical energy. The peasants depicted in Millet's paintings, *Men Digging*, *Man with a Hoe*, and *The End of the Day*, are dropping with exhaustion. Yet they are not agricultural

---

[22] *ibid.*, p. 62.

labourers, but small landowners of bitterly poor soil which calls for unceasing labour and constant effort. Millet, ethnographer-painter, says of these workers:

> I can perceive perfectly well the sun spreading out in the distance, far away over the countryside, its beauty across the clouds. I can see no less well the two steaming horses working on the plain; then there is the rocky spot where an exhausted man, whose laborious gasping has been audible all morning, has tried to straighten up a moment and take breath. All this drama is surrounded by splendour. That is not of my own invention, and the expression the 'cry of the land' is nothing new.[23]

Against the woman's incessant toil one must put the man's physical exhaustion, wearing him out in body and spirit.

The territory reserved for men, therefore, is confined to the work of preparing the fields, whereas the woman's comprehends the kitchen, washing, and the care of small chilren. But let us not give undue importance to this division of labour. In some regions men perform work which elsewhere is entrusted to women. The greatest proportion of work depends on cooperation between the sexes, whether man and wife together, or wider groups of men and women.

INTERCHANGEABILITY AND COOPERATION

So-called domestic activities are sometimes undertaken by men and reputedly male activities are, in some regions, carried out by women.

If there is one job with feminine domestic connotations, then it must be bread-making. Bread was an essential element in the peasant diet. It was made every week, ten days or fortnight.

> *Quand une fille sait pétrir et enfourner, elle est bonne à marier*
> When a girl knows how to knead and bake, she is fit to marry (Bordelais)
>
> *Femme qui fait cuire du pain ou qui fait la lessive est à moitié folle*
> A woman who makes bread or does the washing is half mad [reference to the hard labour involved] (Gascony)

---

[23] Jean-François Millet, letter of 1863, in André Fermigier, *Jean-François Millet*, p. 50.

When these operations are broken down – kneading, putting the dough into the bread-tins, lighting the oven, baking – it appears that they may be carried out by either men or women; that one or the other play different parts in the process, even within the same region; and that the men therefore take on a task which is nonetheless reputed to be feminine and domestic. For instance, in Mantois and Vexin, bread-making was entrusted to the housewife.[24] In Brittany, the men were involved in the process of heating up the oven,[25] whether it was a question of the communal oven or of the domestic ovens lit turn-and-turn-about in the little hamlets, within the framework of neighbourly help. In the Mâconnais, there is an even greater confusion of tasks. 'Men and women both made bread,' writes Suzanne Tardieu,[26] who has collected a wide variety of answers from her informants: 'My mother and I made the dough,' said a woman in La-Chapelle-de-Guinchay; 'there were women who mixed the dough, but usually it was the men' (Vergisson); 'the men did the kneading' (Vergisson); 'I did it, and so did my husband' (Laize, Blanzy). Throughout the technical process, which Suzanne Tardieu photographed and analysed in detail, it was a man making the bread.

Here, it is not a regional model but a family tradition which is developing, or, rather, a distribution of jobs which each couple determines for itself. This interchangeability makes one wonder about the stereotypes which nineteenth-century observers assembled, and about a redefinition, perhaps even an elimination, of the term domestic.

Certain activities were carried out by either men or women, depending on the region. Everything to do with livestock was dealt with in this way. While sheep were rather regarded as being the man's province – though how many popular songs speak of shepherdesses, and how many shepherdesses has Millet painted, with their knitting in their hand! – cows could be the responsibility of either one or the other. Animals whose products were destined for domestic consumption, such as cows, when there were only a few of them, were cared for and milked by the woman, in this small Breton household or that household in Central France. Even when aimed at the market production of butter, milk and cheese, the dairy could still be entirely within female hands, as in the grazing areas of the Auge region

[24] Eugène Bougeâtre, *op. cit.*
[25] Alexandre Bouët and Olivier Perrin, *op. cit.*, p. 172.
[26] Suzanne Tardieu, *op. cit.*, pp. 374–5.

described earlier. In contrast, in Central France, in the Aubrac region which covers the departments of Cantal, Lozère and Aveyron, it was the men who took the cows in the summer to the high pastures, which they call 'mountains'.[27] They would set themselves up in the *burons* – dairies in the high pastures – and make a cheese called *fourme de Laguiole* which would be sold at the end of the summer season. This is rather an extreme example, since the economic system of production is here separate from the household and Aubrac cheese-making is a form of agricultural craft, so to speak, comparable to the workshops of potters or weavers. All that we would demonstrate here is that the cow is not an incontestably feminine animal in the way that the chicken is.

Care for livestock is the point of convergence of male–female complementarity. The cows were cared for by the women, but the byres were looked after by the men, who turned the litter and cleaned out the manure.

The question arises – can such activities still be referred to as domestic? The men took a large share in them; they entered directly into the system of production. In a desire to categorize every task absolutely, have not observers overlooked an essential factor, in the relative interchangeability of tasks from one region to another, and particularly in the advanced cooperation between the sexes, within the same work process? And here, it is very much a question of mutual help between members of the household outside the framework of the mutual help furnished by neighbours and kin when there are major jobs to be done.

Let us look at Millet's painting, *Planting Potatoes*. A man and a woman work together in a luminous atmosphere of tranquillity and tenderness. he works backwards turning the soil, and she follows in the same rhythm throwing in handfuls of the seed-potatoes she carries in her apron. The donkey behind the tree waits in the shade, with a basket on its back where the baby has been put. 'I wanted to show the touching way these two intimately associated people worked together, and to make their actions accord so perfectly that they seemed but a single labour.'[28]

Millet was a somewhat sober observer of peasant life, and the warm atmosphere of work in unison with which the painting is imbued, was

[27] L'Aubrac, vol. III.
[28] E. Moreau-Nelaton, *Millet par lui-même*, vol. II, p. 110, in Jean-Claude Chamboredon, 'Les deux manières de Jean-François', p. 17.

doubtless the reflection of some scene he had observed, perhaps in his infancy.

Where is the folklorist who has mentioned that men and women planted potatoes together? They would have spoken of growing potatoes as a male task, without calling attention to the woman's presence in the fields. In all these cultural processes, the woman was eminently present, not only during the major undertakings, but also in the day-to-day activities which had to be carried out.

Why have observers overlooked this participation of women in agricultural work? Though some folklorists might see the woman as constantly working out of doors – particularly those doctors who reproached mothers and nurses with abandoning their babies to go and work in the fields – other observers tended rather to concentrate exclusively on the technology of agricultural operations, and neglected to ask who did what. Moreover, female participation in work in the fields was so much taken for granted in the rural environment that it was hardly mentioned; it was engraved upon the peasant mentality, which ceased to be aware of it: women no more mentioned their occasional help in tilling or sowing than they did the care they devoted to their children. As for the observer, a woman working in the fields seemed so incongruous to him that he just did not see it. Yet the meticulous research carried out in 1945 and 1946 demonstrates this permanent cooperation, a principle of the organization of rural labour as ancient as the organization of the peasant family itself, which grew up in the sixteenth and seventeenth centuries, and which had only begun to change under the recent development of new agricultural systems, from the 1950s onwards.

On small family farms, in which activity was governed by the rhythm of the agricultural tasks, and which the researchers visited in 1945 and 1946, cooperation continued throughout the year, and was particularly evident during the great labours of the summer. In order to bring out the nature and extent of this cooperation, however, it would be necessary to examine an hourly timetable of work.

Take a farm of around 17 hectares, in the Tarn-et-Garonne, at Miramont,[29] farmed by the owners, a couple, with their son, their daughter-in-law and two helpers. It is a mixed farm, and a brief description of the distribution of tasks can be drawn up as follows: the father and son worked in close cooperation, working the land, looking

[29] EAR, no 27.

10 *Harvesters in the Beauce region: the men carry the large scythes; the women use sickles to collect the sheaves.*

after the grassland, the crops, the upkeep of the vines and the fruit-trees, and were responsible for feeding the larger livestock. The mother and daughter-in-law did the cooking, kept house, fed the poultry, and did the milking. The two servants changed the litter for the cattle and fed them; they maintained the roadways, cut the hedges, and transported the manure. In fact, the division of work seems much less clear if one looks at their timetables in detail: cooperation stands out in a synoptic presentation of tasks. In summer, the women spent little time on domestic activities. They were in the fields with the men in the afternoons, and in the mornings if they had the time. Their particular sphere was that of milking – the animals' litter being prepared by the men – and care of the poultry. The additional time which the men devoted to the fields was spent in preparing meals. Throughout these long days when 20 hours were spent working, at least 14 hours were spent together, sometimes 16 hours if the women spent longer in the fields. This farm was observed in 1945, and had not changed since it was built in 1835, and one can assume that the organization of labour had hardly changed either.

SUMMER TIMETABLE		
Father and son	*Mother and daughter-in-law*	*Servants*
4 o'clock		
Rise	Rise	
5 o'clock		
Coffee	Preparation of breakfast	Rise
Care of animals	and of snack	Breakfast,
Harnessing		Clean pig-sty
6 o'clock		
Leave for fields		Leave for fields
7 o'clock		
	Housework.	
	Preparation of lunch	
9 o'clock		
	Care for poultry	
	Milking	
10 o'clock		
Snack	Either in the house,	Snack
	or in the fields	

1 o'clock

Quick meal at the farm. It was occasionally taken out into the fields

1.30

Washing up

2.30

Leave for fields

6 o'clock

Return from fields
Care for poultry
Milking
Preparation of dinner

8 o'clock

Return from fields		Return from fields
Care for stock		Care for stock

9 o'clock

Dinner	Dinner	Dinner
	Washing up	

12 o'clock

Bed	Bed	Bed

At Imbsheim, in the Lower Rhine,[30] a smallholding of 7 hectares spread its interests over cereals, wheat, barley, rye, fodder beet, a few vines, and potatoes: all products consumed by the occupants of the household, whether men or beasts. Only products from the stock-farming entered the commercial circuit. The household was made up of a couple, their daughter and a servant.

WINTER TIMETABLE

Madame K	*Monsieur K*

7 o'clock

Rises	Rises

8 o'clock

Prepares fire	Cares for cattle
Cares for pig	
Milking	

9 o'clock

Breakfast	Breakfast

[30] EAR, Imbsheim.

10 o'clock

Housework

Fields: transports manure, fodder, beet

11–12 o'clock

Preparation of food

1 o'clock

Lunch

Lunch

2–3 o'clock

Sewing or washing

Repair of materials

4–5 o'clock

Milking

6 o'clock

Cares for pigs

Cares for cattle

7 o'clock

Preparation of dinner

8 o'clock

Dinner

Dinner

9–11 o'clock

Sewing

Accounts, reading

During the summer, there were two great periods of activity: hay-making and harvest.

HAY-MAKING TIMETABLE

Madame K

Monsieur K

4.30

Rises

Rises

5 o'clock

Prepares fire
Cares for pigs
Milking

Cares for cattle

6 o'clock

Breakfast
Housework
Preparation of snack
and of lunch

Breakfast
Leave for fields
Mows

8 o'clock

	Cattle out

9 o'clock

Turns hay	Farm

10 o'clock

Snack	Snack

11 o'clock

Hay-making	Turns hay

12 o'clock

Quick lunch at the farm

2 o'clock

Turning and stacking hay	Stacking hay Cattle home

6 o'clock

Milking Cares for pigs	Cares for cattle

8 o'clock

Dinner	Dinner

9 o'clock

Sewing	Reading

11 o'clock

Bed	Bed

HARVEST TIMETABLE

Madame K	*Monsieur K*

6 o'clock

Rises	Rises

7 o'clock

Prepares fire Cares for pigs Milking Breakfast	Cares for cattle Breakfast

8 o'clock

Prepares packed lunch	Prepares wagon and baskets

9 o'clock

Leaves for fields   Leaves for fields
Harvesting   Harvesting

12 o'clock

Lunch in fields   Lunch in fields

1 o'clock

Harvesting   Harvesting

5 o'clock

Home   Home

7 o'clock

Prepares dinner   Presses grapes
Cares for pigs   Cares for cattle
Milking

8 o'clock

Dinner   Dinner

11 o'clock

Bed   Bed

Men and women follow the same alternation of periods of rest and labour through the annual cycle of the seasons. During the dead period of the winter they both have a shorter working day, in which the feminine tasks of sewing and washing appear as the equivalent of the masculine task of repairing. The animal domain is separate: the woman looks after the pigs and cows, the man after the cattle.

Bedtime remains the same, summer and winter, and the day is prolonged by rising earlier in the morning; the timetable of the farm at Tarn-et-Garonne shows that the men and women were together from eleven in the morning until six o'clock in the afternoon. During the harvest, their common work-time was even longer, from nine in the morning until six in the afternoon: with the accumulated fatigue of the day, and the foreknowledge of more on the morrow, the evening was cut short, and the restful activities which would usually take place then probably made way to discussions on the quality of the vintage.

Cooperation was a daily affair, lasting for longer or shorter periods depending on the state of work in the fields. These examples go to show that the woman had a normal and continuous place in the fields.

Confining the domain of female work to work around the house, and, inversely, loading all the work in the fields on to the man

provides altogether too schematic a view. There was some overlapping of territories and tasks, despite certain areas of dominance.
This cooperation implies a distribution of tasks in working techniques.
During ploughing, for example, the woman could help: the man held
the plough and opened the furrow, while the women led the team.
During hay-making, the big scythe, which was heavy to handle, was a
man's tool, as well as everything that went to maintain it, the
whetstone in its sheath, the hammer and hand-anvil to straighten the
blade. The woman gathered the sheaves with a sickle and bound them;
she helped with stacking the ricks. One can find the same sort of
division of labour in workshops as well. In the clog-maker's, the man
would carve the clogs, while the woman rubbed them down. The
division of labour rarely depends on matters of physical strength but,
rather, on a model of distribution of roles, authority and responsibility.

> Unloading bundles of hay from a cart was done by women, though it
> was heavy work performed with pitchforks. The farmer stood next to
> his cattle, without lifting a finger, but keeping a watch out for any
> errors which could cause an accident.[31]

In an analysis of this cooperation, it is difficult to draw up a general
table which would hold true for the majority of rural households; the
degree of cooperation, and the amount of feminine contribution to the
work on the land depended on the composition of the household and
the particular stage of its evolution, on its economic level, on the time
of year, and finally perhaps on cultural models which are the most
difficult of all to come to grips with.

A large household, employing a number of servants, might relieve a
woman of her participation in work in the fields; this is a variable
linked to the economic level of the farm. In the same way, the presence
of children already able to contribute to the labour force would enable
the woman to devote herself exclusively to her household duties.
Thus, in a Bigouden village in Brittany, there is a distinction between
the women 'who are driven by necessity to the fields and who, side by
side with the men, or alone in their furrows, valiantly tackle the job;
they are ruddy-skinned, with calloused hands, and go home in the
evenings with their shoulders bowed and their step heavy, having
manfully accomplished the daily task,' and, on the other hand, the

[31] André Varagnac, *op. cit.*, p. 188.

'mistress of a large farm who never went to the fields. Her husband, her servants, and her sons were sufficient to work the soil. She kept house, that was her job. The floor well sanded, the furniture waxed, the brass shining, the cupboards filled with well-kept clothes, abundant hot meals ready when wanted, her domain was without fault.'[32] In the case of servants, the term 'mistress of the house' takes on its full meaning, since there are orders to be given, tasks to be assigned, and decisions to be taken to direct the few servants who relieve the woman from her more taxing duties. But the mistress must observe the crucial rule of conduct: she must rise first in the mornings to organize the day's work, as can be seen by looking at the timetables set out above. From the end of the eighteenth century, this precept was numbered among the pieces of advice given to the good farmer's wife 'who must be the eyes of the house, rising first and going to bed last.'[33]

A folklorist making observations in the Basque country notes the physical strength of the women, who would walk forty or fifty kilometres a day: 'They showed themselves quite as good as the men at working in the fields; they harnessed the oxen, and led them, goad in hand. They drove the cart to the market, or the plough along the furrow. They took the oxen by their horns, mastered them, and made the beasts slow their step or accelerate, according to their wishes.'[34]

Female physical strength was not peculiar to the Basque women. The preceding descriptions have shown us the need for it. Whether the tasks are feminine ones, like washing, or whether they are associated with masculine tasks, like hay-making or harvest, the woman must be endowed with solid physical strength, and, if possible, good health, both indispensable to the success of her household. The man relies on the woman to help him, and he relies on a healthy and robust woman. The criteria for choosing a wife based on the externals signs of health – being 'ruddy', being strong — are here explained. Not only do proverbs mistrust feminine beauty:

Fille jolie, miroir de fou
Pretty girl, madman's mirror (Val d'Aosta)

Il vaut mieux dire laide allons souper que belle qu'avons nous à souper
It's better to say hag let's go and eat than beauty what is there for us to eat (Franche-Comté)

[32] Anna Selle, *op. cit.*, p. 114.
[33] L. Roze, *La bonne fermière ou éléments économiques*, p. 45.
[34] Mme d'Abbadie d'Arrast, *op. cit.*, p. 42.

and the curiosity associated with idleness:

> *Fille fenestrière rarement ménagère*
> Gazing out of the window rarely made a good housewife (Champagne)

but they set great store by physical strength and readiness to work:

> *Le corps vaut plus que le dot*
> The body's worth more than the dowry (Gascony)

> *On connaît la femme au pied et à la tête*
> You can tell a woman by her head and her feet (Languedoc)

> *Femme vaillante, maison d'or*
> A valiant woman, a house of gold (Gascony)

> *La femme courageuse fait la maison bonne*
> Dauntless woman makes good house (Catalonia)

> *Une ménagère qui travaille bien vaut sa peau plein d'argent*
> A hardworking woman is worth her skinful of money (Catalonia)

> *Brave femme dans une maison vaut plus que ferme et que cheptel*
> A dauntless woman in the house is worth more than farm and livestock too (Languedoc)

The high value placed on a body in good health is easily explained in a society in which everything depends on physical strength. The inability to work, caused by sickness, was a calamity. A woman who could carry out physically exhausting tasks as well as having a pregnancy every two years, breast-feeding the youngest child and looking after the toddlers, was certainly a 'treasure'. One can also easily understand the rate of female mortality in the traditional rural environment, before the advent of contraception.

It is known that during the nineteenth century, contraceptive practices had effectively made their way into a number of rural areas of France, and that in the north, in Normandy, rural households were less burdened with children. Nonetheless, in a number of regions fertility was still close to the biological maximum, and the multiple tasks attendant upon looking after young children were added to those of looking after the farm. Mme d'Abbadie d'Arrast gives a very good picture of the harshness of the physiological function of motherhood, particularly in the Pays Basque, where heavy physical work was performed by the women.

For the peasant woman in particular, how burdensome and painful the numerous obligations of motherhood become, with the ties of nursing, and the care of small children; while the father knows only the delight of being fussed over by the children when he returns from the fields. An extra mouth to feed, one of these little brat's mouths, what was that to him, what sort of increase of work did that impose on him? Less than nothing. Whereas the mother, whether in the house or out, busy about her duties, coming and going, had to carry these little ones in her arms, or dragging along at her skirts. When she was pregnant, there could be no letting up; she worked every day, because she had to.[35]

Nevertheless, these tasks 'went without saying'. They were never mentioned by the women interviewed by the researchers, even at Saint-Véran in the Hautes-Alpes, where the families were still very large, even in 1945. Looking after the little children went without saying, it was a duty and a delight, both of which were assumed more or less unconsciously by the women and transmitted in the mother's gestures with her daughter, or the grandmother's with her grand-daughter.

This overlapping of the tasks performed by members of the house-hold varied with the seasons. In the winter, the man was more often at home, and more available. During the long evenings where several families gathered together, the jobs were sometimes undifferentiated: men and women together shelled nuts, stripped corn or tobacco; though most often, it is true, the women worked at their spinning or mending, while the men whittled poles, played cards or dice, or just simply talked together. Finally, the degree of cooperation varied from one region to another, and from one regional culture to another, but that is a delicate question which entails a consideration of roles and territory as well as of tasks, and it would not be possible to venture a hypothesis on the subject without widening the scope of this analysis.

This first level of approach to the organization of labour has shown the integration of all the members of the household in farming activities and, in particular, the substance of female cooperation: the woman is not relegated to secondary, non-productive tasks as was often previously stated when using ethnocentric classification. On the contrary, her labour was essential to the life and survival of the farm, and thus of the household, in a production context which depended, even in the nineteenth century, even during the early stage of mech-

[35] *ibid.*, pp. 91–2.

anization, on the necessity for an extensive labour force. In fact, though the winnowing machine represented a technological improvement on the winnowing basket, it still required as much human energy to separate the wheat from the tares as the old-fashioned sieve used to do; the first reapers and threshers were always surrounded by a number of agricultural labourers feeding it material to thresh; and one had to await the invention of the washing-machine before looking after the linen became less of a wearing task than it was when washed in the traditional way.

A woman in the rural environment had no status unless she was married: unmarried she was, more or less, the servant of one of her married brothers or sisters. It was through marriage that she acquired her position as an adult in society, and her right to the responsibilities which she shared with her husband. Marriage rites demonstrate this accession to a new status, as is shown by this folklorist, when he compares the young girl and the married woman in a particularly flowery passage:

> Marriage in the Mâconnais is not liberation by painful servitude. Farewell to dancing, farewell to pretty dresses, farewell to that cheerful gaiety surrounded by attentions. From one day to the next, the wife must show herself as serious as the young girl was radiant. From one day to the next, the dignity of a wife must turn that broad smile into a sober look, quench the dancing flame in those bright eyes, steady the bearing of that giddy step. This metamorphosis is revealed and commented on in the haunting melody sung every evening to the fiancée by the old women, informing her, in a traditional way, of all her various duties.[36]

What these various duties in fact meant, was that the woman had the responsibility of managing all the goods accumulated once a year. In the family economy, 'once-a-year agriculture filled the house substantially, and little by little everyday use emptied it'.[37]

Day to day management rarely placed the woman in an eminent position within the household, but she could share the responsibility with her husband. At the level of the household, they were interdependent and complementary, as was noted by Olivier de Serres: 'And just as Tradition conferred on the woman responsibility for the home, and on the man responsibility for the land, so also . . . it was the

---

[36] Gabriel Jeanton, *op. cit.*, pp. 14–30.
[37] Olivier de Serres, *op. cit.*, p. 98.

mother of the family who would care for the disposal of provisions for everyday use, making the consultations necessary for a well-run household: it being occasionally the case, as things fell out, that the man would interest himself in the least concerns of the household, and the woman in the most important.[38]

The future of the household depends on the complementary and interdependent labour of the married couple, and many a rural household could join in the remark made by a café owner in Paris who, a native of Aubrac, ran a small café and tobacconist's with his wife: 'In this job, there have to be two of you, and well united.'[39]

[38] *ibid.*
[39] Jean-Luc Chodkiewicz, *L'Aubrac à Paris*, p. 226.

4

The Man, the Wife, and the House

An analysis of tasks has shown that a distribution of territory assigning the house to the women and the fields to the men would be over-simplistic, and would have to be modified according to the region, seasons, type and level of economic organization of the farm.

It must also be related to popular attitudes which, linking the material and the symbolic levels, shows the ambivalence pervading male and female appropriation of territory, whether outside (see chapter 5) or inside the house.

WOMAN'S HOUSE OR MAN'S HOUSE

It has been accepted that the house tended to be the woman's domain, with the women's tasks in the fields being circumscribed most often by their movements in and around the house – housework, cooking, caring for the farmyard, and the byre – whereas the man's territory was very much the fields. Charts of movements taken down by researchers in 1944–45, in which the thickness of the line denotes the numbers of comings and goings between different parts of the farm, demonstrates this well-known fact (see figures 12 and 13).

Were the man to be in the house, it would be during the passive periods of the annual cycle of labour: in the winter, or during the daily cycle; at mealtimes, to sleep, or else to do some mending, though that would be in a room separate from the dwelling-place. The communal room was not his kingdom. He was most often in the barns, the cart-shed or the byre. Thus, in the Tarn, at Lavit, the researcher noted that the man running the farm was most often to be found 'in the byre. As soon as he got up he went there and only breakfasted after having cleaned and fed his stock. He was in and out throughout the day. Looking after them, taking them out to grass, harnessing them to go to the fields. Inspecting them before going to bed. He would get up and go to them in the night if they were in calf.'[1]

In the summer, at Saint-Véran, the men even slept in the granary, or went there for their afternoon rest (occasionally joined by the women). The communal room was a 'gynaeceum'.[2]

The woman's power over the house extended beyond the tasks performed within it. This was because, within the house, the communal room was a place for receiving people, for show; the good name of the family was involved. The cleanliness of the house, the way in which one was received, the welcome offered, the way in which the servants were treated, all reflected on the whole household and family.

As the central base for her work, and the emblem of its qualities, the house represented the territory attributed to the woman, who is compared to the animals and domestic utensils occupying the framework of her daily perspective.

Femme sage reste à la maison
A sensible woman stays at home (Val d'Aosta)

Jamais femme ni cochon ne doit quitter la maison
Neither woman nor pig should leave the house (Dauphiné)

La femme et la poêle à frire ne doivent pas bouger de la maison
Neither woman nor frying pan should move out of the house (Provence)

These proverbs are normative: they formulate a desire, since knowledge of what happened in practice has shown the more or less frequent presence of the woman in the fields. The distance between the two levels – norm and practice – is very noticeable here. The woman's outside work necessarily leads her out of doors, but the norm, particularly in proverbs from the south – we will return later to a regional opposition which is manifested in this discussion – is to keep her at home. The house would benefit from the woman's attentions and from her protective presence; the woman shut indoors would not

[1] EAR, no. 24.
[2] Henri Raulin, *L'architecture rurale française, le Dauphiné*, p. 63.

suffer outside aggression; she would not go and join those women whose power as a group was so feared by the society of men; she would also avoid contact with other men.

The house is feminized, just as the woman finds herself made like a house.

La femme est une maison dont tout homme a la clé
A woman is a house to which every man has the key (Provence)

11 *The 'Taste Poule' or 'hen feeler', an engraving by Weivix, late sixteenth century.*

The feminization of the house and its inhabitants, in opposition to the masculinization of the outside world, is very clear-cut in traditional rural society, and the man who stays at home and looks after his outbuildings, the garden, farmyard, etc., is loaded with epithets which ridicule him by feminizing him. The man who is naturally inclined to look after things around the house, and thus to put himself in the position of a woman within his household is related symbolically to the farmyard – feminine territory par excellence – and the female sexual cycle of the hen-woman. The folklorist Eugène Rolland has gathered a number of epithets describing the feminized man:

> The man who looks after the details of the household which are normally the concern of women, such as looking after and counting the eggs and the hens, putting the hens to brood, feeling them to see whether they are going to lay soon, that is to say, wasting his time on trivialities and idiocies, is called derisively:

> *Tâte poule*, French
> *Tâtâ-dzeneille*, canton of Vaud
> *Tate mes glaines*, Picardy
> *Tâteux de poule* (a finicky man), Normandy
> *Cati de poïèts* (n'er do well), Walloon
> *Coquefredouille*, Franche-Comté (*coque*: egg; *fredouiller*: to feel)
> *Metteur de poules à couver*, French
> *Metou de poule à coué*, Bessin
> *Nijou de poules, anijotou de poules*, Côtes-du-Nord
> *Cocoponète* (simpleton, busybody), Bessin
> *Poneau* (literally meaning 'layer'), Morvan
> *Chan pona, chan covis*, Pays messin (Jean)
> *Chan coquegnon*, Pays messin
> *Jean cocotte*, Lorraine, Morvan
> *Coucounié*, Corrèze
> *Coquatié*, Morvan
> *Cacaraca* (= hen-pecked husband), Provence
> *Jorène, Djorène* (chicken, feckless), Plancher-les-Mines
> *Gaougallino* (that is, cockerel-hen: the simple-minded husband of popular legend who does the washing, the cooking, makes the beds, milks the goat, and looks after the eggs and the silkworms), Pays comtadin
> *Jocrisse qui mène les poules pisser* French.[3]

---

[3] Eugène Rolland, *Faune populaire de la France*, vol. VI, pp. 30–31. Rolland's sources have been omitted in this quotation.

To this list can be added the term *chauffe-la-couche*[4] or *miton*.[5]

In addition, masculine and feminine status is not without ambiguity, a fact recognized by traditional society. There is a hazy area of masculinity/femininity in the case of the man who becomes a son-in-law. He loses his name, taking that of his wife's house's lineage; but he resumes his status as a man when, in due course, the management of the household is passed on to him from the father. In exotic societies, on the other hand, there is often a special status reserved to characterize infertile women, who are hominized.[6]

The appropriation of territory and, in particular, the appropriation of the house by the woman is related to a logical organization of responsibilities. Folklorists may assert men's power over women in ideological statements which bear analysis, but more acute observers have noted the proportion of responsibilities which fall to the woman. Above and beyond the tasks she has to accomplish, the qualities which make her a 'good housewife' reflect directly on the household, its reputation and its honour. Just as the husband bears the family honour in the outside world, from the most socially formal occasion to the most intimate environment, so the woman exerts a twofold power over both her household and her husband. The part she plays in the reputation of the household and the manner in which she manages everyday affairs, compose the primary level of this power but, insensibly, in analysing her sphere of activity, one is drawn into the symbolic level which is an indissoluble part of the question. The good housewife becomes a sorceress and the woman's body involved in the work is seen to be the site of taboos which, if broken, bring down misfortune on the farm and its inhabitants.

On the other hand, masculine qualities, which appear to be taken for granted, are never questioned; masculine power always moves in a beneficent direction, whereas the woman's power is double-edged, maleficent or beneficent, according to the times and to the circumstances. That is why one must enquire into the portrait of the good housewife, the *bonne ménagère*, whereas the man's abilities – and one must say 'man', since the term *ménager* no longer exists – go without saying.

---

[4] N. Goffart, 'Glossaire du Mouzonnais', p. 99.

[5] S. Jossier, 'Dictionnaire des patois de l'Yonne', p. 138.

[6] 'The infertile woman must neither plant the garden nor carry the seed.' Pierre Bourdieu, 'Le sens pratique', p. 61.

THE GOOD HOUSEWIFE AND THE WICKED WOMAN

On dit bien vrai qu'en chaque saison les femmes font et défont les maisons
How true it is that in their season women make and break up the home
(Anjou)

Sans être des maçons, les femmes font et défont les maisons
Without being masons, women make and break up the home (Provence)

Une femme fait une maison et une femme la ruine
A woman makes the home and a woman breaks it up (Catalonia)

The woman is the home and its reputation rests in her hands, a
reputation close to honour, to its good name, a capital reputation for
the economic conduct of the household. Let us listen to the '*Simple*'
speaking of his wife, Victoire:

> Even when the servant-girl did all the heavy jobs, Victoire still had a lot
> to do. There were the children, there was the farmyard, the meals, a
> good part of the housework, not counting the times when there was a
> lot of milk, butter and cheese to be made. There was enough to do to
> wear out a stronger woman than her. Clever as she was, she knew how
> to get the best bargain for all the produce she took to the Bourbon
> market every Saturday. She was very economical, and often chided the
> servant-girl for using too much soap, too many lights, too much
> firewood. It even came about that people began to criticize our house . . .
> My work was not well thought of; they said the mistress of the house
> was mean and a busybody. Servants, young men and girls alike,
> thought twice before getting a job with us. We had to pay them over the
> odds.[7]

The woman's economic power in the household was the more
important in that it was she who, in most households, held the
purse-strings. Of course, little money circulated, a great deal being
produced and consumed in a closed circuit, but the money necessary
for day-to-day purchases most often came from the products of the
farmyard and the byre, which in turn derived from female industry.
Rents were paid once a year through the products sold at market.
Thus, on a day-to-day basis, the husband depended on his wife for the
small change he needed to buy a drink or get his tobacco. As holder of
the purse-strings, and distributor of the small sums of money necessary

[7] Emile Guillaumin, *op. cit.*, p. 200.

for day-to-day living, she was in a position to mistreat her servants and ridicule her husband in the eyes of the village community. Guillaumin describes another household which was a local laughing-stock:

> The woman who had taken over the management of the household was making him (the husband) expiate all his former sins. Deprived of all pocket money, the poor man killed time, miserably; he could be seen wandering from the carpenter's to the farrier's, stopping to talk to the rare passers-by. Sometimes, someone would say to him ironically, knowing perfectly well he hadn't got a penny piece: 'Are you going to buy a round, monsieur Gouin?' . . . Madame Gouin penny-pinched over even the smallest things, over heating and lighting, over the soap, the butter, even over the salt and pepper. At mealtimes, the same bottle of wine would furnish the table for a week. The servant-girl shared her third of the loaf with the dog, and could not hope to make up her food on the pittance she was paid. Three servants in a row left the house afflicted with anaemia.[8]

It was difficult to strike a balance between avarice and economy, which was a particularly highly prized quality. It was to the woman that this day-to-day expenditure fell, a task which was all the more important in that little money circulated.

Femme économe et alerte vaut son pesant d'or
An economical, alert woman is worth her weight in gold (Poitou)

Femme économe fait la maison bonne
An economical woman makes for a good house (Champagne)

La femme doit être comme la fourmi et non comme la poule
A woman should be like the ant and not the chicken (Catalonia)

Qui a grande poêle, fin tamis et femme dépensière montre son cul nu dans la rue
Whoever has a big frying-pan, a fine sieve and a spendthrift wife stands bare-arsed in the street (Languedoc)

Femme qui fait des gâteaux, pauvre ménagère
A woman who makes cakes is a poor housekeeper (Provence)

Si tu te maries, prends un râteau, ne prends pas une fourche
If you wed, marry a rake, not a pitchfork (Franche-Comté)

---

[8] *ibid.*, pp. 301–2.

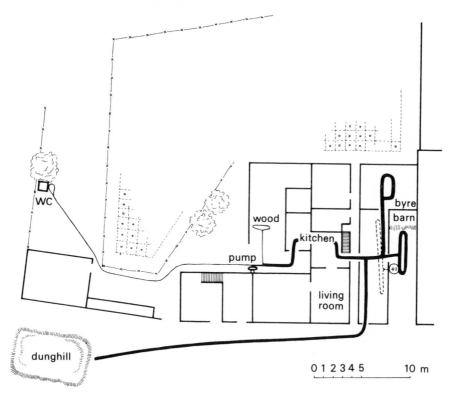

WC

byre
barn

wood

kitchen

pump

living
room

dunghill

0 1 2 3 4 5   10 m

12   *Route covered by man on a farm at Riche, Moselle.*

Proverbs use a wide variety of metaphors to assert the importance of economy in a woman's management of the household. They range from the most abstract, such as those from Poitou and Champagne, to those from the south, which draw on a wealth of comparisons with animals, or domestic utensils (in a big frying-pan you waste things, a fine sieve makes too white a flour), with the cost of food (sugar, associated with feast-days, should be used sparingly), and with agricultural implements (the rake which gathers in rather than the pitchfork which scatters). Household economy is the result of a difficult balancing act. One must not waste things, but at the same time one must avoid the reputation for avarice which makes it difficult to hire servants. Between foresight, charity and waste, there was scant room for manoeuvre, and every year one's reputation was open to question.

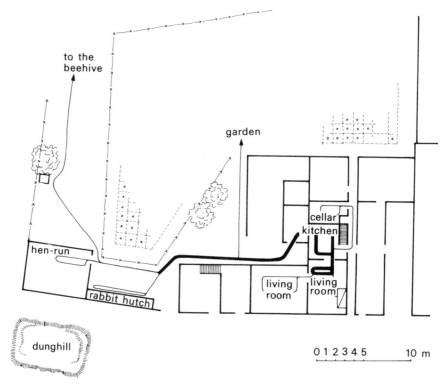

13   *Route covered by woman on a farm at Riche, Moselle.*

Economy in the home, but charity towards the world outside, towards the poor unfortunates who haunted the hedgerows and in whom certain accumulated wealth could excite envy. It was a question both of generosity and of protecting the household.

> Hospitality and charity were not empty words in the countryside of earlier days: their frequency implied a good many impoverished households. They were not only virtues, but strict duties, to ignore which could engage a redoubtable collective responsibility. There were too many narratives recounting the comings and goings of divine and sacred figures in humble disguises, for neglect in matters of hospitality and charity not to be feared by a village community which was always ready to explain natural calamities in terms of the faults of an individual.[9]

[9] André Varagnac, *op. cit.*, p. 188–9.

In fact, the woman also 'makes' the home, insofar as she protects it from everything that could endanger the farm and its inhabitants. All the practices aimed at keeping the young child in good health – magico-religious or empiric mixtures, and the practices of pilgrimage which were indissolubly linked with the maternal care of a young child[10] – fell to the woman, as well as the rituals aimed at protecting the household from evil spirits from outside.

To the popular mind, the universe was scattered with bad luck ready to attack the people and livestock on the farm. 'Conserving the live capital – the men and beasts of the household and the perishable goods: this meant waging a struggle day and night against a world of invisible dangers.'[11] Certain rituals of domestic protection fall jointly on the father and the mother of the family. 'It is the father who, at Candlemas, puts little crosses of holy wax on the outside walls of the byre; he traces a cross on every cow's horns to protect them from illness. On the same occasion, the father of the family lets fall a few drops of wax onto the hair of each of the children, to protect them from sore throats. The housewife marks all the doors and windows throughout the house with the sign of the cross made in wax.'[12] In the same way, at Christmas, the complementary ritual action of man and wife can be observed: 'In the Angoumois, Aunis and Saintonge, the master of the house brings in a large log, the *Cosse*, which he scatters with water and salt before putting it in the hearth. Before going to Midnight Mass . . . the father of the family goes and fetches the big log called the *terfeu* because it has to last three days. He puts it solemnly in its place and the 'mistress' blesses it with a box branch, so that the hearth may never grow cold.'[13]

But, more often present in the house than the man, the woman is seen, more than he, as protector of the hearth. The rituals to be fulfilled occur at the high points of the ceremonial calendar, at Christmas, as we have seen, and on Palm Sunday. With one and the same action, the woman extends the protection of the palm over living and dead. Thus, in Mantois and Vexin:

> On Palm Sunday, the housewife will make crowns of box wood; she has them blessed, and, on coming out of Mass, she takes them to the

[10] Françoise Loux, *op. cit.*
[11] André Varagnac, *op. cit.*, pp. 189–90.
[12] *ibid.*
[13] P. L. Menon and R. Lecotté, *op. cit.*, p. 187.

cemetery and lays them on her family tomb; she also takes branches of box home with her and fixes them over the lintel, while a twig is reserved for putting up over the earthenware container for holy water which is hung over the marriage bed . . . On Easter Saturday, the housewife goes to church to fetch the freshly consecrated holy water. She puts some of the holy water in the stoop over the bed, the rest she keeps in a flask. A scattering of holy water prevented fire and diverted lightning during a storm.[14]

In Touraine, the fields, livestock and even the work-tools received this benediction. 'The housewife, bringing back from the church branches which had been blessed, divided them, so that the workers could go and plant a shoot in each field that had been sown. The cow-girls put a branch over the byres, and the shepherds put them over the shelters. The farmer's wife decorated the old holy-water container over her bed with them.'[15] Certain saints protected the house from the elements, and particularly from lightning, which was much feared, since it could set the thatch alight. To obtain this protection, the mistress of the house often called upon Saint Barbe, 4 December, by lighting a candle which had been blessed at Mass, and going through the byres and the granary with it.[16]

The farmer's wife, alone, was responsible for the farmyard, and we have already seen how often popular thinking equates her with a chicken. The rituals surrounding the farmyard or involving eggs surrounded the symbolic action of the female, protector of hens whose eggs in turn protected the whole household. Thus, 'the farmers' wives in Bresse went on market day to the church dedicated to Saint Denis (a saint reputed to protect the farmyard) and asked him for good health for their hens: some even brought their sickly chicks to church . . . Farmers' wives in Lorraine gave crumbs of holy bread to their chickens.'[17]

The farmyards, thus protected, produced eggs with therapeutic powers. 'At Vénizy, in the Yonne, the *roulées* were eaten by the family. They were made of eggs laid on Good Friday which the mistress of the house had carefully preserved because they had the property of guarding from fevers, since they never perished.'[18] The

---

[14] Eugène Bougeâtre, *op. cit.*, p. 178.
[15] Jacques-Marie Rougé, *Le folklore de la Touraine*, p. 63.
[16] ATP research into the traditional calendar, Basses-Pyrénées, Aïnhoa.
[17] Charles Moiset, *op. cit.*, p. 33.
[18] *ibid.*, p. 29.

preventive power of these eggs was also to be seen behind the collections made by little children during Holy Week. At Ormoy, also in the Yonne, they sang the following ditty as they stood before each house:

Filles et femmes qui gardez la maison,
Donnez des oeufs à ces petits garçons;
Donnez-leur en autant que vous pourrez,
Vous serez de Dieu récompensées.[19]
Women and girls who look after the house,
give these young boys some eggs;
give them as many as you can,
God will reward you.

All these rituals related by folklorists in a fragmentary way must be studied as a whole in order to be able to reconstruct the coherent feminine image which they express. The woman protects the hearth through actions and prayers which are sanctified and authorized by the Church, and which fit into a much wider panoply of empirical and magical rituals. Calling the sacred into play was only one of the protective strategies to which they could have recourse. But most of all this power had a reverse side. As well as being protective and defensive, it had a counterpart which was active and destructive: if the woman in question did not carry out the appropriate gestures, she could bring down misfortune on her household; she could by word or deed do harm to her own household or to others.

She could, first of all, harm others. If misfortunes are seen as always coming together, striking people, and stock, and the entire household, then it is clear that they are the work of a conscious and malignant will. In order to be rid of it, this malevolent influence had to be thrown back on to the sorceress.[20] Thus, neighbourly relations were based on mutual aid, and the woman had to chase ill luck from neighbouring houses, as in this ritual observed in Baugeois:

The farmer's wife who wanted her cows to give abundant butter to the detriment of the other farmers' wives, had to get up on the first of May, before dawn, and walk through the fields or along the paths where her neighbours' cattle grazed, dragging her milk-strainer on a string and

---

[19] Paul Sébillot, *Le folklore de France*, vol. III, p. 221.
[20] Jeane Favret-Saada, *Les mots, la mort, les sorts, la sorcellerie dans le Bocage.*

muttering 'milk and butter, come all to me, and not at all to my neighbours'; similarly, when a woman's cows gave little milk, and her neighbour's gave a great deal, she would charge her neighbour with having 'drawn it off'.[21]

There is, thus, an imperceptible shift from the image of the good mother to that of the sorceress, and this ambivalence characterizes the image which rural society has of the feminine personality, and the fear in which it is held.

The woman's malevolent powers can also work directly against her household and her husband, and this power is all the more disturbing in that it is mediated through the daily tasks, whose tools become transformed into instruments of harm. The good housewife and mother spinning beside a cradle becomes a sorceress riding astride her distaff. The hard-working washerwomen are transformed into *Maoues Noz*, 'Women of the Night' – nocturnal spirits who do the washing to expiate some serious crime committed during their lifetimes.[22] When she does the washing at reputedly forbidden times, the woman can bring down misfortune on herself and on those whose clothes she is washing: during Holy Week, if the ban is not respected, it is said in the Brive region 'that the men of the house are exposed to the risk of death; in the Gex area, it is the head of the household who risks death.'[23] In the Yonne, there is a saying that *qui coule la lessive le vendredi, veut la mort de son mari* (whoever does the washing on a Friday, wants her husband to die).[24]

The housewife can summon the devil if she does not conform to the rulings familiar to the whole social group.

There are several things which must not be done in the home after the sun has gone down. It is forbidden to sweep. A few embers should be left alight under the cinders in case some deceased inhabitant might wish to return to the house where they once lived (Lower Brittany) . . . In Anjou, one is supposed to leave a bucket of water out in the kitchen every night, so that if someone in the house should die during the night, their soul might go and wash in it. The housewife who had omitted to do this would see the sinful soul which had been unable to cleanse itself

---

[21] Claude Fraysse, *op. cit.*, p. 156.
[22] Paul Sébillot, *Le folklore de France*, vol. II, p. 49.
[23] Paul Sébillot, *Légendes et curiosités des métiers*, p. 262.
[24] *ibid.*, p. 266.

return as a will-o'-the-wisp . . . The devil can also appear when a woman looks in her mirror after sunset.[25]

Proverbs comparing a woman to the devil are making more than a metaphorical allusion. Through these rituals, we can see that the woman has the power of summoning the devil, and that she herself can be the devil.

Si petite que soit la femme, elle a plus de fourberie que le diable
However small the woman, she can outcheat the devil (Provence)

Quand le diable ne peut pas le faire, il va chercher la femme
When the devil cannot manage it, he goes and fetches a woman (Aveyron)

In traditional society, a woman has no status outside marriage. This is the only institution which enables her to fulfil herself as a social being; the old woman is treated as a servant, or else excludes herself by retiring into holy orders, or by submerging herself in the anonymity of the town. The man makes a woman, he socializes her, he makes her exist as a social and cultural being. Nonetheless, the woman remains a natural being, and it is from this that she draws her fundamental power. The woman's body – with its own cycles relating to natural cycles, ruled like the phases of the moon, and pregnancies which seem like so many aberrations – appears mysterious and fearful to a man, since its power belongs to a sphere which is foreign to him.[26]

Education aims at watering down this female power just as the attribution of female tasks aims at keeping her in her place. But women are a constant threat of death and a source of social disruption. Because of a fear of their menstrual soiling, they are surrounded, throughout their activities, with a host of interdictions.[27] To circumscribe their movements, to limit their influence on the village society, this is the concern of the community.

The profound fear implicit in the ambivalent image of the woman is deep-rooted. An analysis of sixteenth-century engravings, which would reach identical conclusions if extended to other centuries, shows that one of the most widespread representations of women in

[25] Paul Sébillot, *Le folklore de France*, vol. I, p. 137–9.
[26] Yvonne Verdier, 'Les femmes et le saloir'.
[27] Yvonne Verdier, *Façons de dire, façons de faire*.

addition to that of the wife-and-mother or the mother-and-housewife
is that of the dangerous woman.

> French sixteenth-century society considered the woman to be danger-
> ous; she threatened society through her sexuality, through her associa-
> tion with nature and with the animal world and through her leanings
> towards evil.
>   Her body was an instrument of sin and the fear of female sexuality
> was not only that of perdition, but also a fear of contact with the
> obscure forces which she represented. She was an inexhaustible source
> of moral, social and supernatural difficulties. In the engraving, the
> immodest woman, the old woman and the sorcerer are the three
> principal visions of a conception of the woman as a powerful, malevol-
> ent and dangerous creature . . . Fear of feminine sexuality has a threefold
> source. She is feared as the source of the spiritual defilement with whom
> one potentially recreates in each sexual act the original sin. She is feared
> as the source of social disorder and, as a being belonging to the animal
> world, she threatens the order of society and, of the universe since she
> can subjugate man and make him share in the animal world. The fear of
> female sexuality works at three levels: religious and moral, social, and
> cosmic.[28]

The husband was in the end the most vulnerable target for this
dangerous power and, though nineteenth-century society had lost
traces of the magical semi-rituals which the wife could carry out with
regard to her spouse, the unconscious fear remained. *Les evangiles des
quenouilles*, relating the discussions which took place during the
escreignes (meetings where women came together in the evenings to
gossip and laugh while spinning, during the fifteenth century[29]) are
full of disturbing advice:

> When a woman gets up in the night to piss before the cock has crowed
> for the third time, and she straddles her husband, be it known that, if
> any of his limbs are stiff, they will never relax if she does not return to
> her place by way of the same place where she straddled over him . . .[30]

If a woman wishes to prevail over a husband who beats her, she must
take all his shirts and, when the priest is reading the Passion on a Friday,

---

[28] Sara F. Matthews-Grieco, *La conception de la femme dans l'estampe française du XVIe
siècle*, p. 93 and 123.
[29] *Les Évangiles des quenouilles*, p. vi.
[30] *ibid.*, p. 66.

she must put them beneath the altar, and make him wear them the following Sunday. Know that, as long as he wears this shirt, he will be gentle and courteous to his wife.[31]

In those days, the woman feared the man's blows more than at the time which concerns us, but one might imagine that such a husband, beating his wife, would suffer her magical vengeance, notably in the form of sexual dominance.

SEXUALITY AND TENDERNESS

If there is one area charged with symbolic thinking, then it must be the area of sexuality. Of all the maleficent powers which a man is led to fear in his wife, the most redoubtable are her sexual appetites, which threaten to subjugate him to her power. There are numerous proverbs dealing with this deep-seated fear.

An excessively amorous woman was dangerous:

Quand le poule recherche le coq, l'amour ne vaut pas une noix
When the hen seeks out the cock, love isn't worth a fig (Limousin)

Un coq suffit à dix poules, mais dix hommes ne suffisent pas à une femme
One cock is enough for ten hens, but ten men are not enough for one woman (Pays Basque)

Femme couchée et bois debout, homme n'en vit jamais le bout
A lying woman and standing wood, a man will never see the end of them (Anjou)

Bois debout et femme renversée font plus de force qu'un cheval à la montée
Standing wood and a woman on her back are more tiring than a horse on a hill (Provence)

Through the metaphor of the hen and the farmyard or by playing on the double meaning of the standing wood, these proverbs underline the strength of the woman and the domination of the male which ensued. This sexual power endangers the social order since, in this private, but socialized and controlled domain, the model demands that she should submit. When the sayings deal with the subject in metaphors, using the comparative register of the farmyard, the semantic slide is almost imperceptible. From the hen-woman who wants to be

---

[31] *ibid.*, p. 74.

in charge, proverbs pass on to the hen-seductress who pre-empts the cockerel. To these seductresses who seek to diminish masculine power through the power of their bodies, society promises a violent death, for their charm comprises a real danger of subversion and threatens the advent of a topsy-turvy world.

Quand le coq a chanté la poule doit se taire
When the cock has crowed the hen should be silent (Picardy)

Le ménage va bien mal quand la poule fait le coq
The household is going very badly when the hen plays the cock (Provence)

Poule qui chante le coq et coq qui pond, c'est le diable à la maison
A hen crowing like a cock, and a cock laying eggs, means the devil's in the house (Upper Brittany)

Des femmes qui sifflent, des poules qui chantent comme les coqs, des coqs qui font les oeufs, il faut s'en défaire le plus vite que l'on peut
A whistling woman, a hen crowing like a cock, and a cock laying eggs, are all to be got rid of as quickly as possible (Val d'Aosta)

On a practical level, and despite the recent studies which have been devoted to the subject, it must be recognized that sexuality is an area about which we know very little, particularly in the rural environment. In the hypothesis put forward here, we would like to treat sexuality and tenderness between man and wife together. It seems important not to dissociate the two relationships since they are neither interchangeable nor exclusive. Tenderness cannot be reduced to a gratifying sexual relationship, but can be made up of mutual respect, of a common assumption of tasks and responsibilities, of an association in a common ideal. On the other hand, the manner in which sexuality becomes a sort of leitmotiv in discussions of the family and the way in which it is treated by historians shows a curious conception of sexual behaviour. Historians are especially concerned with the sexuality of young people (is it allowed or not, do they do it or not?), and, where adult sexuality is concerned, they are most interested in the advent of contraception and its effect on conjugal relations. Thus, having begun by setting out the theological doctrines in this area,[32] which condemn love in marriage and seeking pleasure in the sexual

[32] Jean-Louis Flandrin, *Familles, parenté, maison, sexualité dans l'ancienne societé*, pp. 156–9.

act, Jean-Louis Flandrin judges that 'the revolution in the conjugal system cannot occur until after that in the economic system: for only then will it be possible to marry for love without threatening the hierarchic structures of society.'[33] Further on he asks whether, 'in practising coitus interruptus, the man was not imposing his will on the woman.'[34] If these documents suggest that men in bourgeois families had greater concern for their wives, there is nothing which makes it possible to draw any conclusions about the rural environment. Edward Shorter does not have any qualms about drawing such conclusions, however: 'Most men of the popular classes were probably indifferent to their wife's pleasure,'[35] but 'from 1850 to 1914 almost all couples became eroticized (that is to say), sexual activity and attraction began to play an independent role among the factors contributing to a couple's staying together. The triumph of sexuality in conjugal life is manifested for instance in the definitive assertion of the wife's right to orgasm.'[36] Such hypotheses are difficult to sustain, particularly because these historians have based themselves primarily on demographic sources, constructed by science, or on ecclesiastical sources, which reproduce the language of an external and dominant category seeking to impose its views on a dominated society.

Ethnological documents dealing with sexuality in traditional society are exceedingly rare,[37] though a latent sexuality imbued the whole of peasant life: 'It is enough to have been at a country wedding to understand the natural, one could almost say the innocent, way in which the crudest jokes were made and received. In the nineteenth century, bourgeois proprieties greatly modified the tone usually allowed at these affairs, for high society under the *ancien régime*, just like the people, accepted ways of speaking and acting which would not be tolerated a century later unless presented in the most allusive and ambiguous manner.'[38]

Proverbs speak of human sexuality and animal sexuality; novelists and painters, less shackled by taboos than folklorists, have been able to evoke this fundamental aspect of peasant life. Thus, in Guy de

---

[33] *ibid.*, p. 169.

[34] *ibid.*, p. 213.

[35] Edward Shorter, *op. cit.*, p. 300.

[36] *ibid.*, p. 303.

[37] Michel Valière, 'Préparation d'une enquête sur la sexualité en Poitou', p. 2, provides an exception.

[38] André Varagnac, *op. cit.*, p. 153.

Maupassant, in a passage which serves as a preamble to sexual relations between a valet and a servant girl, one is made to feel the relationship between human and animal sexuality:

> In front of the door, the manure-heap gave off a ceaseless light trembling steam. Hens paced over it, crouched on its flank, and scratched in it a bit with one foot to find worms. In the midst of them, the cock stood, proudly. Every moment, he chose one of them and walked around her with a little chirrup to call her. The hen rose nonchalantly and received him with a tranquil air, bending her legs and supporting him on her wings; then she shook the dust out of her feathers and resumed her post on the midden, while he crowed, enumerating his conquests; and cocks answered from all the neighbouring yards, as if they were sending each other, from farm to farm, amorous challenges. The servant-girl looked at them without thinking . . .[39]

Let us also look at Millet's painting *The Meridian*, which shows us two reapers, a man and a woman, lying asleep . . . 'We sense that these two beings stretched out together for the midday rest would also lie together at night, the placement of the sickles and the clogs echoes that of the bodies, and the woman's position shows her submission.'[40] Peasant life is impregnated with sexuality, and there is no problem about education in this area. When they are very young, the children learn about reproduction by observing the farmyard life around them, the cow being taken to the bull, calves and lambs being born. In small houses where old and young all cohabited together, it is likely that sexual relations were more easily known than behind the closed doors of separate rooms. This was certainly something which worried the folklorists. Some of them saw in it a sign of the inferiority and bestiality of the peasant: 'Family life lived entirely in common, with parents and children crammed together in a single room, is, from a moral point of view, a bad thing; the children are made to witness disturbing sights, and it could lead them to a bestial promiscuity.'[41]

The observers feared, as much as an initiation into adult sexuality, the presence of infant sexuality, of incest or homosexuality between brothers and sisters: 'The small number of rooms and the confined space within them, making it necessary to put several beds in a room,

---

[39] Guy de Maupassant, 'Story of a Farm Girl'.

[40] Jean-François Millet, *Exposition du Grand-Palais*, p. 218.

[41] Henri Pullès, 'Les maisons types dans la région de Carcassonne', in Alfred de Foville, *Enquête sur les conditions de l'habitation en France*, p. 257.

and to put them close together, presents serious moral dangers. The parents, as a rule, sleep in the kitchen, while the children and servants of both sexes sleep in other rooms, often in just one room.'[42] On the other hand, peasants are elsewhere presented as being invested with all the sound 'natural' virtues, capable of protecting 'morality': 'Despite the members of the family being crammed together in a small space, there was no falling off in morality. I have lived among them and I never heard even the breath of scandal. An active life, pious habits, a god-fearing father and mother, none of this lent itself to any relaxation in morals.'[43] If peasant sexuality was not seen as bestial, this was because the observer was comparing it with an even more bestial sexuality, that of the 'low', working classes. The remarks made by an observer in the Tarn-et-Garonne show this attitude well:

> We do not claim to be sure that our peasants still remain in the innocence of that golden age; but their morality is infinitely greater than that of the workers in the towns. Religious belief and the traditional authority of the father of the family may be held to account for this to a great extent, but equally, it is incontestable that the fact of living in a large room where the whole family sleeps together under the eye of the head of the household, in large beds provided with canopies and generously curtained, does not present the same difficulties as for those crammed together in a narrow garret who have been depraved by immoral example and the lax language of the street, and who are deprived of paternal care.[44]

We do not know whether parents saw their sexuality as something to be hidden from the children; anyway, the bedroom was not the only place in which one could make love. There was the barn, where the men often went in summer while the women invested the house: it was the place for the afternoon rest, and for meetings; and there were the fields. In the Hautes-Alpes, at Saint-Véran, there was an area called the *bois d'Amour*.[45]

Peasant society was imbued with a permanent sexuality, which was

---

[42] 'Maisons de la région de la Meuse, vallée de l'Ornain (canton de Gondrecourt)', in Alfred de Foville, *op. cit.*, vol. I, p. 91.

[43] M. Martin, 'Maisons du Drac et du Valgaudemar, Hautes-Alpes', in Alfred de Foville, *op. cit.*, vol. I. p. 193.

[44] J. Momméja, 'Air de Montauban, Tarn-et-Garonne' in Alfred de Foville, *op. cit.*, p. 278.

[45] Henri Raulin, *op. cit.*, p. 63.

related to that of the animals. It is difficult to go beyond that as a statement; to know whether the experience of feminine sexuality was one of frustration or of pleasure; to know whether the husband was concerned for his partner's enjoyment, or whether coitus interruptus had any effect on these relations. Might one suggest that traditional peasant sexuality was less influenced by ecclesiastical repression than earlier writings have implied, that it was a constant theme in peasant life – the pregnant cow, the growing corn, the laying hen – but that it was less fundamental than it is today? The relationship of the nineteenth-century peasant couple was quite different from that of the modern urban couple. Some socio-sexologists claim that, today, a sexual relationship which does not satisfy both partners is an indication of the failure of the marriage and a reason for divorce. That is perhaps an oversimplified view of the modern couple, but it is definitely true that the success of sexual relations is not emphasized to anything like the same extent in the rural couple. Today, and even more so in earlier times, the peasant couple are committed to the same end: the success of the farm. A good harvest, the purchase of land are causes for a deep satisfaction shared by man and wife together. Is it not a proof of ethnocentrism to emphasize sexual relations? Let us leave the *Simple* with the last word on this difficult subject, in which, more than elsewhere, the ethnological approach is insufficient. In *La vie d'un Simple*, bourgeois and peasant behaviour are contrasted. The way in which the bourgeois man and wife exchange tender words is judged by the peasant to be 'a bit stupid. If a married couple talked to each other like that in the country, everyone would be amused by it. Perhaps we love each other as much as they do, but we are not so generous with soft words.'[46]

SOLIDARITY BETWEEN THE COUPLE ON THE FARM

From the eighteenth century onwards, the principle of the solidarity of the household, of the necessity of keeping the wife abreast of the management in order to ensure the survival of the farm, the central concern, in the case of one or other of the couple dying, was already established.

> However much the overall management of a farm, the sheep, the horses, buying and selling, in a word, the whole business of the farm,

[46] Emile Guillaumin, *op. cit.*, p. 311.

might be principally the concern of the farmer, he should nonetheless not neglect to tell his wife as much of it as possible. I think it is even his duty to do so, if he does not wish to fail in one of his matrimonial and paternal duties. For is it not true that his wife might lose him any day? Suddenly widowed, what would she do if she knew nothing of the farm, and of its central concerns? Even assuming she thought of marrying again, the decencies of widowhood would demand a certain lapse of time, during which she could find herself in very real difficulties, and having to turn for advice to her servants, who can never have the point of view of a master.[47]

All these learned discussions from the end of the eighteenth century, like the earlier ones of Olivier de Serres, were drawn from the observation of the behaviour of peasant families, at the same time creating a frame of reference for their conduct in the nineteenth century. The woman in the country was powerful: through her activity she participated fully in production; she was the protector of the hearth. Man and wife more often appear united than disunited. Farm contracts were often drawn up in their joint names. Thus, 16 March 1873, a farm lease was granted before a notary in Pont-l'Abbé, South Finistère, to 'Jean-Marie Le Berre and Marie Cossec, his wife, authorized by him, farmer, living in the village of Kermatheano in the commune of Saint-Jean-Trolimon, purchasers here present and having jointly and together accepted . . .' The wife here is legally responsible for the farm. Numerous rituals testify to this position.

On farms where the mistress of the house did not participate in the major agricultural labours, there was a ritual to associate her with them. In Touraine, 'the reapers gave the mistress who came out to meet the procession the final sheaf, called the *javelot*, or javelin.'[48] In Upper Brittany, 'the last sheaf was decorated with flowers and with an oak branch. It was always made into the shape of a person. If the farmer was married, the sheaf was made double; there was a large person, and a smaller one, like a doll, which was placed inside the larger one. This was then called *Mère Gerbe*, Mother Sheaf. It was presented to the mistress of the house who then undid it and gave out drinks.'[49]

Identification of the household was often carried out by means of the name given to the house, to the extent that the surname was

[47] L. Roze, *op. cit.*, pp. 41–2.
[48] P.-L. Menon and Roger Lecotté, *op. cit.*, p. 127.
[49] Paul Sébillot, *Coutumes populaires de la haute Bretagne*, p. 307.

completely lost in ordinary usage. In certain regions of the South, the name of the house was more important than that of the family, and was transmitted through men and women alike, depending on who inherited it. Sometimes, a house took on the name of its occupant. Thus, in the Corrèze, at Bugeat, there was a farm called the *maison Arfeullière*,[50] though M and Mme Arf were only tenant farmers. The name might also come from a previous occupant. At Piolenc, in the Vaucluse,[51] a farm worked by its owners was called 'La Lusiniane' after the name of a previous owner, Mme Lusinian, who had been widely renowned in the region for her intelligence and hard work, and who had owned and worked the farm in the previous century.

Thus the name of the house is no longer specifically masculine, and often the family or household name tends to be that of the farm. The family name transmitted through men by law was in fact little used in everyday speech, and, therefore, to see in that name an example of male supremacy or a form of the preponderance of masculine lineage would be misleading. In the Bigouden region, for instance, Mme Hélou was unknown to her fellow villagers, partly because there were a limited number of patronymics, and that alone was not enough to identify her. The woman kept her first name and her father's surname, by which she had been known before she married, and to this was added the name of the farm she worked. To her fellow villagers, this particular Mme Hélou was Victorine Tannel from Kervouec, or even just Victorine Kervouec. In other regions, the wife loses her identity and takes on that of her husband: in Beauce and in Perche, 'in the village, the married woman takes a feminized form of her husband's name: la Planchenaude is Planchenaud's wife, and la Rouillone the wife of M Rouillon.'[52] On the other hand, if the man is foreign to the region, he often takes his wife's name, e.g., Ernestine's man, 'Génie (Eugénie)'s man, Mélie (Amélie)'s man . . .' In the same way, children were often called by their mother's name, e.g., Louise's lad, Norine (Honorine)'s girl.[53]

Our knowledge of systems of naming, and of the use of surname and first name in the rural environment is still too limited to make it possible to draw up a table of regional variations. Such a study would doubtless tell us a great deal about man–wife relations and about the

[50] EAR, no. 6.
[51] EAR, no. 19.
[52] F. Chapiseau, *op. cit.*, p. 157.
[53] P.-L. Menon and Roger Lecotté, *op. cit.*, p. 107.

way in which those relations functioned with regard to the community at large. The system of address between husband and wife is also a reflection of that symbiosis between family life and work life. The terms husband–wife, or man–wife, which have a religious or an administrative connotation, were not widely used. The terms used referred to the farm. In the South of France, in Provence, 'the wife called her husband *vous* and called him only by his surname, in the same way as the eldest child in each family, whether boy or girl, was called by the family name and never by their first name.'[54]

In Touraine, the wife was called *compagnie* (companion), and when she died, they spoke of 'losing one's companion'.[55]

In Beauce, in Normandy, according to Menon and Lecotté, the farmer's wife was called 'the mistress' and called her husband 'the master'. Instead of seeing this as a sign of equality between the couple, the observers maintained that these appellations were a proof of female inferiority: 'The marriages in our community were usually happy ones. The wife always had the profoundest respect for her husband and spoke of him only in the third person, just as in polite society. In speaking of him, she referred to him as *le niotre* or *not homme* (our man). She served at table and remained standing while he ate.'[56]

If the wife called her husband 'our master' was she not employing a plural which globally encompassed the farm, the household and its members, rather than the royal 'we'? The man called master was the man in charge of men and animals. For 'our master' there was a corresponding 'our mistress'. Certain writers have noted the use of the terms *bourgeois* and *bourgeoise*, in Normandy for instance,[57] which have no connotations of authority, nor do the terms *patron* and *patronne*, which apparently were introduced quite late, in the nineteenth century. These reciprocal appellations were not for the exclusive use of the man and his wife. With the exception of the children, and that is an area which still needs to be checked, they were the terms used by all the members of the household. Neither familiar nor tender, implying no intimacy, they were terms used by everybody, and referring the speaker to his farm.

Did the married couple use *tu* or *vous* to each other? The variety of usages appears to be very great. Thus, Abel Hugo notes: 'In the other

[54] Paul Lafran, *Le folklore de Saint-Chamas en Provence*.
[55] Jacques-Marie Rougé, *Le parler tourangeau (région de Loches)*, p. 45.
[56] Lucien Gueneau, 'Us et coutumes du Morvan', p. 106.
[57] Abbé Léonor Blouin, *Moeurs et coutumes de basse Normandie*, p. 123.

countries of the Aveyron, couples of every class said *tu* to each other from the moment they were married. In the Mauges, on the other hand, as soon as the wedding ceremony was over, a couple which had previously said *tu* now said *vous*. The wife from then on only spoke to her husband with deference and respect.'[58] Jeanton speaks of *vouvoiement* in the Mâconnais as both a sign of distance and of 'the outstanding dignity of marriage'.[59]

Thus, from wherever one starts to unravel the web of social relations woven between and around the rural couple, relationships within the household appear to be in balance, but once the man and wife are outside the setting of the household, segregation between the sexes appears a great deal more clearly marked.

[58] Abel Hugo, *op. cit.*, vol. II. p. 202.
[59] Gabriel Jeanton, *op. cit.*, p. 60.

5

The Man, the Wife, and the Village

Les femmes à la maison comme les chats, et les hommes à la rue comme les chiens
Women in the house like cats, men in the streets like dogs (Catalonia)

The sexual division of territory within the house is reproduced in the segregation of external territories: the organization of male and female village sociability is an example.

Proverbs are normative here too: they state the norm rather than describing the practice. Thus, they refuse the woman the right to go out and move about outside without a reason, for fear that these absences might stop her fulfilling her duties.

Miroir de rue, fumier de maison
Mirror of the street, dunghill of a house (Provence)

Toute femme qui passe trop longtemps hors de chez elle, sa maison n'est pas solide
Any woman who spends too long away from home does not have a steady house (Provence)

Ni maison d'angle ni femme au balcon
Neither a corner house nor a woman on the balcony (Catalonia)

Mieux vaut tourte de pain sur la table que miroir à la fenêtre
Better a loaf of bread on the table than a mirror at the window (Brittany)

It is, strictly speaking, more a question here of the street, and of gossiping with other women, than of work outside. As well as condemning the neglect of her daily tasks, traditional society mistrusts the power acquired by the woman as soon as she finds herself with other women. Now, the work of the farm is not always carried out in the enclosed world of the household, but calls for mutual help between neighbours; this marks out, for men and women alike, the primary framework of village sociability and describes the community's sexual territories. Work and sociability are often two aspects of the same activity.

WORK AND SOCIABILITY

The men would be in the fields or at the forge, but they were also in the café, on the communal playing-field. The women were at the laundry, at the spring, at the communal oven, in the breadshop. It is the exterior extension of their domestic tasks which takes the women out of their houses. They go out for household reasons: water must be fetched, the dough must be taken to the baker or the linen washed at the river each week, as well as the 'great laundries' which only take place two or three times a year. These last form major female festivals, to some extent comparable to hay-making and harvest for the men – works employing a number of hands and ending with a meal.

Frequently throughout the year the women would go to the stream or the river, and all our male folklorists note, in half-amused, half-condemnatory tones, the social role of this meeting-place and the kind of conversation carried on there.

The wash-house 'is also a tribunal, a highly popular court of justice, in which indulgence is banned and where all the men pass some wretched moments. These strapping wenches undress them in a trice, soap them from head to foot, rinse them off, scrub down the lather with a scrubbing-brush and then on with beating them! Bang! Bang! Here's for you, père Amedée! Bang, bang! Take that, Zephyrin old fellow!'[1] A Breton folklorist uses the same terms: 'The washing is rinsed, twisted, and beaten at the wash-house where the tongues are quite as active as the washerwomen's beetles; it is the seat of feminine justice, with little mercy for the menfolk. Soaped from head to foot, soaped again, and rinsed down, they go through some bad times . . .'[2] 'The wash-house is one of the principal places of gossip in our region, Women of all ages meet there, and soaping and beating their linen

[1] Henri Massoul, *La vie paysanne dans la Haute-Loire*, p. 18.
[2] Alexandre Bouët and Oliver Perrin, *op. cit.*, p. 51.

often seems only a secondary activity, so enthusiastically do they exchange scandal, and tell each other of the loves, marriages, births and other major events of the district.'[3]

The kind of news which was spread at these 'feminine' meetings was in fact of a fairly particular nature: it was related to the major biological or social events of the human cycle. There was less discussion of political than of family matters and the intimate relations between young people or adults: the shameful pregnancy of such-and-such a young girl, or the donkey-ride old father so-and-so would suffer at the next Carnival. Traditional society confided to the woman speech on personal, almost taboo subjects, involving the body. No man would go near the wash-house, such was the dread of this group of women, whose power was increased by force of numbers.

Individual female power was reinforced by the collective power of the group of women. Nothing was more feared, nor felt to be more excluding, than a group of women gathered together at the wash-house or the bake-house. The women spoke together, criticizing, denouncing, insulting, slandering, relating family histories, deepening rivalries, and, through all this, supported that whole part of social relations which is expressed through a violent and slanderous speech, of which they seemed to have a monopoly. To the woman alone, face-to-face with a man, corresponds this female society, face-to-face with male society, a society which feels threatened by its very existence because of the kind of remarks made within it.

The folklorists, conscious of this sense of exclusion and threat, defend themselves in turn by passing a derogatory judgement on the gathering, and the subjects of conversation current in wash-house and bake-house, as if to diminish their importance and exorcize their fear of them. The women 'very much enjoy these days (of group work); they are for them real pleasure jaunts, spending a few hours together, with nothing to do but chatter and outdo each other with all the true and false news of the region. The bake-house, like the wash-house, thus becomes a school of slander and gossip and Breton women, who elsewhere, when it comes to working and suffering, seem to have something masculine in their character, appear purely feminine there.'[4]

Proverbs confirm the nature of the remarks exchanged and show us women, at once exhausted by their work and furious with a husband whose shortcomings they have become all-too familiar with. Is this

---

[3] *ibid.*, p. 170.
[4] *ibid.*

not the way to interpret the aggressiveness against her husband which proverbs ascribe to the washerwoman?

> *A la fontaine, au moulin, au four et au lavoir, les femmes disent tout*
> At the spring, at the mill, at the bake-house and at the wash-house, women tell everything (Provence)

> *Quand les femmes viennent du ruisseau, elles mangeraient le mari tout vivant*
> When women come from the stream, they would eat their husbands alive (Gascony, Provence)

> *Quand la femme vient du ruisseau, elle mangerait l'homme tout vif*
> When a woman comes from the stream, she would eat her husband alive (Limousin)

In some regions, female work gatherings function along the same lines as the wash-house or the bake-house. Ulysse Rouchon describes their organization as well as the topics discussed on such occasions. Known as *covize* in the Auvergne, or *covegis* in Velay, they consisted of gatherings of women from the same district, similar to the summer evening spent together in a *veillée d'été*.

> While the labourers worked in the fields, and the artisans in their workshops, while the blacksmith was bent over his anvil, and the carter followed the ruts . . . the housewives felt the need during the good weather to pool their extra-domestic activities, such as mending clothes, or that additional craft so dear to their expert fingers, lace-making. Pass through our villages then, one weekday, in the afternoon. You won't see many people in the streets, except when it's time to drive the cows to pasture, but if you go past a little square or a courtyard, you will hear from a distance a confused murmur, the clatter of bobbins on the pavement, snatches of conversation, laughter, occasionally the strains of a song and often the responses of a prayer. You are going to find youself before a *covegis*.
> Under the shade of a tree, arranged against a wall away from the road, there would be a dozen of them facing whoever lived in the farm, but keeping an eye on everything that was going on. The mothers would bring their toddlers to scratch in the dirt with the chickens from the neighbouring houses; some would have cradles set on the ground beside them; there were dogs curled up, dreaming their dreams with their noses in the dust. The housewives were filled with curiosity and an appetite for news from the region guided their conversations. *Souvas*, of which charity was the principal ornament. Perhaps one of them had

mentioned a forthcoming marriage, or expressed fears of an imminent death, this would form the pretext for more or less sympathetic comments, bitter-sweet reflections, unkind deductions. The genealogy of the subject is rehearsed, and it is rare enough that it doesn't present the opportunity for some untimely joke or bitter slander . . . It happens almost unconsciously and yet time passes. When the conversation languishes some good soul will propose a rosary, and decade will follow decade.[5]

Women could also meet at the spring, which was the site for a certain amount of gossip, but without the ease of the wash-house. The steps of the church, coming out of Mass or Vespers on a Sunday, were both a time for display and for social contacts. These meeting-places were only ever inside the village, putting into contact families which already knew each other.

To this female sociability, exclusive of men, set within the territory of the village and organized around the elements of water and of thread, there corresponded a male sociability, set around fire or alcohol. The village smithy

was the forum in the region to which only men were admitted. It was the counterweight to the wash-house, tribunal of feminine justice. There were always one or two benches set out in the workshop where the old men of the village would go and sit, and surrounded by idlers when the major tasks in the fields were done. It was a place to chat and to get warm. One could pick up the news and a whole variety of information brought from the most far-flung hamlets. The school-master (one of the few inhabitants who used to buy a newspaper) would conduct political discussions there.[6]

Extended by the sociability of the cafe (which was occasionally part of the smithy and run by the smith's wife), male gatherings discussed themes complementary to the female register.

For the women, the family, the intimate, the hidden, the sexual; for the men, the social, the public, the technical, the economic, the political. In the Auvergne, according to Ulysse Rouchon, there were no political debates: on Sundays

---

[5] Ulysse Rouchon, *op. cit.*, p. 140–41.
[6] P.-L. Menon and Roger Lecotté, *op. cit.*, p. 152.

While the women took the road home chatting with their neighbours, the men dawdled happily along, and not always to discuss business. They felt a real satisfaction in the sensation of being freed of their daily burdens, and of being able to swap over a bottle of wine their impressions of the recent markets, the harvests, the weather, or some recent incident or other. They hardly touched on politics, for, as well as being fairly ill-informed, they had a horror of giving themselves away by stating a personal opinion which might compromise them.[7]

Nonetheless, the nineteenth century saw the development of male sociability organized around the bar, which accorded politics an increasing place, and which, in many respects, was opposed to the sociability of the *veillée*, spent with neighbours at home:

Bar	*Veillée*
Opening out onto society	Peasant isolation
Masculine segregation	Family unity
Written French culture:	Oral culture: virtue, coffee,
newspapers, vice, absinthe,	traditional wisdom,
left-wing politics	moral order[8]

The development of male alcoholism in the rural environment went hand-in-hand with this male sociability: it was a phenomenon which could have adverse effects at the level of the household. A husband who drank away all the resources of the farm undermined his strength and his ability to work, and beat his wife and children, bringing about the ruin of his household. This abuse of alcohol could, on the other hand, lead the woman to take charge of the management of the household, and control her husband's excesses: she could make him lose (social) face by going to fetch him home from the bar, forbidding him to drink, etc.

GATHERINGS AND FESTIVALS

Female sociability was linked to work, and was only slightly institutionalized: gatherings like the *covegis* were customary, and had no statutes to organize and regulate them. The men of the village, on the other hand, liked to settle the framework of their meeting-places, and to institutionalize them. Was it just a question for them of 'physically

[7] Ulysse Rouchon, *op. cit.*, p. 138.

[8] M. Agulhon, G. Désert, and R. Specklin, *Histoire de la France rurale*, vol. III, pp. 354–5.

getting away' away from the single family room, filled with the noise of squalling brats and all the women's household affairs'?[9] What profound need impelled men to organize themselves into the societies which appear to have been very widespread throughout the whole of rural France in the nineteenth century, cutting across the whole mosaic of cultural and regional types, whether chambers, associated with brotherhoods, corporations, political, religious, or leisure societies? Was it as a defence against a female society which was regarded as aggressive or threatening? 'The most obvious reason for the existence of the *Chambre-Cercle* is that it formed an exclusively male gathering in an enclosed space in which the community of men shared an awareness of its power and communicated to its members a reassuring sense of participating in it.'[10]

The association provided a physically enclosed space, to which women did not have access: the café, the playing area, the club room. The religious brotherhoods, whether *Pénitents du Sud* or *Charités de Normandie*, shared in this organized male solidarity, in which meals taken together occupied an important position, even if the reasons impelling the men to join together were above all Christian and charitable.

In the Norman brotherhoods of *Charité*, which had as their aim the burial, with great pomp, of the dead of the village, and the free burial of members of the brotherhood, in a reciprocal arrangement, the Christian ideal of charity was the official reason for the society.[11] In the nineteenth century, there was not a parish in the region which did not have its own charity. Now, the statutes of the society laid down specifically that it was a brotherhood, a society for men. Women were admitted as members, but they could not fulfil any of the functions assigned to a *chariton*: they could not participate in funerals and were excluded from the statutory meals which the brothers took together several times a year. The brothers could meet in their charity house.

The very fact of having a place reserved for them, a sort of 'men's house' – whether chamber, charity house, Penitents' brotherhood chapel, café or just the forge – appears to have answered a deep-felt need of male village sociability. In the same way, the women were excluded from these groups, and from music, or gaming societies, as

[9] Lucienne Roubin, *Chambrettes des Provençaux*, p. 125.
[10] *ibid.*, p. 123.
[11] Martine Segalen, *Les confréries dans la France contemporaine: les Charités*.

well as from boxing, shooting, or bowling clubs.[12] Supremely male societies, some of these associations placed themselves under the horned sign of Taurus in order to elevate the cuckolds and to feast them once a year. Thus, among many examples, let us cite the Brotherhood of Horns, in the Ille-et-Vilaine, at Rimou, which comprised between 1,200 and 1,500 members. 'On payment of an initial subscription, the members had the right to one part of the 52 masses said each year, and to one horn of a small loaf of bread made with four horns,'[13] thus making the symbolic sign of their shame disappear through a thoroughly material consumption. All these societies were more than just a reaction to female solidarity. It would be reducing the phenomenon to see them simply as a defensive attitude. They gradually came into being out of the community institutions which kept a parish, or town, or trade, running; the religiously aimed brotherhood was separate from the parish, and the political or gaming society was able to base itself on those traditional groups which had always been male. It would be necessary to know the different kinds of societies which led to the diversity seen in the nineteenth century in order to have a better understanding of their nature and the need which they satisfied within the male group.

The rare female societies were essentially religious and operated within the sphere of Catholic life, taking on above all devotional functions. They did not usually have anywhere specific to meet, but, influenced by their male counterparts, they were often called 'brotherhoods'.

In some regions, although they did not go so far as to institutionalize the arrangement, the women would organize themselves for a celebration of Saint Agatha, the patron saint of wives, mothers and nurses – the martyr who had her breasts torn off with tongs. The women would gather together, but only married women, and sometimes even only married women who had had children, that is to say, 'complete' women. After having attended Mass, they would meet to share a meal together. 'At Saint-Pierre-d'Albigny, in Savoy, the women meet in groups of about ten or fifteen, and eat preserves, fruit and *agathes*, and discuss men's relationships with women. They sing songs, and celebrate women's special qualities, like the cunning and subtlety which enables them to prevail over the brute force of their menfolk.'[14]

---

[12] Hélène Tremaud, *Jeux de force et jeux d'addrese*.

[13] Adolphe Orain, *Folklore de l'Ille-et-Vilaine, de la vie à la mort*, vol. I. pp. 233–4.

[14] Arnold Van Gennep, 'Le culte populaire de Sainte-Agathe en Savoie', p. 77.

14 *Division of male and female territories during a wedding in Lower Brittany: the 'men's side'.*

15 *Wedding in Lower Brittany: the 'women's side'.*

Elsewhere, in imitation of the male brotherhoods, they had veritable banquets at which they drank coffee. In Champagne, the feast of Saint Agatha was the occasion for a reversal of roles, as in the engravings of *A Topsy Turvy World*: 'If women met a man before Mass they would take his hat, and only give it back when he paid a forfeit.'[15]

Studying the contemporary revival of this festival in Dauphiné, and particularly in Diois, which links tradition and modernity in this renaissance, Henri Raulin has noted that the sphere in which this custom is carried out came in contact with but did not overlap the sphere of influence of the 'Chambers'.[16]

These annual manifestations of female autonomy were also marked at times of role reversal, such as Carnival. Men and women came together at village festivals and Carnival, when the traditional division of roles and territories was abolished. Separated at the village level throughout the year, they could come together at a time of the breakdown of customary behaviour.

In Alsace, on the day before Shrove Tuesday,

> Only the women had the right to go and drink in the inns; if a man was there, or went in, they would seize his hat or his bonnet, and he would only get it back by buying some bottles of wine.

> *Spitze Schu und Knöplein dian,*
> *Die Frau ist meister und nicht der Man.*
> Pointed shoes with knots in front,
> The woman's the master and not the man.[17]

In the Yonne:

> Shrove Tuesday was also the occasion for a different kind of rather interesting custom. In several areas (Méré, Varennes, Branches, Neuilly) the woman became the absolute mistress of the house for that day, up until the time of the ringing of the midday Angelus. The man was reduced to the role of domestic servant, and the woman took full advantage of the situation to use her power despotically. She would make him sweep out the rooms, clean the dishes, etc. The husbands, however, did not willingly succumb to this temporary suspension of their authority, and frequently enough, to be rid of their chores in the house, they would ask the *curé* permission to ring the midday Angelus

[15] André Varagnac, *op. cit.*, p. 95.
[16] Henri Raulin, *op. cit.*, p. 24.
[17] J. B. Weckerlin, *Chansons populaires de l'Alsace*, vol. II, p. 61.

at eight in the morning: permission which was often granted. At Neuilly, it was the youngest married man whose job it was to ring the Angelus. His haste to do so was a gauge of what stage his honeymoon was at.

At Germiny, on the morning of Shrove Tuesday, there was a custom called *courir l'andouille*. A group of women ran through the streets, carrying a pole with a rag on top. Any man they came across was chased, and, if he was caught, smeared with the rag. Then the group would go and visit the relatives of young couples married during the year and sit down to eat *andouilles*, [chitterling sausages] there.[18]

In the Franche-Comté, women were in authority during the month of May. In the fifteenth century, they had their own form of justice, which was administered by the wives of mayors and magistrates, and throughout the whole of May they were 'outspoken', and their husbands should not beat them 'if they did not wish to incur severe blame'. The month of May is the month of love, the women's month in traditional French society; here, more particularly, an ancient custom deriving from germane law authorizing female justice, could still be seen 'in full vigour at Salins in which it was carried out in the most solemn manner in 1815 and in 1840.'[19]

The organization of tasks and roles within the family, and the degree of sexual separation of territories must be related to forms of village sociability. At the level of political institutions, the difference in the positions of men and women in village society is very marked. There were no women mayors or town councillors in the nineteenth century, still fewer female county councillors or deputies. In such matters, the dominant ideology and the existing model of male authority combined to withdraw all political power from the woman, or at least all visible, official power. A Breton informant, a woman, told me that her mother forbade her father to put himself up for election to a town council of anti-clerical tendencies. In a region in which 'red' and 'white' did not get on together, her daughters were threatened with being sent away from the convent school where they were studying. But if the man maintained the political mediation between the family and society, the woman was responsible for religious relationships with the Catholic community which she em-

[18] Charles Moiset, *op. cit.*, p. 22.
[19] Désiré Monnier, 'Autorité des femmes en Franche-Comté, moeurs et usages anciens', pp. 101–4.

bodied within the domestic group. In the nineteenth century, the female role became increasingly clearly marked following the male disaffection with religious practices, at least in certain regions. The man was content to take part in the ceremonies which marked the major rites of passage, baptism, marriage, and burial, or the cycle of the year: Christmas, Easter, Pentecost and All Saints, a festival observed by the entire village community in combination with the cult of the dead.

This male disaffection with the Church can be explained by political and religious impulses. The local power of the priests was increased in the years following the Revolution: 'the Restoration made a supreme effort to revive a failing Catholic faith in rural areas, a faith intimately bound up with the Royalist cause: clericalism was substituted for Christianity.'[20] But while it was mandatory, up until the July Revolution, for households to attend Mass as a body, the men stopped doing so as soon as it ceased to be obligatory. Social and psychological reasons reinforced the political impulse.

The man was the principal agent of the development of birth control through the exercise of coitus interruptus, which was forbidden by the Church. In many regions of France, the woman thus had sole charge of the religious life of the family, both because of this male disaffection and because a lot of the practices concerning the protection and health of the family for which she was responsible were an important aspect of religious activity. At community level, the woman mediated between the Church and the family. She took charge, within the family, of the religious education of the child, and she was the only faithful attendant at Sunday Mass and at the religious obligations regularly imposed by the Church.

The famous *Angelus* by Millet remarks on this difference between man and wife. Millet wrote about this painting, which was completed between 1855 and 1857: 'The *Angelus* is a painting which I did while thinking of how, when I used to work in the fields, my grandmother, when she heard the bell ring, would never fail to stop us in our work and have us say the Angelus for the poor dead, piously and with our hats in our hands.'

As the catalogue of the Millet exhibition explains, 'the true key to an understanding of this painting lies in the differences between the man and the woman praying. The man is not praying: he is twisting his hat

---

[20] Eugène Bougeâtre, *op. cit.*, p. 178.

in his hands waiting for his wife to finish. At Chailly, as in all the villages of France, it was by and large the women and children who filled the church on Sundays, while the men stayed talking in the square or in the farmyard . . .'[21]

Millet's painting is thus not an exaltation of Christian sentiment, but underlines the feminization of religious life. It also implies that the woman is able to speak, knows how to address God and can manipulate symbolic powers. The other elements of the painting underline the contrast between the role of the woman and that of the man. On the man's side there is only a fork, the symbol of labour, but on the other side Millet has accumulated the objects which symbolize the woman's function in gathering for her family the fruits of that labour, etc. The catalogue makes mention of a letter from Gambetta, dated 1873, and reprinted by the École de Paris 11 June 1889. Gambetta put forward a social interpretation of the picture which, according to him, forces the spectator to 'meditate on the still all-powerful influence of religious tradition on the rural populace . . . The task is done, the barrow is there, full of the day's harvest, they are about to go home to their cottage for the night . . . They wait, counting the strokes of the bell, just as they had done the day before, just as they would do the next day, in an attitude too natural not to be customary, for the rite to be finished so that they might resume the path leading to the village.'[22]

The church is the only place, outside her house, permitted to the woman, and not linked to her daily tasks. Proverbs make use of this sacred territory to evoke women's hypocrisy, and perhaps to comfort men for their abandonment of religious practices:

> *Les femmes sont des saintes à l'église, des anges dans la rue, des diables au logis*
> Women are saints in church, angels in the street, and devils at home
> (Languedoc)

> *Dévote à l'église, et diable à la maison*
> Devout in church, and a devil at home (Languedoc)

FAIRS AND MARKETS

The distance between action and speech is nowhere more clearly shown than in the way in which women went to markets, while men

---

[21] Jean-François Millet, *Catalogue de l'exposition du Grand-Palais*, pp. 103–4.
[22] *ibid.*

went to fairs. This extra-village distribution of space corresponds to the sexual segregation of territories in the house and in the village.

The true opportunity for an opening on to the outside world is offered to the mistress of the house by the weekly market. Once a week she sells the products of her industry in the nearest small town of the locality: chickens from the farmyard, butter, cheese, and cream. Let us not have too much regard for Mme d'Abbadie d'Arrast when she writes: 'No-one knows better than the Basque housewife how to get the best price for her cattle as well as for her eggs, her chickens and her cheeses,'[23] for as much could be said for the Breton housewife, or the housewife from Normandy. This market has a twofold importance. It is seen first of all as providing for the household small regular sums of money to be spent on daily purchases; these sums of money often had a specific name: in the Haute-Loire they were called *campanage*.[24] In addition, the market provided the woman with an opening on to the world outside, beyond the world of her village community. Although it was only a specifically female market, where our sellers had only to do with other women coming to make purchases, one must not overlook the effect on peasant women of finding themselves in regular contact with the customs of the town, and its language, and it is perhaps there that one should look for the underlying cause of the changes in the rural family observed towards the end of the nineteenth century, with the girls leaving for the towns, encouraged by mothers who knew of the existence of a different way of life from their own.

The excursion of women into the outside world in the nineteenth century has perhaps been slightly underestimated. The development of beautiful peasant costumes and jewellery – a sign of increasing wealth – can be seen, surely, as a desire on the part of the peasant woman to assert herself in relation to the townswoman? The indi-vidualization of peasant culture expressed in their furniture and their costumes certainly passed away through this constant rubbing against urban culture, by means of these female contacts. Male fairs were of a different order: livestock markets were meetings of technicians, all country men, whether buyers or sellers. It was not a question of an opposition between urban and peasant culture. What was involved was a homogeneous group, drawn from the farming community,

[23] Mme d'Abbadie d'Arrast, *op. cit.*, p. 43.
[24] Ulysse Rouchon, *op. cit.*, p. 100.

sharers in a common knowledge, and actors in the same economic sphere.

The same specialization can be generally applied to the cereal markets where grain was sold to the miller or the broker. It also applies to the specialized fairs, the hirings, where masters engaged their servants. The markets took place frequently, the fairs two or three times a year.

> It was the men who went to the 'fair', not only to buy or sell stock, but to 'keep abreast' of the mechandise so as to have a better understanding of what was going on. This understanding was the fruit of long observation and an extensive experience which they had started to acquire even in childhood by working with their fathers and listening to them. Above and beyond understanding the animals, their defects, their illnesses, and their age, it was necessary to know where and when the stock would sell best so as to know when to take them to one fair and when to another.[25]

Observers were very struck by the distinctive nature of these male and female markets, which were sometimes held jointly: 'In the markets of Le Puy, the women who come to sell their goods take a scratch meal at a bench, while their husbands sit in the bar, or gamble away the hard-earned fruits of their labours and their sobriety'.[26]

Married women did not generally attend the livestock markets, since they lacked the technical knowledge of the commercial trans-actions taking place. Nonetheless, in certain cases, their presence there was necessary; for example, when they had to take over the manage-ment of the farm, if they were widowed, or if their husbands had temporarily emigrated. In certain regions renowned for their strong women, such as, for instance, Brittany, the women attended the fairs and took part in all the discussions, and this participation seems a good indication of the distribution of roles within the household itself. The market is the place where the family prestige is put on show before the whole community. The sale of an animal is a prestigious transaction which involves the good name of the household and the family. It was an operation which involved knowing how to be diplomatic and how to be patient. It was a transaction which, in the final analysis, called

[25] P.-L. Menon and Roger Lecotté, *op. cit.*, p. 131.

[26] J. Merley, *La Haute-Loire, de la fin de l'Ancien Régime aux debuts de la troisième République*, p. 57.

into play part of the economic balance of the household. The husband who goes to market and strikes a good bargain comes back haloed with a glory which is all the more prestigious because it is exceptional when set against the unvarying routine of day-to-day domestic affairs.

Courbet painted these Franche-Comté peasants *Returning From the Fair* in terms of a sexual hierarchy. The master, with a townsman's hat perched on top of the peasant's kerchief which protects his hair, is mounted on horseback and leads the bullock he has just bought. Beside him walks the manservant; behind, on foot, their baskets on their heads, walk the women with, perhaps, the mistress and the maidservant side by side. In the foreground, another villager is bringing home a young pig. In a world where there were few transactions and in which the only important economic operations took place at the fair, the return from the fair was the supreme moment when the man should display his superiority and his authority, whatever the actuality of his day-to-day relationship with his wife. Thus, the wife found herself kept apart from the commercial aspect of the fair, as well as from the licentious celebrations which frequently accompanied them.

Qui abreuve son cheval à tous gués, mène sa femme à tout festin, de son cheval fait une rosse et de sa femme une catin
Whoever lets his horse drink at every ford, and takes his wife to every festival, makes his horse into a nag, and his wife into a whore (Languedoc)

Qui prête les boeufs et le cheval et laisse sa femme courir les fêtes reste cocu et sans bêtes
Whoever lends out his cattle and his horse and lets his wife go around the fairs will be a cuckold and without stock (Catalonia)

Qui veut à toutes pierres son couteau aiguiser, à tout pèlerinage sa femme mener, à toute eau son cheval abreuver, au bout de l'an n'a qu'un mauvais couteau, une putain et une haridelle
Whoever sharpens his knife on every stone, takes his wife on every outing, and waters his horse at every stream, at the end of the year will have a bad knife, a whore and a nag (Provence)

Celui qui va aiguiser son couteau sur toutes les pierres, celui qui conduit sa femme à toutes les foires et fait abreuver son cheval à tous les ruisseaux n'a au bout de l'an qu'un méchant couteau, qu'une mauvaise femelle et une haridelle
Whoever sharpens his knife on every stone, whoever takes his wife to all the markets, and whoever waters his horse at every stream, at the end

of the year will have a poor knife, a wicked woman and a nag
(Languedoc, Anjou)

These proberbs are a reflection of the deep-rooted suspicion felt
towards anything foreign, a well-known theme in studies of village
communities. In the markets and pilgrimages which bring together a
crowd exceeding the framework of mutual knowledge, social control
is abolished. The proverb usually depicts the woman as a weak being,
susceptible to temptation, judges her lost, and the reputation of the
household lost with her. More than a practical interdiction, these
precepts mediate, through the image of the woman offered in the
proverbs, the agony of the community when faced with the unknown.

6

Male Authority –
a Folklorists' Tale?

Peasant culture recognizes that the good name of a household depends on the husband and wife whose tasks and roles are complementary, interdependent and closely interwoven. We are far from the notion of a dependent and inferior woman. Yet statements about male authority and female subordination abound. Songs, proverbs, and sayings all create an image of the couple which is far removed from actual practice.

We must question why this inconsistency should exist. Are the women authoritarian? Or are they, on the other hand, totally dominated creatures? In putting forward propositions of this sort, haven't the folklorists confused several levels of behaviour? And is there, in the field of male/female roles, one, single model, or are there several regional ones?

THE AUTHORITARIAN WOMAN

A certain number of popular nineteenth-century engravings show the wife in an aggressive stance with regard to her husband: '*M. Brise-Ménage et Mme Carillon*' (Mr Home-breaker and Mrs Nag), '*La dispute de la Culotte*' (The Quarrel over the Trousers), '*La grand querelle du ménage*' (The Great Domestic Quarrel). The quarrel often has as its origin the wife's refusal to give her husband some pocket-money to go to the bar. Against the stick wielded by the husband is set the distaff or grid-iron held by the wife; the instruments of her daily activities, the instruments of evil witchcraft, were also the instruments she used in defence or attack, in their most material form. The married couple

LA FEMME A LE MOUSQUET LA QUENOUILE LÉPOUX
ET BERCE POUR SURCROIT LENFANT SUR SES GENOUX

16 *Role-reversal in a print by Rabier-Boulard, Orléans,* circa *1820. The woman bears the insignia of masculinity: hat, pipe, walking-stick, gun; the man, wearing a wig, is spinning and nursing the baby.*

fight over a pair of trousers, the symbol of authority; sayings and expressions refer to the same range of metaphors: in Upper Brittany a dominant woman is said to have 'the whip and the reins',[1] or to 'wear the trousers'.

Proverbs pick up this same image; trousers, as we know, with their importance in certain marriage rituals, remain the ultimate symbol of authority:

Tiens le pantalon si tu veux la paix
Keep the trousers if you want peace (Corsica)

Ni pantalon la femme, ni jupes l'homme
Neither trousers for the woman nor skirts for a man (Catalonia)

---

[1] Paul Sébillot, 'Additions aux coutumes de la haute Bretagne', p. 99.

This female demand threatens the family order and the social order. It belongs in the same absurd world as the fish catching the fisherman, and the hare shooting the huntsman. In the engravings of *The World gone Topsy-Turvy*, the symbolic power of objects is everywhere. The wearing of trousers, of a hat, the gun and pipe which masculinize the woman, while the man is feminized rocking the child and spinning. Here, too, proverbial sayings belong to the same attitude of mind and contribute to the coherence of the represented universe:

Le chapeau doit commander la coiffe
The hat must master the bonnet (Brittany)

Un homme qui file et une femme qui conduit les chevaux composent un ménage ridicule
A man spinning and a woman leading the horses make an absurd household (Picardy)

The woman dominating her husband is not criticized as much as the man that is too weak to dominate her. Thus proverbs denounce men who have lost the masculinity of authority: *L'homme est indigne de l'être si de sa femme il n'est pas le maître* (A man is not worthy of the name if he is not master of his wife) (Catalonia), just as the rituals of the charivari express social control over the husband who has not been able to instil proper respect for the model of male superiority. The charivari makes mock of the battered husband, guilty of weakness, and old engravings showing the husband being maltreated by his wife bear the legend: 'He's deserved it.'

Is the inevitable conclusion, then, that authority lies in the hands of the men? Let us first of all recognize that this was not necessarily so, since women dared to claim authority for themselves. One might even put forward the hypothesis that in the nineteenth century a greater consideration was accorded to women. With regard to the numerous proverbs recognizing the husband's right to beat his wife:

Qui veut battre sa femme, trouve assez de raisons
He who wants to beat his wife can always find a reason (Provence, Gascony)

De l'âne, du noyer, du genre féminin, n'en attends rien de bon qu'un bâton à la main
From a donkey, a walnut or a woman expect no good unless you've a stick in your hand (Provence)

Les femmes sont comme les côtelettes, plus on les bat, plus elles sont tendres
Women are like chops, the more you beat them the tenderer they are
(Languedoc)

Jean-Louis Flandrin has noted the later appearance of proverbs which show a certain withdrawal from the use of physical force:[2]

Battre sa femme, c'est battre sa bourse
Beating your wife is like beating your purse (Franche-Comté, Limousin)

Qui frappe sa femme frappe un sac de farine, le bon s'en va, le mauvais reste
Beating your wife is like beating a sack of flour, the good flies out, the bad remains (Provence)

And if a sixteenth-century proverb still quoted in Anjou states that: *Bon cheval, mauvais cheval veut l'éperon, bonne femme, mauvaise femme veut le bâton* (Good horse or bad, they need the spur, good wife or bad, they need the stick), in the nineteenth century it was more often quoted in a form which drew a distinction between 'good' and 'bad':

A mauvais cheval les éperons, à mauvaise femme le bâton
The bad horse needs the spur, the bad wife the stick (Gascony)

In the same way, popular engravings of the nineteenth century dedicated to these themes show redress in the balance between these roles. In the *Dispute de la culotte* (Quarrel over the Trousers), the couple are shown standing on an equal footing, each beating the other, whereas in certain sixteenth- and seventeenth-century engravings of *La femme mise à raison par son mari* (The Woman brought to her Senses by her Husband), she is shown in a submissive attitude, her hands clasped, on her knees before her husband. Whether authoritarian or submissive, acting through her beneficial powers or weaving evil spells, the rural woman is recognized as powerful in proverbs which draw on the most deep-seated aspects of peasant mentality:

Un cheveu de femme tire plus que trente paires de boeufs
One hair from a woman's head can lead more than thirty pairs of oxen
(Catalonia)

---

[2] Jean-Louis Flandrin, *Familles, op. cit.*, p. 121.

Une femme peut faire sortir par la chatière ce qu'un homme ne pourrait faire entrer par la grande porte
A woman can get out through the cat-flap what a man could not get in through the front door (Franche-Comté)

Une femmelette porte plus hors de la maison dans son tablier qu'un homme avec un chariot n'en peut porter dedans
The little woman can carry more out of the house in her apron than the man could carry in in a wagon (Val d'Aosta)

Rural society, opposing the interior and exterior territories, and using metaphors with physical connotations such as hair (the part for the whole), or sexual connotations such as the apron, recognizes feminine power. In order to defend itself against it, it builds up a symbolic speech in which the woman is laden with every fault, is intolerable to men, and exercises a malign influence.

Il n'est point de vice que les femmes et les guenons ignorent
There isn't a vice which women and she-monkeys don't know about (Languedoc)

De femme et de cheval il n'en est point sans vice
There isn't a woman or a horse which is without a single vice (Provence)

Femme sans vice, curé sans caprice et meunier fidèle, c'est un miracle du ciel
A woman without vice, a straightforward priest and an honest miller, are some of heaven's miracles (Languedoc)

Il n'y avait en tout que deux femmes supportables, la première s'est pendue, la seconde est au diable
There were in all only two bearable women, the first hanged herself, the second belonged to the devil (Champagne)

La femme est tête sans cervelle, serpent, diable pour la maison mais telle quelle, horrible ou belle à tous plus ou moins il en faut
A woman is a head without a brain, a snake, a devil in the house, but for all that, beautiful or hideous, everyone more or less needs one (Provence)

Proverbs which share in this conception of the woman and reinforce it use a very aggressive form of speech towards the woman, reflecting the mingled fear and respect in which she is held, and casting her out into the demoniac universe to which her body's rhythms relate her. Proverbs dedicate the woman to the devil or to death, without even passing through the mediation of the animal or vegetable world: their violence is all the more increased:

Les femmes ne sont pas des gens
Women aren't people (Provence)

Les femmes c'est pas du monde
Women aren't of this world (Anjou)

A qui Dieu veut aider, sa femme lui meurt
Whosoever God wishes to help, his wife dies on him (sixteenth century)

Deux beaux jours a l'homme sur terre quand il prend femme et quand il l'enterre
Man has two good days on earth, when he takes a wife and when he
buries her (Languedoc, Provence, Pays Basque, Gascony)

Deuil de femme morte dure jusqu'à la porte
Mourning for a dead wife lasts just as far as the door (Franche-Comté,
Catalonia, Gascony, Anjou)

It is within this symbolic context that one must attempt to assess the
statements made by folklorists. Have they not confused the level of
actual practice with that of representation?

It is the same from one text to another. Local scholars go into analyses
of roles, in terms of hierarchy and superiority. One might ask whether
the ethnocentrism of the observers' approach is not particularly
evident here. As participants in the dominant bourgeois ideology, the
folklorists did not question its models, and looked for them implicitly
in the peasant culture they were observing. Now, the male/female
hierarchy was particularly strongly marked in the bourgeois civilization of the nineteenth century. The woman was inactive, making no
sort of productive contribution to the household. She served as a
support for the social prestige of her husband, and as a foil for him in
his social relations. Moreover, the so-called female domestic tasks
were fulfilled by hired workers: washing, cooking, housework, were
all done by servants. The tasks were thus devalued. There only
remained to the woman the education of her children, which for the
most part was shared with governesses, tutors or educational establish-
ments. The man supported the household, through his activity or
through his inheritance, and it was he who administered his wife's
affairs. He effectively held the authority, in the sense that he made the
important decisions about life at work and in the family. This model of
domination by the husband over the wife is something which the

folklorists think they can also see in the peasant culture which they are observing, or rather, they are so deeply obsessed with it that they do not even discuss the question. For them, everything is a sign of female inferiority. Take, for instance, narratives of the woman's place at table during meals. This account is given by Gabriel Jeanton, the folklorist of the Mâconnais:

> In the Mâcon region, as in Bresse, it was a well-established custom for the women of the house never to sit at table, even when strangers were invited. They maintained the attitude of servants and ate out of their bowls away from the family table, in a corner of the room near the fire, or even in the kitchen in houses wealthy enough to have a separate room dedicated to cooking. This custom was general forty years ago [around 1880], even in the most civilized villages in Bresse, where we have frequently witnessed it. It has not even disappeared completely in the Mâcon region, and we were present, in 1921, at a meal given by one of the wealthier landowning families of the Montagne, where only the men joined in . . .

Lamartine had already mentioned [this custom] in his own time, as testified by this passage from *Le tailleur de pierres de Saint-Point*, Ch. VII, 6:

> Then, taking out of her basket all that she had put in it, she spread out a cloth on the grass, and standing up, leaning against a tree, she watched me eat and drink. Even though I said to her, 'Sit down, Denise, and eat something with me' she laughed and said: 'No. It was alright before when we hadn't spoken and I was only your cousin; but now I am your betrothed, and you will soon be my master, and I must serve you and not sit and eat before you.' It was the custom of the country, sir, and there was nothing I could say.[3]

Now, this was not just the custom in the Mâcon region: it was a mode of organization of labour that was to be seen throughout French rural society. In Brittany, for instance, where even the diet was still fairly distinctive in the nineteenth century, and in which village solidarity involved numerous collective undertakings – such as clearing land, packing down the threshing floors – during which the men and women danced together, the meal which all these workers took was not eaten together: 'The men finish eating and in a few minutes the piece of land they are clearing is swarming with workers . . . The women take their place around the pot of stew after their lords and

[3] Gabriel Jeanton, *op. cit.*, pp. 59–60.

masters.'[4] What the folklorist sees as a sign of hierarchy is only the physical impossibility of the women being able to eat, at the same time as the men, the meal which they also have to cook and serve. In the same way, on everyday occasions, the fact that meals had to be served hot and on time meant that the woman could not eat them until she had fed the workers coming in from the fields. This being so, let us not share the opinion of that observer from the Lorraine who saw in it an expression of female reserve. In fact, Louis Marin stated that:

> The modesty of these women is very great. Right up until the beginning of the nineteenth century, having the meal to prepare, they did not sit at the table with the men and only came to sit down with their guests when it came to the dessert.'[5] A woman observer in the Pays Basque gave a different interpretation: 'If the woman does not sit down at table, this is in no way a sign of inferiority and servitude; it is because she is faithful to her role of housewife, and gives the family their food first. She then eats after the others, most often standing up or sitting in the chimney corner.'[6]

If one chooses to see in this absence of the woman from the family table a symbol of her inferiority, is this not due to an ethnocentric approach? Nineteenth-century observers relegated to an inferior rank the tasks of preparing and giving meals: they employed the term 'serving', with its connotations of 'servant'; the rural woman is seen as a servant because she brings the plates to table. Now, the mother of the family is responsible for the meal: it is a task which requires her presence if it is to be carried out well. Rather than considering that she is inferior because she does not sit down, does not the housewife see herself as fulfilling her task properly in not doing so, and see in that a source of pride, similar to a well-kept house and a fertile farmyard. What is important to learn is not so much the way in which observers appraise the exterior of a situation as the manner in which the actors themselves perceive it. And that is the heart of the difficulty: peasant speech is communicated through the voice of the folklorists.

In this way, the general assessment made by the folklorists in the nineteenth century, who provide us with interpretations of the too-silent peasants, was made in terms of a hierarchy of roles and status within the peasant famly. Furthermore, in observing these relation-

[4] Alexandre Bouët and Olivier Perrin, *op. cit.*, p. 273.
[5] Louis Marin, *Regards sur la Lorraine*, pp. 88–9.
[6] Mme d'Abbadie d'Arrast, *op. cit.*, p. 55.

ships through the distorting lens of their own bourgeois model, they looked for signs of this hierarchy. Curiously enough, these observers often remarked that male superiority was observed elsewhere than in the region under consideration, thus shifting to some distant location what they thought to discover before their eyes. The texts which follow are revealing. Thus, a folklorist in Berry believes women to be maltreated in the Cévennes, while imposing on the head of the family his own interpretation of his feelings: 'The master in Berry saw the mistress of the house as an inferior. He did not, it is true, conduct himself towards her with the harshness of the Cévennes peasant who, returning from market, walked ahead leaning on his stick and smoking his pipe while his wife followed behind laden like a donkey. In the Marche, too, it is the women and cows which work, while in our plains of Berry, it is the bullocks and the men.'[7] But a folklorist of the regions of Marche and Limousin questions this view of things:

> Some writers have asserted that women in the Limousin are in an inferior and humiliating position. Seeing her labouring hard at work inside and out, they have concluded too readily that she was treated as a servant and not as a companion. Laisnel de la Salle [another observer of Berry] quotes this remark by a Berry sharecropper: 'I have had the misfortune this year to lose two bullocks and my mule, not to mention Jeanne, my woman, who died at the beginning of the season.' And he goes on: 'Our neighbour in the Limousin places his wife even lower down in affections, putting her in his daily prayer some way down after his chestnuts and his beetroots:

> *Monsieur sen Marsau*
> *Nostra boun foundatour*
> *Pregatz per nous nostre seinhour*
> *Qu'il veuilla gardar*
> *Nostra castanhas*
> *Nostra rabas*
> *Nostra femma*

> Monsieur Saint Martial
> Our good patron
> Pray Our Lord for us
> To guard
> Our chestnuts
> Our beet
> Our wives.'[8]

[7] Hugues Lapaire, *op. cit.*, pp. 35–6.
[8] Michel Coissac, *Mon Limousin*, pp. 176–7.

The writer can modify the picture, through being able to call on an extensive knowledge of actual practice. Once again we come up against the question of the relationship between what is said – in this prayer, as in the proverbs – and what is done, and even what is thought!

> In the country, there is a vast amount to do and where resources are too limited to be able to employ a servant, then the wife, just like her husband, must buckle down to the work. In some regions where the men and boys emigrate, it is the women, the old men and the children who do all the agricultural work. It is beyond question that in these cases the peasant woman sometimes has a hard and difficult task, often beyond her strength, but that is the exception and it is said that these days the peasant cherishes his wife rather more.
>
> It would often be unfair to assert that the woman does not enjoy any consideration when it is usually she who looks after and runs the household. We must acknowledge that she does not always have the theoretical and practical knowledge to manage an organized interior, but after all she was in charge. Moreover, when the young bride enters her new house, she is usually well received and the 'best room' is often reserved for the young couple by the old parents.[9]

If folklorists find the model they expect, but in which the wife is excessively badly treated, then they feel obliged to contrast peasant barbarity with their own, more polite customs. Often, they refer this example of savagery to some foreign source. Here is the answer to an inquiry conducted in the Deux-Sèvres just after the Second World War: 'North African customs are particularly to be found in the southern part of the Gâtine region and especially at Verruyes. The head of the household is always the master . . . The women do not sit at the table, but serve the head of the household.'[10] Moorish customs explain this practice, which is common throughout France!

On the other hand, when they find dominant women, writers are astounded and see in the discovery a sign of the superiority of the region they are studying over the other regions of France. Thus:

> The women of Lorraine: they have gradually taken charge of the whole of the family economy, buildings and gardens; with regard to the

[9] *ibid.*

[10] ATP inquiry into the traditional calendar, at Verruyes in the Deux-Sèvres, no. 528 *bis*, April 1946.

general running of the farm, they tell the husband, sons and workers what they should be doing at the different hours of the day. They oversee not just the farmyard and the rabbit–runs, but the horses and pigs too; they decide on purchases and economies; they receive any money coming in and keep a tight hold on the purse strings; thrift being one of their main qualities, one might often see, between 1880 and 1900, the father of the family, wishing to play cards with his friends on a Sunday, asking his wife for forty sous, and then a hundred. This happens, doubtless, in a number of provinces in France, but nowhere to such a degree as in Lorraine, and above all, without having to trim it to suit the tender susceptibilities of the man. And yet in the Lorraine, women have achieved all this with such discretion that their husbands trust themselves entirely to their advice and have the deepest admiration for their wives' role. The Lorraine woman is very much involved in public affairs. Under the *ancien régime*, until the Revolution of 1789, they voted in the communal assemblies held on Sundays after Mass.[11]

Some observers, whose evidence has not always been regarded sufficiently critically by historians, see women, on the contrary, as being inferior. Abel Hugo can be numbered among these, no matter what region he was discussing.

He wrote about Mayenne:

Always living alone, and not having those daily contacts with other men which modify and soften the character, the peasant from the lower Maine shows, in all his customs, a veritable savagery . . . The way of life of these peasants is rough and hard, and their customs harsh. Work relations between the two do not engender those abuses and that laxity which one can see elsewhere, but women are held there in an inferior position which often renders their condition very wretched indeed. The wife of a master farmer did not think it right to give orders to the young working men, nor even to her sons when they were no longer children. If she was a widow, she rarely remained in charge of affairs; she either remarried, or left her farm, unless one of her children was old enough to take over running things out of doors. Thus in every aspect of daily life, women are in a subordinate position; during meals they never sit down with the men, except on the days when they share in their labours, as during the harvest, or on solemn occasions, such as weddings, baptisms, etc.; but as a rule, they eat standing up, or sitting in a separate corner, constantly stopping to look after the men . . . Peasant women living in a very dependent manner and never leaving the daily round of

[11] Louis Marin, *op. cit.*, p. 91.

their domestic occupations acquire a sort of wildness and shyness which they do not even seek to overcome. They are nonetheless good, gentle, charitable and intelligent, and in the unhappy civil wars which ravaged the region, they often gave proof of their courage, devotion and virtue.[12]

He describes a similar situation in the Sarthe:

> The old customs persist in this region; the saying, *du côté de la barbe est la toute-puissance* (the side of the whiskers is all-powerful), still keeps all its force. The farmer's wife, called the mistress, and calling her husband 'master', never sits at table with her men servants, however tired she might be. She cooks for them, serves them, and eats standing up, as do all the women and girls without exception. The master sits at the table with the men and they all eat in a mess together like Abraham with his servants and slaves. If the mistress is brought to bed, they ask: '*est-ce un gas?*' ('is it a boy'). If the opposite arrives, they say: '*Ouen, ce n'est qu'une creature*' ('it's only a creature' . . . a girl) . . . We are back among the customs of the Hurons and the Iroquois. Thirty years ago (things have improved since) the cow and the mare were better looked after than the women or girls. If one of the animals was sick, they quickly fetched medicine and the vet; if their wife or daughter were taken ill, they said 'she's like to die of it' and left the poor creature to cope with her fever with her flagon of cider.'[13]

These texts tell us more about the folklorist's own ideology than they do about peasant behaviour. His sources are not at all reliable and are very far-removed from ethnological inquiry. Hugo copied memoirs or questioned local notables whose observations were deeply coloured by ethnocentrism. Faced with peasant behaviour, the folklorist reveals an ambivalent attitude: on the one hand they were savages, Hurons, Iroquois who had such small respect for their wives that they refused them the help of a doctor, or made their wives serve them, while on the other hand they were 'good savages', because their women, treated worse than the beasts by their menfolk, possessed the 'natural' virtues which the bourgeois women would do well to copy. They were gentle, devoted, courageous, charitable, and even intelligent!

In the case of Brittany, we have the opportunity of comparing

[12] Abel Hugo, *op. cit.*, vol. II, pp. 234–5.
[13] Abel Hugo, *op. cit.*, vol. III, pp. 74–5.

Hugo's ethnocentrist vision with the view of an ethnographer who was familiar with the culture he was discussing. As elsewhere, Hugo sees Breton women as dependent (see Introduction, p. 4): 'The women, in their households, are the chief servants . . . The sex, it must be admitted, had nothing seductive about it, nothing that might excite love,' etc., all of which Hugo took from a report by Captain Connier in 1829. Pierre Jakez Hélias, ethnographer of his family and his culture, notes, in contrast, the importance of the Breton woman at every level of family and social life:

> The men of the Bigouden region were ruled by their wives with a rod of iron, without a doubt. When a Bigouden couple went out together in public, the woman would make her husband walk ahead so as not to be led astray. He strutted along, his thumbs stuck in his waistcoat, his chest puffed out like the cock of the walk. But he only had to show the slightest inclination to turn to the right, towards the bars with their cronies and their card-games, and immediately, his lady wife would lift her umbrella and poke him in the elbow with it imperiously from behind. And he would turn, with a sigh, to the left, towards home. There were nonetheless occasions when he had to go and have a drink at the bar to keep up his position. At such times it was the *patronne* (Ar Vestrez) who, in a quiet voice, ordered her husband's drink . . .
>
> Bigouden women are renowned for their appetite for authority which they assert loudly or dissimulate under a false humility according to circumstances, using at will a loud voice or ready tears.[14]

In this way, outside observers reinterpret according to their own code gestures and behaviour which have quite a different meaning, or else are surprised to find a woman whose activity is complementary to her husband's, and interdependent with him in terms of the responsibility for the farm. 'Women in earlier times knew how to link persuasion with the firmness which brooks no denial. Everyone thus obeys the voice of the woman, and the first to obey is the farmer himself.'[15] The protagonists of *La vie d'un Simple* are shown daily sharing their cares and their decisions. Living with a sour stepdaughter 'much grieved my wife; she wept about it when we were alone; we spoke of it far into the night.'[16]

---

[14] P. J. Hélias, *Le pays bigouden*, p. 8, reprinted in *Le cheval d'orgueil*, p. 246.

[15] Abbé Léonor Blouin, *op. cit.*, p. 127.

[16] Emile Guillaumin, *op. cit.*, p. 275.

Far from any concept of hierarchy, man and wife shared responsibility for the way the farm worked, within an organization of labour which implied a fairly strict but not a rigid division of tasks. A way of life evolved, probably long ago, which can be defined in the same way at both extremes of traditional pre-industrial society. The economic code of the good farmer's wife involved shared responsibilities: 'If the outdoor, and the major seasonal tasks, in a word all of the farming and marketing, devolved primarily on the farmer, affairs within doors were very much the farmer's wife's particular sphere; it was she who was the principal agent, constantly present, the necessary overseer of the farmyard and of the hired help; it was in the end upon her, and upon her care, her vigilance and her capacity that the prosperity of the farmer most often depended.'[17]

At the other end of this chronological chain, Roger Béteille, describing daily life in Rouergue before 1914, makes mention of this cooperation with all the modifications that this type of relationship implies.

> It is accepted that the responsibility for the management of the farm is held jointly by the master of the house and his wife, but that it is he who must have the last word. In particular, it is the husband who takes the major decisions: the distribution of crops on the farm, buying and selling. It would, for example, be fairly badly regarded for a married woman to go and sell cattle. On the other hand, if she is a widow, and excels in this through necessity, then she gains general approbation . . .
>
> Her husband's reputation, the prosperity of the family and of the farm are intimately dependent on the skills of the married woman.[18]

But even if the wife beat her husband, ordered the servants about, decided the crops and the harvests, the rural household must still maintain the image of male authority with regard to the social groups, so as to observe the norm which ensures the reproduction of the social group.

The head of the family had the sole function of representing the household in its entirety, he was its spokesman and its incarnation. Anything that happened to him affected through him all those living on the farm, people and animals alike. This was the case with those magic powers which came from the outside:

---

[17] L. Roze, *op. cit.*, pp. 11–12.
[18] Roger Béteille, *La vie quotidienne en Rouergue avant 1914*, p. 88.

The one the sorcerer aims at is the head of the farm (whether or not it is agricultural), who is also the head of the household. It was always he who was said to be bewitched, even if he himself was not affected at all, while his wife or his rabbits were clearly suffering from the violence of a sorcerer . . . Whatever the element attacked, it is never being attacked for its own sake, but in the function of its relation to the head of the farm or of the family, because they are his crops, his cows, his rabbits, his chickens, his children, his wife . . . the 'I' of the one bewitched is made up of the whole, comprising himself and his possessions, that is to say, the whole which is socially linked with his name.[19]

This explains the image of the couple in Franche-Comté painted by Courbet returning from the fair. It is very much a question of maintaining an image of a normative relationship which the folklorists have confused with actual practice.

The authority of the father of the family is accepted by all without question; everyone is aware of it, and everyone observes it in the hierarchy of domestic respect, highlighting it, incidentally, through the banning of the familiar *tu* between man and wife, and between children and parents . . . The father freely gives over (to the mother) the education of his children on condition that he is ensured those external signs of a constant respect, for no one would try, particularly not in front of a stranger, to show any signs of initiative without his consent.[20]

These family relationships having been established, and the folklorists' discourse to some extent demystified, is it possible to conclude that there is a model of family relationships which can be applied to the wide variety of French peasant cultures?

GENERAL MODEL, REGIONAL MODELS

Is it legitimate to construct a model of the relationship between husband and wife which is applicable to all cultures? This would come to the same thing as saying that the relationship between husband and wife is determined by work relationships, and to give economic factors primacy over the social and cultural factors. Now we know that the model of the inheritance of goods, the legal status of the

---

[19] Jeanne Favret-Saada, *op. cit.*, pp. 252–3.
[20] Jean Merley, *op. cit.*, pp. 230–1, reiterating a quotation from Ulysse Rouchon, *op. cit.*, vol. I, p. 23.

married couple, and of the wife in particular, occupy an important position in the variety of models, and that the cultural heritage of the past has left deep impressions on the organization of traditional peasant society, but it is not possible for us to make the same sort of subtle comparative analysis with regard to the nineteenth century as has been made to the sixteenth.

In Northern France, we can observe at this date a weakening of lineage ties, combined with the pre-eminence of the couple: that is, where one should place the quarrel over the trousers. In the south, on the other hand, the supremacy of lineage was maintained until much later, and the couple remained based on a much wider family entity. The authority of the husband is much harder to contest because it has descended to him through the line: 'The mother, such a marked presence in the customs of Orléans or Paris, in the regions of the south remains, by contrast, in the background, and now more so than ever, amid the insignificance of all the household tasks.'[21]

In the nineteenth century, our only exhaustive corpus of evidence, that of proverbs, also presents a picture of the southern woman which is rather different from that of the northern woman of Brittany or Lorraine. Being fully aware of the caution necessary for dealing with proverbial discourse, one must be content to put forward only hypotheses in this domain: proverbs from the South emphasize more often the seclusion of young women and wives than do northern proverbs, and, in series devoted to marriage, they often associate marriage for love with grief; they emphasize particularly the antagonism between kin through marriage, and supremacy of the male, physically enforced (through beating his wife). There are also a good many more of them which evoke feminine beauty, but so as to warn against it. In the domain of authority, their language is violent and categorical, without using the mediation of metaphor. *L'homme est indigne de l'être si de sa femme il n'est le maître* (A man is not worthy of the name if he is not master of his wife) (Catalonia) is a proverb which is concerned with asserting the essence of virility, while the Breton proverb: *Le chapeau doit commander la coiffe* (The hat should master the bonnet) proposes, through the less brutal means of metaphorical language – taken here from the code of clothing – a more or less accepted model, which each couple internalizes and follows according to its own tastes.[22]

[21] Emmanuel le Roy Ladurie, 'Système de la coutume. Structures familiales et coutumes d'héritage en France au XVIᵉ siècle', p. 841.

[22] Martine Segalen, 'Le mariage, l'amour et la femme dans les proverbes du Sud.'

Female seclusion has as its corollory the withdrawal of women at social functions and from the social representation of the household with regard to the outside. Going to the fields – excluding any consideration of the physical exhaustion entailed by the work carried out there – is already an appropriation of male territory, as Anton Blok has shown in his studies of the social organization of those Sicilian villages which are the headquarters of the Mafia's operations.

> The peasants prided themselves on exempting their mothers and sisters from working the land . . . A man who allowed his women to work outside the house put his honour at risk, in two ways: directly, by showing that he was incapable of maintaining his family himself, and incapable of observing the cultural role assigned to him, a role establishing the superiority of the males with regard to the inferiority of the females of the family; and indirectly, because it would be more difficult for him to control their behaviour in the sphere of sexual relations. Whence the cultural emphasis placed on the seclusion of women: the fields are forbidden to most peasant women, and they are rarely seen in public.[23]

In Brittany, on the other hand, proverbs emphasize the presence of girls outside: *Montrous-vous les filles, qui n'se montère n'est vu* (Show off you girls, who isn't shown isn't seen).[24]

Participation in outside activities is the sign of a relative sharing of the social representation of the household, and, according to the cultural area, the woman might or might not go to the market and participate in the economic bargaining whose crucial importance has already been noted.

No Northern proverb forbidding a woman to go to market, on pilgrimages, attend festivals, etc., has been noted. She might also participate in the political affairs of the village, as she did in the Lorraine; she could participate in or be excluded from relations with the municipal authorities, notaries, etc. Thus, in Brittany, it is the woman who traditionally arranges all the business affairs.

The technical organization of work, more or less extreme sexual segregation of territories, the responsibility for the social representation of the household, the system of inheritance of goods, and the ancient cultural heritage deriving from German and Latin civilizations

---

[23] Anton Blok, *The Mafia of a Sicilian village, 1860–1960*, pp. 49–50.
[24] Paul Sébillot, *Coutumes populaires de la haute Bretagne*, p. 87.

all combine in each society to produce a specifically regional model. That of Mediterranean societies seems clearly less favourable to women, as this observer of Provençal society has acutely noted:

> The man was the sole master of the house, particularly before 1900. The woman used the formal *vous* to him and only addressed him by his surname. I was always taken aback by our grandparents' way of speaking to their husbands using their surnames . . . The woman was the servant who obeyed her husband, while he exerted a veritable tyranny over her. The subordinate role of the woman could also be found in administrative life. A woman could never be a witness before a notary, that is, a woman of the people. It took the Great War and a shortage of men to make the lawyer call on her to witness her notarised acts. Children born at the end of the century conserve the memory of their mother as an unhappy wife.[25]

One should specify the territorial limits of the South of this subject woman: they would comprise Provence, Gascony, and Languedoc, while the Pays Basque is a region of 'strong women'.

A good deal of work is still required to draw up a geography of matrimonial behaviour. This would clearly be necessary in order to understand the weight of social and cultural considerations placed upon twentieth-century French agriculture, as it has proceeded along the road to modernization since the 1950s.

---

[25] Paul Lafran, *op. cit.*, pp. 166–7.

7

The Rural Household
and Change

While the nineteenth century was a century of improvement in terms
of agricultural yields and of important technical progress, it was not a
century of profound, deep-seated change. It was only after the industrialization of the country that the economic, technical and social
conditions of agricultural labour found themselves utterly changed in
the years following the Second World War, and, since then, the
changes have speeded up as agriculture has been restructured. Now,
the disappearance of the traditional organization of labour, which has
been the concern of the preceding chapters, again poses the whole
question of the balance of roles within the family and within the rural
household which had previously been regulated by centuries of
practice. Yet the framework of the family farm persists. So we must
look at the question of the rural household faced with the changes
brought about by the integration of the agricultural system of production with industrial society. What are the links between technical
changes and changes in the family? What is the interrelationship
between the development of mechanization and rural celibacy, for
instance? What sort of family farms are we moving towards, and what
sort of family roles will be lived out on them? There are a host of
questions to be asked about the problems of tradition and change, and
the position of one with regard to the other. In attempting to analyse
the chronological development of these changes in the nineteenth and
twentieth centuries, are there certain constant factors which can be
brought out? As, for instance, in the way new forms of community
organization of labour have taken over from the mutual help of family

and kin, or workers' cooperatives have taken the place of the communal mill or bake-house.

However, such similarities are, more often than not, very superficial, compared with the changes which these new organizations have brought about in the relationship between the household, the farm, and society as a whole.

ECONOMIC DEVELOPMENTS AND CHANGES IN THE HOUSEHOLD

On the eve of the First World War, despite very marked improvements, French agriculture was in the main still highly labour-intensive. After the growth it experienced during the first fifty years of the nineteenth century, it simply marked time during the 1880s. Farms were too small, and investment too small-scale, for French agriculture suffering from the 'owner's complex. All the resources were directed at acquiring extra pieces of land rather than moving towards capital investment in equipment.'[1] In 1914,

> The world of the peasant remained a harsh world in which the poor man worked as hard as he could, because stopping work meant the end of any possibility of self-support and running all the risks of charity. There was no possible recourse to the State or society; the only recourse was to the family group. Whence the tenacious presence of the family system in the peasant mentality, whence too – perhaps – some of the conservatism and even universal traditionalism of that mentality.[2]

The 1914 war subjected the rural family to its first major shock. The men left; the women took over with an ease which was surprising only to those who had seen them simply as bourgeois women transplanted to the fields. They took on the management and upkeep of the farm just as they had often done throughout their lives, when their husbands died or emigrated. Returning from the war, the men resumed their positions, and the rural household underwent the first wave of mechanization, which did not as yet threaten the traditional organization of labour, since a large labour force was still necessary and all the major agricultural work still continued to be carried out within the traditional network of mutual aid. Nonetheless, rural society developed

[1] Maurice Agulhon, Gabriel Désert, Robert Specklin, *op. cit.*, vol. III, p. 460.
[2] *ibid.*, p. 501.

rapidly; emigration and the breakdown of traditional social frameworks led to a crisis in the years between the wars.

The combination of mechanization and the need for investment mobilized all the economic resources of the household. Everything was directed towards the purchase of a tractor, the comfort of the house was neglected, for lack of means, and, in the pre-war years, the morale of rural female society found itself in an extremely critical condition. What generations of women had borne with courage and pride, they could bear no longer. After all, the farmer's wife in the nineteenth century was well aware of the differences in the way of life and in social status which separated her from the bourgeoisie and the gentry. At the beginning of the twentieth century, the awareness of these differences became intolerable, while the feeling that they could be bridged led, irresistibly, to a radical solution: emigration. In 1933, a female observer of 'rural women' analysed this critical situation, and wrote about it in terms that were hardly likely to stem this exodus, which had all the appearance of a rout. Her narrative took a very different form from any that we have looked at up till now, from Olivier de Serres to the nineteenth-century folklorists.

The woman was seen as being deprived of her role as producer.

A woman's normal work is one of collaboration. The man's task is the production of the means of subsistence; the woman's the utilization of resources, and all the chores which demand care, precision, and perseverance. Keeping the man on the land by creating for him an agreeable interior, where he can find, after a hard day, the relaxation and modest comforts he has earned; charming rural life with her gaiety, courage and good humour; ennobling it through her moral influence, her example, her virtues, and her prayers; finally, bringing up numerous children to a love of the land and of their father's occupation. This is the peasant woman's great mission in life; this is the task which no-one else can fulfil, and which she is increasingly letting slip.[3]

But this moralizing speech seemed singularly ineffective, even to its author, when she saw the extremely hard labour the women endured. For instance, in a part of Brittany which was still only partially mechanized, the women regularly worked 13, and occasionally 17 or 18 hours a day, at the same time as bringing up numerous children. The disparity between rural and urban women had never been so

[3] Comtesse de Keranflech-Kernezne, *La femme de la campagne*, p. 21.

great. As improvements in education opened up opportunities in the outside world, it became the less-gifted children who were left behind on the farm. As for the young girls 'without a corner to call their own, often sharing their beds with a younger sister or a servant girl . . . employed as farmworker and servant, without wages,'[4] small wonder that they were drawn to the towns – preferring factory work to this sort of slavery, and a place to live with 'all modern conveniences' – and that they should refuse to marry a man from that culture. Might we not assume that the mothers themselves encouraged their daughters to leave? The outcome of this one-way emigration was a profound crisis in the rural family. Succession was no longer assured from one generation to the next, and the main aim of the household-farm – that of transmitting patrimony – lost its meaning. Male celibacy acquired an often dramatic significance in certain regions. In serious instances, it became a reason for young men to leave, preferring to abandon the farm altogether. Today, regions in which celibacy has reached a critical level are those in which there are smallholdings which cannot cope with both the investment demanded by the farm and the dwelling, and in which material conditions remain precarious: 49.1 per cent celibacy in Limousin, and 31.6 per cent in Finistère, for example. A high rate of celibacy can be seen to be associated with low agricultural yields and high school attendance for girls, as in Limousin, Brittany, the region of the Rhône-Alpes, Franche-Comté, and the Midi-Pyrénées; a less marked rate of celibacy is recorded in regions where the yield is close to the national average and education is poor, as in Lower Normandy, the Loire, or Poitou-Charentes. Finally, the lowest rate of celibacy prevails in the Paris region, in Champagne, and in North Picardy, areas of intensive farming where the agricultural yields are above average.[5]

As for the couples who stayed on the land between the wars, they became more inward looking then ever in order to resist the crisis which was marked and maintained by the rural exodus, and by the destructuring of traditional solidarities. This gradual rise in the individualism of the couple can be traced through changes in the habitat. All the same, modernization of the dwelling-place follows a long way behind alterations to the farm buildings. In this sense, the house is a factor of rigidity and a brake to economic progress. Some buildings became obsolete, others lost their functions. Farms visited just after

[4] *ibid.*, p. 22.
[5] Gwenhaël Jegouzo, 'L'ampleur du célibat chez les agriculteurs'.

the Second World War by the architects of the Musée national des arts et traditions populaires were often ill-suited to the technical and economic conditions under which they were worked. Certain very specialized buildings were too extensive: at Rosières, in the Ardèche, the dwelling-place made up part of a farm of 20 hectares of chestnuts, 11 hectares of mulberries and olives laid out in 1822.[6] But, with the abandonment of silk-worm rearing, the breeding houses were no use to the new viticultural products which the farm was involved with in 1945.

In the Lower Seine, at Marcanville, the typical *cour masure* structure of the Caux farmyard was ill-suited, in 1944,[7] to agricultural functions. Originally a grazing rather than a crop farm, it had subsequently been converted to a cereal culture, badly suited to the widely spaced distribution of the buildings. Movements were difficult, journeys from place to place long and time-consuming. The placing of buildings, which had previously provided advantages of security against the risk of fire, had lost its purpose. The disparity between the working tool as represented by the farm and its new economic function imposed the need for modifications and improvements to – that is to say, investment in – the farm buildings long before any concern for making changes in the household dwelling. In the Tarn-et-Garonne, at Cazals,[8] 'the house is the ancestral dwelling,' writes the architect-researcher, 'which is handed on unchanged to the children. Everything is done to improve the animals' quarters. There is thus a difference in the phase of development, the dwelling being almost everywhere much older than the barn and outbuildings.'

Nonetheless, according to social level and cultural customs, the dwelling-place did change as well. In the Morbihan, at Belle-Ile,[9] the large communal room which had previously been a common feature on this sort of small farm was subdivided into several small rooms. One of them served as the best dining-room, used only for family festivals. Sometimes – as in Plédran in the Côtes-du-Nord – the improvement of the dwelling amounted to nothing more than a wooden partition, which, by cutting off the vestibule, sheltered the communal room from draughts.[10] Elsewhere, in the Eure, at Gouville, changes were carried out simultaneously on the farm and the dwelling-place.[11] The first buildings, put up in 1833, consisted of the 'best

[6] EAR, no. 2. [7] EAR, no. 5. [8] EAR, no. 3.
[9] EAR, (Le Palais). [10] EAR, no. 11. [11] EAR, no. 15.

room', the communal room, the bedroom, the washroom, and the dairy. In 1903 there were added an outhouse, a dormitory, a dining-room for paying guests, two children's rooms and a lavatory, a barn, a sheep-pen, rabbit-hutches, and a smithy; towards 1920, a grain-barn was added: the changes are all leading in the direction of greater intimacy within the household and of separation of generations. It might well be assumed that such intimacy was something that was sought after. But social level and cultural practices did not always impose the need for such separation. Thus, in 1945, in the Lot, at Engarenne,[12] the architect found himself faced with a big house made up of two parts. The older dated from the Revolution. A second wing had been added in 1876, at right-angles to the earlier building. The other changes were, above all concerned with the farm buildings: in 1880, the old barn-byre was replaced; in 1913, the trough was extended; in 1914 a hen-house was built. Two improvements related to the dwelling: in 1934, the scullery-washroom was built, and, in 1939, the main room was enlarged. By 1945, the house was nearly too big for its inhabitants, and one wing was virtually unoccupied. There lived in it a couple, their married son and their baby, and another unmarried son. These people occupied only the communal room and two rooms of the old wing. The young couple slept in one room with their baby, while the old couple shared their room with their bachelor son. In the new wing, only the best dining-room and a guest-room were put to occasional use. Sleeping together was common, not from lack of room, but from the time-honoured custom of sharing sleeping-time. The development of the rural household, as the dwelling-place reveals, was a complex process involving economic, social and cultural factors. Three factors in particular determined the type of changes which took place in the peasant interior: a desire for display, a desire for intimacy, and a desire for comfort which bears witness to the emergence of a new family mentality. The desire for display accompanies the increasing wealth of the peasant and shows – in the house as the mark of this new comfort – the sign of a wish to imitate a higher social class. It is marked by the appearance of chilly, rarely used rooms, furnished as 'dining-rooms', with furniture given to the young couple as wedding presents. These rooms are hardly used, except on the occasion of large family gatherings, or for entertaining a guest outside the communal room. Show is also revealed as another

[12] EAR, no. 1.

aspect of the desire for intimacy; the reception room marks a separation between the stranger and the family. Receiving someone in the dining-room is both a way of honouring the visitor by showing him the household in its social representation, in the room where the treasures of the household – wedding presents, photographs – are on display, but it is also a way of making the visitor feel a stranger. Intimacy is marked by the appearance of separate areas or rooms for sleeping, by a wish to distance the generations, to segregate the area of sexual relations, and for the couple to have a place of their own, where their clothes and personal objects are kept, somewhere that is not shared by other members of the household. However, though the rooms are rarely used during the daily cycle – they are merely a place to sleep – they reflect a new aspiration of the couple to become more inward-looking, a desire for on the part of the husand and wife to be autonomous with regard to the rest of the household. And, as if to preserve this new-found intimacy, the beds were often taken from the big room into the separate room with its curtains and its bedside table.

TECHNICAL AND STRUCTURAL CHANGES: A REDEFINITION OF TASKS AND ROLES

The rise of the couple in the rural environment is demonstrated in the development of family structures and mentalities, and there can be no other family in which so many profound changes have been observed in recent decades. These changes affect the organization of family labour and the distribution of roles within the household. Now, more than ever before, the pre-eminence of the husband is undisputed, in that he is the head of the farm, and priority is given to the farm in the ideal of modernization, aggrandisement and ceaseless restructuring. The agricultural worker, perhaps more ready than ever to share with his wife the responsibilities of the farm, is prevented from doing so by existing agricultural structures. But if the 'quarrel for the trousers' has been well and truly resolved, recent years have seen the development of a consideration of the position of the woman in agriculture, a position which she has lost due to the technical and structural upheavals which have taken place in the agricultural arena. In effect, the grandmothers of the present generation of farmers' wives were *patronnes*, mistresses; their mothers were the 'lost generation', but farmers' wives of today no longer know where to place themselves or what to do, so contradictory are their aspirations and so difficult are the conflicts of their daily lives to live with. We have just described the rift between the modernization of agricultural equipment and domestic equipment but it is beginning to disappear. There is another one: the rift between the need to break out of their isolation and the disappearance of the old forms of sociability. The major domestic operations carried out communally by a group of women at the wash-house or the bakehouse have disappeared. The weekly contact with the market in the town has been cut off by the collection of milk at home. A whole sector of traditional female sociability has thus disappeared. Naturally, these 'modernizations' should not all be regarded as being negative. It is true that they have lightened the physical tasks of the woman, but they have, on the other hand, cut off opportunities for meeting and for entering into the community which were much appreciated. It is not surprising that in a small Breton community of 660 inhabitants there were eight coffee-cake-bread shops (as well as the butcher). Isolated on their farms, the women found that their daily visit to the corner-shop on the pretext of fetching the bread each day was their only contact with the outside world. The traditional position of women on the farm, a position which was important, and recognized as such, was threatened on the most forward-looking agricultural enterprises. In this sense, agricultural modernization has not resolved the problem of the balance of roles within the rural household, but, rather, has complicated it, as has been shown by a recent study of 'the distribution and characteristics of tasks in specialized agricultural enterprises.[13]

On these farms, which are being rationalized through a simplification of system of cultivation, the concentration of the activity of a restricted number of products, and the notion of the 'workshop' are inspired by the image of the organization of labour in a factory; it is a unit of production making a single product or even simply concerned with a single stage of production. Women's tasks in these types of enterprises are restricted to manual work of a repetitive nature, whose rhythm is dictated by a machine. The very fact that they work in noisy workshops, often at a distance from the farm, at dirty jobs and under pressure of time introduces a conflict between work and family tasks.

Previously, looking after young children presented no problem: the grandmother, servant-girl or older sister could look after them when the mother was not there, if she did not in fact take the baby with her to

[13] Marie-Catherine Becouarn, *Le travail des femmes d'exploitants dans l'agriculture et l'évolution des techniques.*

the fields, in a small cradle put in the shade under a tree. This is no longer possible in a workshop where the pace of work has to be kept up, and boxes of fruit or vegetables sent on their way by train to the markets of the regional capital. On a farm where milking is carried out mechanically and where livestock occupy a much more important position than before, the operation, in spite of, or, perhaps, because of mechanization, takes up from an hour and a half to three hours a day, twice a day, just at the time when the children are going off to school or coming home. Yet it is technical work which is sufficiently complex not to allow of interruptions or distractions. So there is direct competition between the work of the farm and care for the children. In the same way, housework is nowadays more difficult for the farmer's wife. An earth floor took less looking after than tiles, and there is not a woman on the world who believes that modern food products, whether frozen or otherwise, represent any saving in the time spent preparing a meal. On the contrary, what has been termed progress as regards diet – that is to say, a greater variety of dishes, and a decrease in the bread consumption – corresponds to an increase in labour in this area. In the country, as in the town, potato chips are now a staple, and they take time to prepare. In diversifying, by coming closer to urban menus (which themselves are reviving the stews and casseroles of country cooking, but much improved!), cooking in the rural household takes up more time than before.

The farmer's wife today is thus subject to a daily conflict between her work on the farm and her responsibilities towards the upbringing of her children, as well as being occupied with housework which, in spite of all the modern gadgets, takes a good deal longer than before. On specialized farms, women find themselves dealing only with fragmentary tasks; they are there to cope with any urgent need. As one of them puts it: 'I am a stop-gap. If there is an urgent errand, it is logical that I should shift myself and do it because what I am doing is less important than what he is doing. On the other hand, if I need him urgently, he will only come when he has finished what he doing.'[14]

This is because the jobs to be done on a modern farm have become too technical, and the woman has not had the necessary training to undertake them. All that is left for her are the 'stop-gap' jobs, and the woman suffers from proletarianization. Cut off from physical work, she is equally cut off from participation in service tasks: she cannot do

[14] Newsletter from the Association amicale des anciens élèves des écoles nationales d'enseignement technique agricole, no. 56, p. 18.

the accounts either, from lack of training, and participation in decisions is entirely beyond her reach. It is no longer a question, as it used
to be, of short-term decisions affecting only the family farm, but of
long-term strategies, demanding radical revision, heavy investment,
involving several farms, and determined within structural frameworks which extend beyond any one, single enterprise.

According to other interpretations, the woman has not become
proletarianized so much as 'housewifed' in the sense that all participation in the material tasks or management of the farm has been taken
away from her. Just like the urban woman, all she has to do is look
after the home and children.

The model of that first woman corresponds to the medium-sized
farm in the process of modernization, looking for new production
methods and new structures; the non-participant woman is to be
found on the large cereal farms, which have already been specialized
for several years, and where the division of labour is both highly
marked and based on a large labour force. The disappearance of
livestock has completely brought an end to her work there.

Between the family organization tied to a medium-sized agricultural undertaking in the process of specialization, and the very large
farm, there exists an intermediate type which preserves and accentuates the productive role of the woman, and that is the medium-sized
farm which cannot maintain agricultural workers: the complementarity
and solidarity between husband and wife are intense, just as in the past,
as is the constant fear of ill-health, which is only lessened by the
continuance of a network of mutual help. Nonetheless, we may well
consider the development of such undertakings which function har-
moniously on the family level, and ask whether the woman's place
will not become more and more difficult to maintain. Now, while this
situation whereby the woman is excluded is regarded as a crisis, the
link between the family and the farm is becoming increasingly emphasized. At times, just as before, family activities and production are
linked; in terms of inheritance, also as before, but under radically
different conditions. The woman loses her role as manager of the
family budget and, while external organizations of banking or agricultural associations manage the financing of the farm, she finds herself
deprived of the budgetary independence she used to enjoy from the
sale of the products of her farmyard and garden.

Alongside the technical developments whose consequences we have
briefly reviewed here, the development of agricultural production

structures conspire, in a similar way, to deny the farmer's wife her status as producer. In a study of agricultural workers' cooperatives in France, Placide Rambaud noted that the position of women in these new agricultural groupings presented a problem,[15] particularly in the communal farming associations, the Groupements agricoles d'exploitation en commun or GAEC, which most often brought together land belonging to related families, organized production into workshops and entrusted the keeping of accounts to centres of administration. In this way, the newsletter of the Union des ententes et communautés rurales reveals the difficulties which have arisen in this new situation:

> It is the home which must be integrated into the community. Historically, the joint holding of the means of production and the new division of labour between associates have liberated the woman from numerous tasks for which she was previously responsible; they also tend to separate family and farm. In a second phase, women also find themselves eliminated from decision-making; there ensues a kind of employment and isolation. The third stage, that of their integration into the cooperative, has come up against a twofold difficulty: their assumed lack of professional qualifications and, hence, their remuneration. The GAEC are still engaged in seeking criteria to define the status of female workers to which a good many women now aspire: the effective work time, professional competence, responsibility, personal remuneration for labour. Some, a few, are associates; others run specialized workshops, which are occasionally set up alongside the farming enterprise; others deal with the accounts.[16]

Another observer also noted that 'the breakdown or poor performance of the GAEC were all too often laid at the women's door . . . but how can one blame them for weighing down the atmosphere, sowing discord and fomenting quarrels, when it is the only power which remains to them on the farm? . . . Some GAEC salve their consciences by putting women in charge of the accounts . . . under such conditions, this is in no way a mark of power, but the sanction for an inferiorization.'[17]

The rural woman was thus faced with a historical situation which was

[15] Placide Rambaud, Le coopératives de travail agraire en France, p. 47.

[16] Newsletter from the Union des ententes et communautés rurales, 1 January 1953, in Placide Rambaud, Les coopératives de travail agraire en France, pp. 47–8.

[17] Jean Rémy, Travail, famille et développement agricole. Aspects de la vulgarisation féminine, p. 112.

entirely new to her. The technical nature of modern operations demanded a training which was only rarely available to her; and the credo of the schools devoted to the study of the significantly named 'domestic' science took no account of it. Now agricultural women are demanding the training which will give them access to mechanized labour or to the running of the farm, and thus to a technical training and to training in accountancy, which will, in turn, lead to a greater share in the responsibilities.

The traditional role held by the man as representative of the household–farm in the world outside has been reinforced by the development of modern agricultural structures, whether one is speaking of the GAEC, the CETA (Centre d'études de travaux agricoles), the CUMA (Coopératives d'utilisation du matériel agricole), or the institutions which give credit, and which can influence the direction of agricultural policy. Thus an enquiry into the different agricultural organizations of the Allier shows the 'absence' of women:[18]

NUMBER OF WOMEN PRESENT

Crédit agricole (administrative council)	0
Mutualité agricole (mutual society)	
administrative council	3 out of 18 members
local delegates	4 out of 148 members
communal delegates	8 out of 632 members
Chambre d'agriculture (chamber of agriculture)	0
Union organizations	1
Administrative centre	2
Women's associations for agricultural development	9
Women's CETA	4

The existence of agricultural advisory services, since 1966 called associations for agricultural 'development', specifically geared towards women, does not fundamentally alter the situation. Women remain cut off from power on the farm.

These groups have nevertheless provided structural frameworks for women wishing to break out of their isolation, to meet together and to consider their new situation. Women's participation in associations of this type varies a good deal from region to region, and certain cultural constants can be observed in the position of women outside the home. Thus it has been noted that the Breton woman was quite easily able to

[18] Newsletter from the Association amicale des anciens élèves des écoles nationales d'enseignement technique agricole, no. 56, p. 52.

attend training or information meetings, her neighbours readily agreeing to look after the children and her husband encouraging her participation: the Breton woman, as we have seen, has always been open to the outside world. On the other hand, this kind of meeting remains tacitly forbidden to women in the Midi, where contact with the outside world has traditionally been badly regarded. The all-powerfulness of the man is marked by the way in which he can facilitate or refuse his wife access to knowledge, integration into the new structures of production which have been established, and as-sociation in the running of the family farm.

The constraints limiting the power of the farmer's wife today are all the more intolerable in that, in marrying, she makes the choice of remaining on the land, if one excepts very large agricultural enter-prises. In choosing a farmer as husband, she chooses a trade. She seeks to be associated, but in a newly defined framework: she is concerned with the recognition of status.

TOWARDS A NEW DEFINITION OF THE POSITION OF WOMEN IN AGRICULTURE

Women have had a major influence on the upheavals which have taken place in agriculture. They have often been the motive force of pro-gress,[19] even if only *a contrario*. When they stayed on the farm, it was with the desire to improve production and the condition of the family. Their dynamism, tempered by a prudence drawn from a daily prac-tical experience of reality, led them to prefer 'adaptation to mutation'. Often the instigators of the purchase of modern equipment or of the farm's adopting new production structures, today they find them-selves cut off from the running of the farm, while still carrying out an important part of the work on it under difficult conditions. Thus women in agriculture seek status for themselves, and ask that their work should be recognized, evaluated and paid an appropriate wage with the same guarantee of work and social rights enjoyed by all other workers.

In this domain, certain technical measures are urgently demanded of the State: for instance that the exceptional payment (installation bonus) made to young farmers should be paid to the household, even in the case of the wife alone having a certificate of agricultural studies (at present the law lays down that it must be the husband who holds this

---

[19] Marie Moscovici, 'Le changement social en milieu rural et le rôle des femmes'.

diploma); and that farmers' wives should be able to receive social security benefits (such as old age or invalidity pensions). These demands have met with fierce resistance within the agricultural community itself, since they tend to accord to the woman a status in the social representation of the household with regard to the outside world, in this case, the central administration. On the financial level, women demand that the married couple should be represented in production associations on the basis of shares rather than through each individual farm.

At the level of the farm itself, agricultural women seek for themselves some sort of autonomous activity, given that the technicalization of agricultural operations will continue to increase and that they can never resume a complementary position. They are becoming more and more involved in the creation of specialized 'workshops' where they are concerned with the administration, production and management. In a move related to the longstanding assocation between the woman and the farmyard, many have set up poultry-raising concerns. Finally, more than ever, rural couples – and women in particular – are seeking to put an end to a situation which used to be the norm: co-residence with parents.

Separate dwellings for different generations is a new demand. It is well known that coresidence, which in earlier times was accepted without question, even if not all households were involved (there were a good number of regions where one did not find 'complex households') is a situation which is no longer tolerated.

An aid to 'decoresidence' has been considered by the State, but it would need an active policy of home loans in rural areas to get rid of a situation which, it appears, is difficult for both generations to put up with. Other tendencies are beginning to be apparent among agricultural women. Some of them wish to continue to pursue the profession they had before they married: nurse, schoolteacher, saleswoman. But the community often looks askance at the idea of their keeping up a previous occupation, and it is, certainly, difficult to make such a practice compatible with life on a farm; it is as if the tie between the rural household and the land which we defined in the introduction had somehow been reinforced despite all the technical changes. Often the women who give up their earlier professions become agriculturalists: whence their deeply felt wish to be associated in the farm as these rural women demand.

Nonetheless, amid this concert of voices raised in a desire for action and power alongside men, there is a growing discourse expressing specifically feminine desires and needs, and which forms part of a movement concerned with ecology and the quality of life.[20] We are now in a better position to evaluate the social cost of the modernization of agriculture which has been paid by a large part of the agricultural population. At present, everything is given up to the farm, while a number of women judge that the farm should be at the service of the family and not the other way round. Equally, the family agricultural undertaking is perceived as the site of the contradictions between the human values to which these women aspire and the endlessly increasing race for productivity and production towards which French agriculture is tending.

[20] Jean Rémy, *op. cit.*

Conclusion

Farm life in the nineteenth century was not easy, and the relative prosperity earned by the peasants was the fruit of blood, sweat, tears and toil over generations of peasant families welded together around the farm; an understanding of the relationships between man and wife therefore seemed necessary in order to understand at what price the modernization of agriculture has been carried out. Such an analysis must cover all levels of social practice, from the concrete to the abstract, from the banal to the ritual, from the material to the symbolic, with all these levels being integrated, despite their apparent incoherences or contradictions. Thus, practice rooted in economic and social factors has been confronted with the cultural dimension making up the background of the mentality and attitudes of the peasants.

From the polyvalent microholding to the large specialist enterprise, a whole range of situations and organizations of labour within the family may be encountered: the more or less sharply defined division of tasks between the married couple, regular or occasional participation of the wife in the work in the fields; the presence or absence of a paid labour force have combined with the diversity in methods of agricultural production and of modes of organization of labour to produce an impression of diversity which is difficult to synthesize, and which is emphasized even further by the cultural, and particularly the legal, background involved.

Above and beyond these differences, the central point common to all these agricultural households may perhaps rest in the disparity between discourse and actual practice. In response to the deep-seated fear of what, to a male society, appears an incomprehensible and aggressive female nature there exists a symbolic discourse exorcising this potential power which the women themselves help to transmit to their sons and daughters, as it were, tongue-in-cheek. Nonetheless, the peasant woman's status was a relatively favourable one, and the combination of the couple in the household and on the farm proved fruitful, both for individual families and for the progress of the agricultural economy in general.

The upheavals in the economy were as disturbing for the rural family as they had been for the urban family, though they are rarely mentioned, as if the rural household continued to be the preserver of traditional values. Now, while in certain cases the disappearance of paid labourers has seen the return of the woman to working in the fields or the byre, there has also been a movement in the opposite direction on medium-sized types of farm which are turning towards an increasing specialization: here the woman is proletarianized or excluded from the domain of decision-making. Finally, at the other extreme, the wife of the major cereal-producer of the Beauce region or the Ile-de-France lives like a townswoman, or, rather, like a *bourgeoise*, able to combine the advantages of life in the country with the privileges of a social category which can go off for winter sports.

The disappearance of the woman's productive function has been accompanied by the evaporation of the profound fear which she aroused. Her power, whether for good or ill, had disappeared when she became detached from direct contact with the fire and water of which she had previously been guardian and provider; when she ceased to spin and to prepare the food in the cauldron, and was thus deprived of the instruments of her maleficence. The female body has also been separated from the cosmic universe, and the disappearance of the restrictions which periodically enclosed the woman in a network of taboos might be seen, in the final analysis, as the reason for the disappearance of her function as producer, a disappearance which had been attributed to recent structural and agricultural developments and to technical and economic changes.

Will the present crisis, to be seen in the relationship between the agricultural household and the farm itself, be resolved by an even more marked separation of the one from the other? Or, will the old combination of household and farm persist, and, if so, what position would the wife then be able to occupy alongside her husband?

Experts estimate that the family farm is very solidly based: 'Family farms are not survivals from the past; they have not been overwhelmed by industrialization: in France, they still represent 85 per cent of agricultural work, in the USA 75 per cent. They are easily able to adapt to modern economy so long as they have a sufficient initial patrimony, financial facilities and technical progress which correspond to their needs.'[1]

In France in particular,

> The so-called family farm shows a great deal more flexibility today than has been generally assumed and continues to adapt to the demands of the social system without causing too many difficulties. Not only was it possible for the family farm, even more at the turn of the century, to increase the quantity of goods it put on the market, through an increasingly well worked-out application of its own means, but also, since 1955, it has shown that it can improve its performance by turning to the means of production put at its disposal by industry.[2]

The example of the fruit-growers and cheese-makers of the Jura[3] shows the extent to which the traditional family farming structure favoured a development which, it has been generally agreed, was well modified to the demands of a modern economy. Nonetheless, the increase in the number of members of a family who follow a profession outside agriculture has led some observers to believe that 'the identification between family and farm has ceased to be absolute.'[4] and that

> Coresidence is increasingly based on the function of sheltering the young workers until they are in a position to set up on their own. From this point of view, the position of young men and women from agricultural backgrounds is the same as that of young urban workers living at home with their parents. But for the peasant family this change is significant because it means that instead of being a unit of production, as it used to be, it has now become a 'unit of consumption', like other households.[5]

---

[1] Paul Houée, *Quel avenir pour les ruraux?*, p. 127.

[2] Michel Gervais, Marcel Jollivet, Yves Tavernier, *Histoire de la France rurale*, vol. IV, p. 238.

[3] Michèle Dion-Salitot and Michel Dion, *La crise d'une société villageoise, "les survivanciers", les paysans du Jura français*.

[4] Michel Gervais, Marcel Jollivet, Yves Tavernier, *op. cit.*, vol. IV, p. 267.

[5] *ibid.*, p. 268.

Is this really a new situation? The rural family often raised numbers of children who left their agricultural professions and moved away from their birthplace – children who did not inherit and had to find work elsewhere, or the waves of migrants in the last half of the nineteenth century who came from agricultural backgrounds and moved to the towns to find employment. The increasing similarity between the urban and the agricultural family is, from this point of view, nothing new. Moreover, the rural family continues to preserve particular characteristics which testify to its uniqueness. It is dependent on nature, even if that nature has become domesticated, and continues to experience its rhythms, its excesses and uncertainties, even if State aid makes the experience less painful; the biological rhythms of calving and lambing mean that the stock-farmer's profession can never be run according to a clockwork timetable which the laws of nature refuse to observe. Nature continues to keep some secrets: in one modern pig-farm, neither farmer not vet could understand why the sows did not come on heat; an inexplicable loss in profit which was borne with a sort of resignation: 'They are not machines.'

Experts estimate that by 1985 there will be over a million agri-cultural enterprises, of which 700,000 will be small-scale producers employing over a million workers drawn above all from the close family. The dominant type would be the farm of the 40–50 hectares worked by a household with the part-time help of one paid worker.[6] Cooperative forms of work would also develop. One can already see the increase of GAEC based on family ties, whether in terms of associations of brothers and kin, which make up 46.3 per cent of the total, an increase of over 14 per cent between 1968 and 1972, or associations between father and son (31.6 per cent), an annual increase of 1 per cent.[7]

One can see the importance and urgency of the resolution of the family crisis being experienced by certain agricultural enterprises, since the family farm still seems to be something in the future and associations based on family links, like the GAEC, are still developing. Assigning the rural woman a position as producer within the farm is not a demand made by the feminist movement; even if it had been (though it seems that the feminist movement only evokes a weak response in the rural environment and that it takes little or no interest

[6] Paul Houée, *op. cit.*, p. 129.
[7] Placide Rambaud, *Les coopératives de travail agraire en France*, p. 40.

in the agricultural woman itself), it is evident that such a wish derives from the traditional organization of the rural family itself.

The increasing importance and isolation of the couple are characteristics of all families in contemporary society. It is in the rural environment that this modern individualism finds its social fulfilment, in the traditional association of man and wife linked together towards the same goal. This might even be a short-term goal, no longer concerned with the farm being handed on within the family, since many farmers – whether consciously or unconsciously – turn their children away from a wish to take up farming, and direct them towards academic achievement and other activities. Nonetheless, insofar as agricultural labourers are a thing of the past, a man and his wife working together with a common goal and strategy offer an image of a harmonious couple which constitutes a vanishing mirage for a society which is in conflict at every level, even within the heart of the family unit. Hence the importance of what is at stake.

The agricultural woman will regain her lost position either on the farm, or within one of the new structural groupings, or else the rural household, and the entire agricultural world will undergo a profound crisis. One may be sure that the new tendency which has been expressed by some agricultural women – to put a brake on growth and the race to increase productivity – is not something which is going to find an immediate hearing. On the other hand, the achievement of a new status is something which ought to be possible.

The traditional agricultural household consists of a couple based on the dwelling-house, whose strategies were shaped by those of lineage. Man and wife worked together to attain the central aim which was constituted by the survival and transmission of the farm. They shared the functions of production. The integration of their activities was not contradictory to a social life based on a separation of the sexes. Finally, though one would wish to repudiate the prejudice of male domination within the household, the norm must nevertheless be seen as the husband being bearer of the image of the couple and of the household with regard to the community at large.

Today, there is still something fundamentally unchanged in the relationship between man and wife and farm, rather as there still persists, in terms of love or death, an essential relationship which has resisted all upheavals, since social change is always a good deal slower than technical change: the woman on the tractor may have appropriated a male territory, but, once she has returned home, she still continues to do the washing-up and look after the children.

That a book such as this, on the rural household, should conclude with a consideration of particularly feminine concerns – does this mean that the new consciousness of self prevalent among women has also had an effect on the rural family? That would imply that the agricultural household was giving off distant echoes of the family in general. On the contrary, we have sought to show, in these pages, the uniqueness of the rural household which could, drawing on its traditional sources, provide a model of the family combining the work aspirations of men and women with the desire for individual fulfil-ment within the conjugal unit, such as present-day society is seeking.

Bibliography

Abbadie d'Arrast, Mme d', *Causeries sur le pays basque, la femme et l'enfant*, Paris, de Rudeval, 1909, 250 p.

Agulhon, Maurice; Désert, Gabriel; Specklin, Robert, *Histoire de la France rurale*, vol. III. *Apogée et crise de la civilisation paysanne, 1789–1914*, Paris, Seuil, 1976, 568 p.

Alford, Violet, *Les sabots de la vallée de Bethmale*, Art populaire en France, 1933.

L'Aubrac, vol. III, Ethnologie contemporaine, I, Paris, CNRS, 1972, 333 p.

Becouarn, Marie-Catherine, *Le travail des femmes d'exploitants dans l'agriculture et l'évolution des techniques. Etude de la répartition et des caractéristiques des tâches dans les exploitations agricoles spécialisées*, Tours, Université de Tours, 1979, 293 p.

Bérenger-Féraud, L. J. B., *Réminiscences populaires de la Provence. Légendes de la Provence, 1885–1888*, Nyons, Chantemerle, 1971, 410 p.

Béteille, Roger, *La vie quotidienne en Rouergue avant 1914*, Paris, Hachette Littérature, 1973, 254 p.

Blok, Anton, *The mafia of a Sicilian village, 1860–1960*, Oxford, Basil Blackwell, 1974, 293 p.

Blouin, Abbé Léonor, *Mœurs et coutumes de basse Normandie*, Saint-Lô, Le Tual, 1901, 425 p.

Bouchard, Gérard, *Le village immobile, Sennely-en-Sologne au XVIIIe siècle*, Paris, Plon, 1972, 386 p.

Bouët, Alexandre and Perrin, Olivier, *Breiz-Izel ou Vie des Bretons de l'Armorique*, Paris, re-issue, Tchou, 1970, 471 p.

Bougeâtre, Eugène, *La vie rurale dans le Mantois et le Vexin au XIXe siècle*, Meulan, Marcel Lachiver, 1971, 284 p.

Bourdieu, Pierre, *La maison kabyle ou le monde renversé, in: Equisse d'une théorie de la pratique,* Genève et Paris, Droz, 1972, pp. 45–69.

Bourdieu, Pierre, Le sens pratique, *Actes de la recherche en sciences sociales,* February 1976, I. pp. 43–86.

Brunhes-Delamarre, Mariel J., Hairy, Hugues, *Techniques de production: l'agriculture,* Guides ethnologiques 4/5, Paris, RMN, 1971, 70 p.

Burguière, André, *Bretons de Plozévet,* Paris, Flammarion, 1975, 383 p.

Cahiers d'histoire de l'enseignement, *Les Cahiers du Devoir,* Rouen, special issue, 1976.

Chamboredon, Jean-Claude, 'Les deux manières de Jean-François Millet', *Actes de la recherche en sciences sociales,* November 1977, 17/18, pp. 8–28.

Chapiseau, F., *Folklore de la Beauce et du Perche,* Paris, Maisonneuve et Larose, 1902, 2 vol.

Charivari, Le, ed. Jacques Le Goff and Jean-Claude Schmitt, Paris, La Haye, New York, EHESS, Mouton, 1981, 444 p.

Chodkiewicz, Jean-Luc, *L'Aubrac à Paris, in: L'Aubrac,* IV, Ethnologie contemporaine, II, Paris, CNRS, 1973, pp. 196–281.

Coissac, G. Michel, *Mon Limousin,* Paris, Lahure, 1913, 438 p.

Cuisenier, Jean, (ed.), assisted by Segalen, Martine, *Le cycle de la vie familiale dans les sociétés européennes,* Paris, Mouton, 1977, 494 p.

Daugé, Abbé G., *Le mariage et la famille,*Paris, Picard and Bordeaux, Féret, 1916, 294 p.

Dergny, Dieudonné, *Usages, coutumes et croyances,* G. Monfort, Le Portulan, 1888.

Dion-Salitot, Michèle and Dion, Michel, *La crise d'une société villageoise, les survivanciers, les paysans du Jura français,* Paris, Anthropos, 1972, 399 p.

Evangiles des quenouilles, Les, revised edition, Paris, P. Jannet, 1855, 168 p.

Fabre, Daniel and Lacroix, Jacques, *La vie quotidienne des paysans de langue d'oc,* Paris, Hachette, 1973, 479 p.

Favret-Saada, Jeanne, *Les mots, la mort, les sorts, la sorcellerie dans le Bocage,* Paris, Gallimard, 1977, 332 p.

Fermigier, André, *Jean-François Millet,* Paris, Skira, 1977, 151 p.

Flandrin, Jean-Louis, *Les amours paysannes,* Paris, Gallimard-Julliard, coll. Archives, 1975, 255 p.

Flandrin, Jean-Louis, *Familles, parenté, maison, sexualité dans l'ancienne société,* Paris, Hachette, 1976, 287 p.

Fleury, Michel and Henry, Louis, *Nouveau manuel de dépouillement et d'exploitation de l'état civil ancien*, Paris, INED, 1965, 182 p.

Fortier-Beaulieu, Paul, *Mariages et noces campagnardes*, Paris, Maison-neuve, 1937, 367 p.

Fortier-Beaulieu, Paul, Coutumes et cérémonies des Brandons dans le Roannais et en Berry, *Revue du folklore français*, V, 1934, pp. 100–104.

Foville, Alfred de, *Enquête sur les conditions de l'habitation en France. Les maisons types*, Paris, Ernest Leroux, 1894, vol. I, 381 p., vol. II, 338 p.

Fraysse, Claude, *Le Folk-lore du Baugeois*, Baugé, R. Dangin, 1906, 196 p.

Frémont, Armand, *L'Elevage en Normandie, étude géographique*, Association des publications de la faculté des lettres et sciences humaines de l'Université de Caen, 1967, 2 vols.

Gastebois, Victor, *Légendes et histoires du Mortainais*, Mortain, printed by G. Letellier, 1932, 246 p.

Gervais, Michel, Jollivet, Marcel, Tavernier, Yves, *Histoire de la France rurale*, IV, *La fin de la France rurale, de 1914 à nos jours*, Pariś, Seuil, 1977, 666 p.

Goffart, N., Glossaire du Mouzonnais, *Revue de Champagne et de Brie*, 1898, X, pp. 60–110.

Gueneau, Lucien, Us et coutumes du Morvan, *Mémoires de la Société académique du Nivernais,* vol. I, 1886, pp. 39–60, 94–133.

Guillaume, Lucie, Fraternité bretonne, *Revue des traditions populaires,* XVII, 1902, pp. 501–2.

Guillaumin, Emile, *La vie d'un Simple. Mémoires d'un métayer*, Paris, Nelson, 1935, 369 p.

Hélias, Pierre Jakez, *Le pays bigouden*, Brest, Editions de la cité, 1971, 231 p.

Hélias, Pierre Jakez, *Le cheval d'orgueil. Mémoires d'un Breton du pays bigouden*, Paris, Plon, 1977, 576 p.

Houée, Paul, *Quel avenir pour les ruraux?*, Paris, Les Editions Ouvrières, 1974, 248 p.

Hudry, Marius, Relations sexuelles prénuptiales en Tarentaise et dans le Beaufortin d'après les documents ecclésiastiques, *Le monde alpin et rhodanien*, 1974, I, pp. 95–100.

Hugo, Abel, *France pittoresque*, Paris, Delloye, 1835, 3 vols.

Jeanton, Gabriel, *Le Mâconnais traditionnaliste et populaire*, Mâcon, impr. Protat frères, 1920–1923, 4 vols.

Jegouzo, Gwenhaël, L'ampleur du célibat chez les agriculteurs, *Economie et statistique*, 34, May 1972, p. 13.

Jossier, S., Dictionnaire des patois de l'Yonne, *Bulletin de la Société des sciences historiques et naturelles de l'Yonne*, vol. XXXVI, 1882, part 1, pp. 35–153.

Jouhanneau, Eloi, *Mémoires de l'Académie celtique*, 1808, vol. III, pp. 305–310.

Keranflech-Kernezne, *La femme de la campagne*, Paris, Spes, 1933, 278 p.

Lafran, Paul, *Le Folklore de Saint-Chamas en Provence*, Uzès, Ed. Henri Peladan, 1975, 79 p.

Lapaire, Hugues, *Le Berry vu par un Berrichon*, Paris, Gamber, 1928, 335 p.

Laslett, Peter and Wall, Richard, *Household and family in past time*, Cambridge University Press, 1972, 623 p.

Lebrun, François, *La vie conjugale sous l'Ancien Régime*, Paris, Armand Colin, 1975, 179 p.

Le Roy Ladurie, Emmanuel, Système de la coutume. Structures familiales et coutumes d'héritage en France au XVIe siècle, *Annales ESC.*, 4–5 July to October, 1972.

Le Wita, Béatrix, *Les fiançailles à Troyes du XVe au XVIIe siècle,* Master's thesis, 1975, Paris, univ. Paris VIII, 160 p.

Loux, Françoise, *Le jeune enfant et son corps dans la médecine traditionnelle*, Paris, Flammarion, 1978, 276 p.

Marcel-Dubois, Claudie, La paramusique dans le charivari français contemporain, in: *Le Charivari*.

Marin, Louis, *Regards sur la Lorraine*, Paris, Paul-Geuthner, 1966, 216 p.

Massoul, Henri, *Au bon vieux temps. Souvenirs du Gâtinais et de la Brie*, Fontainebleau, impr. de l'Informateur de Seine-et-Marne, 1941, 39 p.

Matthews-Grieco, Sara F., *La conception de la femme dans l'estampe française du XVIe siècle*, Master's thesis, 1975, univ. Paris I, 210 p.

Maupassant, Guy de, 'Story of a farm girl', *Boule de Suif and other stories*, London, Alfred A. Knopf, 1928, pp. 78–97.

Menon, P.-L, and Lecotté, Roger, *Au village de France, la vie traditionnelle des paysans,* Paris, Bourrelier, 1945, 2 vols., 212 p.

Merley, Jean, *La Haute-Loire, de la fin de l'Ancien Régime aux débuts de la troisième République,* Le Puy, Archives départementales, 1974, 2 vols., 667 p.

Millet, Jean-François, *Exposition Grand-Palais*, 17 October 1975–5 January 1976, Paris, RMN, 1975, 311 p.

Millet, Jean-François, *Exhibition catalogue Hayward Gallery (London)*, 22 January–7 March 1976, London, Arts Council, 1976, 235 p.

Moiset, Charles, Les usages, croyances, traditions, superstitions ayant existé ou existant encore dans les divers pays du département de l'Yonne, *Bulletin de la Société des sciences historiques et naturelles de l'Yonne,* vol. XLII, Auxerre, 1888, pp. 5–158.

Monnier, Désiré, Autorité des femmes en Franche-Comté, mœurs et usages anciens, *Travaux de la Société d'émulation du Jura,* 1841–1842, pp. 101–104.

Monnier, M., Vestiges d'antiquité observés dans le Jurassien, *Mémoires de la Société des antiquaires de France,*IV, 1823, pp. 338–412.

Moreau–Nelaton, E., *Millet par lui-même,* Paris, H. Laurens, 1921, 3 vols.

Moscovici, Marie, Le changement social en milieu rural et le rôle des femmes, *Revue française de sociologie,* 1960, 3, pp. 314–322.

Orain, Adolphe, *Folklore de l'Ille-et-Vilaine: de la vie à la mort,* Paris, Maisonneuve, 1897, I, 298 p.

Poette, Charles, *Histoire d'Holmon,* Saint-Quentin, impr. C. Poette, 1885, 568 p.

Rambaud, Placide, and Vincienne, Monique, *Les transformations d'une société rurale, la Maurienne (1561–1962),* Paris, A. Colin, 1964, 272 p.

Rambaud, Placide, *Les cooperatives de travail agraire en France,* Paris, Ecole pratique des hautes études, 1973, 167 p., multigraphié.

Raulin, Henri, *L'Architecture rurale française, le Dauphiné,* Paris, Berger-Levrault, 1977, 277 p.

Rémy, Jean, *Travail, famille et développement agricole. Aspects de le vulgarisation féminine,* Paris, INRA, 1977, 115 p.

Rocal, Georges, *Le Vieux Périgord,* Paris, E. Guitard, 1927, 255 p.

Rolland, Eugène, *Faune populaire de la France,* vol. VI, Paris, Maisonneuve, 1883, 243 p.

Roubin, Lucienne A., *Chambrettes des Provençaux,* Paris, Plon, 1970, 251 p.

Rouchon, Ulysse, *La vie paysanne dans la Haute-Loire,* vol. II, *Les Travaux et les Jours rustiques,* Le Puy, impr. La Haute-Loire, 1935, 252 p.

Rougé, Jacques-Marie, *Le folklore de la Touraine,* CLD Normand, 1975, 299 p.

Rougé, Jacques-Marie, *Le parler tourangeau (région de Loches),* Paris, Emile Lechevalier, 1902, 137 p.

Roussel, Louis, *Le mariage dans la société française,* Paris, PUF, Cahiers de l'INED, 73, 1975, 407 p.

Roze, L., *La bonne fermière ou éléments économiques,* Lille, J. B. Henry, 1767, 205 p.

Sébillot, Paul, *Le folklore de France,* Paris, E. Guilmoto, 4 vol., 1904–1907.

Sébillot, Paul, Additions aux coutumes, traditions et superstitions de la haute Bretagne, *Revue des traditions populaires*, VII, 1892.

Sébillot, Paul, *Coutumes populaires de la haute Bretagne*, Paris, Maisonneuve, 1886, 376 p.

Sébillot, Paul, *Légendes et curiosités des métiers*, Paris, Flammarion, n.d., 638 p.

Segalen, Martine, *Mari et femme dans la France rurale traditionnelle,* Catalogue de l'exposition organisée au musée des Arts et traditions populaires (ATP), Paris, Ed. des Musées nationaux, 1973, 78 p.

Segalen, Martine, *Les confréries dans la France contemporaine: les Charités,* Paris, Flammarion, 1975, 257 p.

Segalen, Martine, Le mariage, l'amour et la femme dans les proverbes du Sud, *Annales du midi*, 1975, 87, 123, pp. 265–288.

Segalen, Martine, Les derniers charivaris *in: Le Charivari*

Segalen, Martine, Le mariage, l'amour et les femmes dans les proverbes populaires français, *Ethnologie française*, 1975, V, pp. 119–162, and 1976, VI, I, pp. 35–88.

Segalen, Martine, Cycle de la vie familiale et transmission des biens; analyse d'un cas, *Ethnologie française,* 1978, VIII, 4, pp. 271–278.

Seignolle, Claude, *Le Folklore du Languedoc*, Paris, Maisonneuve et Larose, 1977, 303 p.

Seignolle, Claude, *Le Berry traditionnel*, Paris, Maisonneuve et Larose, 1969, 312 p.

Selle, Anna, *Thumette Bigoudène*, Ed. du Vieux Meunier breton, Rennes, 1974, 250 p.

Serres, Olivier de, *Le théâtre d'agriculture et mesnage des champs (1600). Extraits*, Aubenas, Lienhart, 1968, 109 p.

Shorter, Edward, *The making of the modern family*, London, Collins, 1976, 369 p.

Solé, Jacques, *L'amour en occident à l'époque moderne*, Paris, Albin Michel, 1976, 307 p.

Sutter, Jean and Tabah, Léon, Evolution des isolats de deux départements français, Loir-et-Cher et Finistère, *Population*, 1955, 4, pp. 645–673.

Sutter, Jean, Fréquence de l'endogamie et ses facteurs au XIXe siècle, *Population*, 1968, 2, pp. 202–24.

Tardieu, Suzanne, *La vie domestique dans le Mâconnais rural pré-industriel*, Paris, Institut d'ethnologie, 1964, 546 p.

Thompson, Edward P., Rough music: le charivari anglais, *Annales ESC*, March–April 1972, pp. 285–312.

Thompson, Edward P., Rough music and charivari: some further reflections, *in: Le Charivari.*

Tremaud, Hélène, *Jeux de force et jeux d'adresse*, Guides ethnologiques, 14, Paris, RMN, 1972, 48 p.

Valière, Michel, Préparation d'une enquête sur la sexualité en Poitou, *Annales de linguistique de l'université de Poitiers*, 2, 1974, mimeo.

Van Gennep, A., *Manuel du folklore français contemporain*, Paris, A. Picard, 1943–1958, 7 vol.

Van Gennep, A., *Le folklore du Dauphiné*, Paris, Maisonneuve, 1946, vol. I, 432 p.

Van Gennep, A., *Le folklore de la Flandre et du Hainaut français*, Paris, Maisonneuve, 1935, 739 p.

Van Gennep, A., *Le folklore de la Bourgogne*, Paris, Maisonneuve, 1934, 204 p.

Van Gennep, A., Le culte populaire de Sainte-Agathe en Savoie, *in: Culte populaire des saints en Savoie,* Archives d'ethnologie française, no. 3, 1973, p. 73–81.

Varagnac, André, *Civilisation traditionnelle et genres de vie*, Paris, Albin Michel, 1948, 402 p.

Verdier, Yvonne, La femme-qui-aide et la laveuse, *L'Homme*, 1976, 2–3, pp. 103–28.

Verdier, Yvonne, Les femmes et le saloir, *Ethnologie française*, 1976, 3–4, pp. 349–364.

Verdier, Yvonne, *Façons de dire, façons de faire*, Paris, Gallimard, 1979.

Weckerlin, J. B., *Chansons populaires de l'Alsace*, Paris, 1883, 2 vol.

Zink, Anne, *Azereix, La vie d'une communauté rurale à la fin du XVIIIe siècle*, EPHE, 6 section, XI, SEVPEN, 1969, 323 p.

Index

Abbadie d'Arrast, Mme d', 108, 151
adultery, 28, 43, 45–7
affection *see* love
Agatha, St (festival), 144, 147
agriculture: effect of changes, 173–7, 179–81, 187, 188–9; women and modernization, 179–87, 191–2; employment figures, 191
alcoholism, 142
Allier, 184
Alsace, 147
Angoumois, 121
Anjou, 124
architecture, rural, 7
Artois, 73
asouade (ritual), 43–5
Astarac, 26
Aube, 83
Aubrac region, 98
Auge (Normandy), 83–4, 97
Aunis, 121
authority: husbands', 2, 9, 25–6, 32–7, 179, 192; in household, 25–37, 155–72; and female conflict, 69; and farm management, 71–2
Auvergne, 141
Aveyron, 136
Avranches, 49

bake-house (communal), 138–40, 180;

see also bread-making
bars, 142
Basque country *see* Pays Basque
Basses-Alpes, 26
Baugeois, 123
Beauce (Normandy), 33, 100, 135
beauty, standards of, 17–18
bedrooms *see* sleeping arrangements
Berry, 42, 163
Béteille, Roger, 168
betrothal, 18
Bigouden region (Brittany), 71, 79, 89, 106, 134, 167
Blanzy, 97
Blok, Anton, 171
Bocage (Normandy), 84
Bouët, Alexandre, 22
Bougeâtre, Eugène, 86–7
Brandons, 30
bread-making, 96–7; *see also* bake-house
Bresse, 122, 161
Brie, 35
Brittany: marriage contracts, 13; nuptial rituals, 29; widows in, 31; communal living, 55; house-cleaning, 89; bread-making, 97; women in, 139, 152, 156, 166–7, 170–1, 175, 185
Brittany, Lower, 5, 40, 124, 145–6
Brittany, Upper, 16, 21, 44, 133
Brive, 124

brotherhoods, 143–4
Bugeat (Corrèze), 134
Burgundy, 32

Carnival, 42–5, 147
Caux, 52, 77, 177
Cazals (Tarn-et-Garonne), 177
celibacy, 176
CETA (Centre d'études de travaux
    agricoles), 184
Cévennes, 163
Chambre-Cercle, 143
Champagne, 119, 147, 176
Charités de Normandie, 143
charity, 120
charivari, 43–7, 157
children: as labour, 61, 63, 65;
    upbringing, 92, 121, 149, 169, 180–1
Church, the, 149–50
class (social): and marriage strategy,
    21–3; and farm ownership, 71,
    77; and modernization, 178
Code Civil, 72
Coïc, Corentine (married to F.
    Tanneau), 61, 66
Coise, 26
community, and couples, 38–41
Connier, Captain, 167
contraception, 23, 108, 128
cooking, 87–9, 181; *see also* meals
cooperatives (agricultural), 183–4
Corcuff, Marie (married to H. Le Berre),
    59–62
Cornouaille, 16, 22, 24
Côtes-du-Nord, 51
couples: personal feelings, 14–18; and
    sex, 20–4; and arranged marriages,
    22–3; and community, 38–9, 41, 53;
    and household, 39, 61; sleeping
    arrangements, 49–51, 53; age
    differences, 58; distribution of tasks,
    80–5, 111; sex and tenderness, 128–32;
    solidarity, 132–6, 189, 192; names and
    forms of address, 133–6; relationship,
    169–72; effect of modernization on,
    176, 179

Courbet, Gustave, 6; *Returning From the
    Fair,* 153, 169
courtship, 16–19
covegis, covize, 140, 142
créantailles (betrothal rituals), 18
cuckolds, 45–6
Cuisenier, Jean, 7n
CUMA (Coopératives d'utilisation du
    matériel agricole), 184

Dauphiné, 33
death, and wedding ritual, 28, 36
Dergny, Dieudonné, 32
Deux-Sèvres, 164
devil, the, 124–5
Diois (Dauphiné), 147
donkeys, and wife/husband beating,
    43–5, 53
Dordogne, 40
durmenés, 44
dwellings *see* houses

eggs, 122–3; *see also* poultry
Elbeuf, 75
emigration, 13–14, 39–41, 175–6, 190–1
Engarenne (Lot), 178

fairs and markets, 150–4
family: rural and urban differences, 1–2,
    39, 190–1; sources for study of, 3–5;
    19th century stability, 8; changing
    strategies, 8, 12; and migration, 41,
    176; collective sleeping arrangements,
    49–51; place of couple in, 53; definition
    and types, 56–7; organization of
    labour, 78, 85; instruction in, 91–2;
    modernization of rural, 173, 179; and
    modern farming, 182, 189–90, 192;
    and economic upheaval, 189; *see also*
    household
farms: importance to household, 61, 63;
    names, 70, 133–4; management
    authority, 71–2; economy and
    ownership, 72–7; production aims,
    78–9; distribution of tasks, 79–84,
    92–5; and solidarity of couples, 132–3;
    and agricultural change, 173–5, 180–5;

buildings and modernization, 177–9; survival of family type, 189–92

fertility, 8, 13

festivals, 147–9

Feuquières-en-Vimieu, 32

Finistère, 12, 23, 176

Finistère, South, 59

Flandrin, Jean-Louis, 15, 57, 129, 158

Fortier-Beaulieue, Paul, 36

Fours, 25

Franche-Comté, 148, 169, 176

GAEC (Groupements agricoles d'exploitation en commun), 183–4, 191

Gaillac (Tarn), 28

Gambetta, Léon, 150

gardens, as women's domain, 43, 93

Gascony, 172

Gâtine region, 164

Germiny, 148

Gers, 46

Gex, 124

gifts, in courtship, 18–19

Gouville (Eure), 74, 177

Great Domestic Quarrel, The (engraving), 46, 48, 155

Guernsey, 45

Guillaumin, Emile, 63, 118; *La vie d'un Simple*, 117–132, 167

Harcanville (Caux; Seine-Maritime), 52, 74

Haute-Loire, 151

Haute-Saône, 29

Hautes-Alpes, 30, 32, 49

Hélias, Pierre Jakez, 167

hens *see* poultry

household (*ménage*): defined, 8–9, 39, 56–77; dependence on parents, 14; and working of farm, 24; authority in, 25–37, 69, 155–72; and couple, 39–41; communal living, 51–3; types, 56–77; and farm economy, 72–3, 106; rural changes, 173–87, 189, 192–3

houses (dwellings): construction, 7; rooms and plans, 52–3, 57, 60, 67, 76;

cleaning, 89–90; as women's domain, 112–17; and modernization, 176–9; and separation of generations, 186; *see also* sleeping arrangements

Hugo, Abel, 4–5, 135, 165–7

husbands: authority, 2, 9, 25–6, 32–7, 155–72, 179, 192; beaten by wives, 43–5, 47; and wife-beating, 44, 47, 126–7, 157–8; vulnerability to female power, 126–7; *see also* men

Idaux-Mendy (Basses-Pyrénées), 52

Ille-et-Vilaine, Rimou, 144

Imbsheim (Lower Rhine), 60, 102

inheritance, 68–70, 72, 74, 182, 192

Isigny (Normandy), 79

Jeanton, Gabriel, 136–161

Joigny (Yonne), 33

Jura, 190

Kiltgang (custom), 23

kinship, 53, 67–9, 78; *see also* family

knitting and sewing, 90–1

labour: wife's initiation into husband's, 32–3, 36; household distribution of, 61, 63, 65, 76, 78–84, 164, 168; and production systems, 72; reserved to women, 85–94; reserved to men, 94–6; cooperation and interchange, 96–111; daily routine, 101–5

La-Chapelle-de-Guinchay, 97

Lagadic, Marie-Jeanne, 13

Laisnel de la Salle, A., 163

Laize, 97

Lamartine, Alphonse de, 161

land, 13, 22; *see also* farms

Landes, 54

Languedoc, 35, 172

Laslett, Peter, 56–7, 59

laundering, 87, 124; communal, 138–40, 180

Lavit (Tarn-et-Garonne), 73, 86, 93, 112

Le Berre, Henri and family, 59–62, 65

Le Bleis, Isidore, 59

Le Drezen, Thumette (married to P. Le Garrec), 63–4
Le Garrec, Pierre and family, 63–5
Le Havre, 75
Le Puy, 152
Limousin, 163, 176
lineage, 170
livestock, 97–8, 105, 113, 152, 181
Loir-et-Cher, 12
Loire (department), 36, 176
Lorraine, 122, 162, 164–5, 170–1
Loudun (Vienne), 46
Louviers, 75
love (and affection): marriage for, 4, 14–20, 23–4, 129, 170; demonstrations of, 16–19

Mâcon, 29, 161
Mâconnais, 97, 136, 161
Mafia, 171
magical practices, 121–3, 126
Mantois, 86–7, 97, 121
maraîchinage (in Vendée), 15, 17
Marc, Corentin and family, 59
Marcanville (Lower Seine), 177
Marche, 163
Marin, Louis, 162
markets *see* fairs and markets
marriage: for love, 4, 14–15, 19–20, 23–4, 129, 170; proverbs on, 6; stages, 11; rates, 12–13; ages of, 12–14; length of, 12; endogamous, 12–13, 23, 53; contracts, 13; and couples' independence, 13–14; arranged, 22–3; and economic realities, 24–5; age differences, 58; and social ascent, 71; son-in-law's, 70–1; confers status on women, 110; *see also* couples; weddings; wives
Mauges, 136
Maupassant, Guy de, 130
Maurienne, 22–3
Mayenne, 165
meals, 87–9, 145–6, 161–2, 165–6; *see also* cooking

men: activities reserved to, 94–6; and interchangeable tasks, 96–111; territory, 112, 115; feminized, 115–16, 157; power, 116; village and social life, 137–9, 141–4; drinking, 142; and role reversal, 147–8, 156; and religion, 149–50; attend fairs, 150–3; celibacy, 176; *see also* husbands
ménage see household
Menon, P. L. and Lecotté, Roger, 135
Midi-Pyrénées, 176
Millet, Jean-François, 6, 77, 96–7; *Angelus*, 149–50; *The Child's Candle*, 92; *The End of the Day*, 95; *The Knitting Lesson*, 91; *Man with a Hoe*, 95; *Men Digging*, 95; *The Meridian*, 130; *Planting Potatoes*, 98; *Woman Returning From the Well*, 85
Miramont (Tarn-et-Garonne), 99
Mr Home-Breaker and Mrs Nag (engraving), 155
money, 117–18
Monnier, Désiré, 66n
Montauban, 31
morality, 20, 49–50
Morbihan, 177
Mortainais, 27
mortality, 8, 12–13, 39, 92

names, farm and family, 69–70, 133–5
neighbours, 44
Neuilly, 147–8
Normandy, 13, 52, 75, 77, 83–4, 135, 176

Oise, 46
Orléanais, 35
Ormoy (Yonne), 123

parents, dominance of, 14
Paris, 176
Pays Basque, 69–72, 107–8, 162, 172
Pénitents du Sud, 143
Perche, 27, 33
Péron, Jean-Louis, 13
Perreux (Yonne), 30
Picardy, 73, 176

Piolenc (Vaucluse), 134
Plédran (Côtes-du-Nord), 51, 74, 177
Plonéour-Lanvern (S. Finistère), 13
Ploudalmezeau (Finistère), 67
Poitou, 119
Poitou-Charentes, 176
Pont l'Abbé (S. Finistère), 133
poultry: as wife's domain, 35, 82, 93, 101, 122, 186; and feminized man, 114–15
pregnancy, 21, 23
Provence, 135, 172
proverbs: as source, 6, 170; and family tensions, 12; ambiguities, 37

Quarrel over the Trousers, The (engraving), 155, 158

Rambaud, Placide, 183
Raulin, Henri, 7n, 147
religious practices, 121–3, 148–50
remarriage, 12, 47, 65–7
Rhône-Alpes, 187
Riche (Moselle), 74
rings, wedding, 27–8
Rivière, Georges Henri, 7
Roannais, 42
Rochechouart (Haute-Vienne), 86
Rolland, Eugène, 115
Rosières (Ardèche), 177
Rouchon, Ulysse, 140–1
Rouergue, 168
Roussel, Louis, 15

Saint-Étienne-de-Lisse (Gironde), 73
Saint-Jacut-de-la-Mer, 45
Saint-Jean-la-Poterie, Morbihan, 50
Saintonge, 121
Saint-Pierre-d'Albigny (Savoy), 144
Saint-Véran (Hautes-Alpes), 51, 74, 109, 113, 131
Salins, 148
Sarthe, 166
Savoy, 70
schools, 91
Sébillot, Paul, 28, 45
Seine-Maritime, 51–2

Sennely-en-Sologne, 39
Serres, Olivier de, 9, 110, 133, 175
servants: living quarters, 49, 51–2; in household, 59–60; and farm work, 61, 63, 75, 89, 101; and cooking, 87; and mistress of house, 107; in bourgeois households, 160
sewing, 90–1
sex, sexuality: prenuptial, 20–4; and marriage rituals, 35–7; female initiative, 35, 45–6, 127–8; and power of women, 126, 127–8; and tenderness, 128–32; *see also* love
sharecroppers, 73–4, 77, 82
Shorter, Edward, 129
Sicily, 171
sleeping arrangements, 49–52, 57, 60, 76, 130–1, 178
societies (and brotherhoods), 143–4
sorcery, 123–5, 169; *see also* magical practices
spinning, 31–2, 90
Sutter, Jean and Tabah, Léon, 12

Tanneau family, 59, 61, 66
Tardieu, Suzanne, 97
Tarn, 30, 77
Tarn-et-Garonne, 82, 131
tenant-farmers, 73–4, 76
Thèse (Morbihan), 86
Tinchebray (Orne), 82–3
tools, 32–3, 36, 94
Topsy Turvy World, A (engraving), 147
Touraine, 42, 122, 133, 135
Treuchtersheim (Lower Rhine), 74
Trosse (Savoyard custom), 23

Union des ententes et communautés rurales, 183

Valenciennes, 44
Van Gennep, Arnold, 5, 24, 30, 32, 34, 70
Vannecroq (Eure), 86
Vaucluse, 83
veillée d'été, 140, 142
Vendée, 15, 17
Vénizy (Yonne), 122

Verdier, Yvonne, 87
Vergisson, 97
Verruyes, 164
Vexin, 86–7, 97, 121
Vieux (Tarn), 73
Vieux-Rouen-sur-Bresle (Seine-Maritime), 91
village: social solidarities, 10; male and female sociability in, 137–44, 148, 154, 180
Villevieux (Jura), 57

washing *see* laundering
water, 85–7
weaving trade, 75
weddings: ceremony, 11; rituals and authority, 25–37, 69, 90, 110; *see also* marriage
widows, 65–7, 72, 165; *see also* remarriage
wife, wives: status, 2, 4–5, 9, 37, 110, 164; and household authority, 25–6, 32–7; and division of labour, 32–4, 80; community rights over, 41–2; beating, 43–5, 126–7, 157–8, 170; adulterous, 45–6; and farm management, 132–3; names, 134–5; *see also* women

Woman Brought to her Senses by her Husband, The (engraving), 158
women: labour and tasks, 2, 79–94, 164, 168; condition of, 9; community of, 25, 42, 88, 137–42, 144, 180; and sexual initiative, 35, 45, 127–8; conflict within household, 68–9; and inheritance, 70; and interchangeable tasks, 96–111; physical characteristics, 107–9; married status, 110, 125; and house, 112–17; infertile, 116; power and authority, 116, 125–6, 133, 155–9, 164, 189; control of money and household management, 117–21, 182; as protector of hearth, 121–3, 133; as sorceress, 123–5; as danger, 125–6, 189; sexuality, 126, 127–8, 132; village and social life, 138–42, 171, 180; eating separately, 145–6, 161–2, 165–6; and role reversal, 147, 156–7; and religion, 148–50; at markets, 150–3; lampooned in proverbs, 156–60; status in household hierarchy, 160–72, 189; seclusion of, 171–2; emigration from land, 175–6; and agricultural modernization, 179–87, 191–2; proposed rights, 185–6

Yonne, 31, 124, 147